PRAISE FOR *GROWING AMERICA*

"When I served as director of public relations for Rotary International in the early 1990s we used David Kidd's Stark Free Tree Program as a model for local Rotary Clubs around the world to follow. It is not surprising that Mr. Kidd writes with the same excitement, verve, commitment and skill that he applies to his tireless environmental activities."—**Martin Kantor**, The Juniper Group, Chicago, Illinois

"*Growing America* is an inspiring story of what one man can do to better himself and his community. David Kidd's spirit stands as tall and as strong as the trees he plants. Do yourself and your world a favor—read *Growing America.*"—**Michael A. Klaper**, M.D.

"David Kidd disassembles the roadblocks that face us all when inertia or fear of failure loom larger than the urgency of active engagement and leadership."—**Jenepher Lingelbach**, author, *Hands-On Nature*

"David Kidd's journey from a poor child to one of America's foremost activists makes us realize that we are the future. He makes Johnny Appleseed pale by comparison when it comes to planting trees, and that is only part of the story. David Kidd is an American hero and his book is fascinating."—**Howard F. Lyman**, author, *Mad Cowboy*

"David Kidd is an inspirational activist. *Growing America* reflects David's refreshing style and demonstrates how one person can make a real difference."—**Ken Margolis**, Director, River Network

"*Growing America* is here just when we need it most. David Kidd's amazing life and page-turner stories inspire the kind of commitment the world so desperately needs. We could use a lot more David Kidds right now—or we could read this book and learn to do what he does."
—**Victoria Moran**, author, *Creating a Charmed Life*

GROWING AMERICA
The Story of a Grassroots Activist

DAVID A. KIDD

DEAR DOUG,

BEST WISHES,

DAVID KIDD

JAN 2012

Lantern Books • New York
A Division of Booklight Inc.

2003
Lantern Books
One Union Square West, Suite 201
New York, NY 10003

Printed in Canada

Cover art donated by Mark Gaynor, Indian River Graphics. Photograph of
David Kidd for cover used by permission: Michael Kanakis.
Top photo on page 146 provided by The Fund for Animals.

Library of Congress Cataloging-in-Publication Data

Kidd, David A., 1951–
  Growing America : the story of a grassroots activist, a call for
renewed civic action / David A. Kidd.
     p. cm.
  ISBN 1-59056-030-2 (alk. paper)
  1. Kidd, David A., 1951–2. Environmentalism—United States. 3.
Environmentalists—United States—Biography. I. Title.
  GE56.K53A3 2003
  363.7'0092—dc21

                                                            2003002054

printed on 100% post-consumer waste paper, chlorine-free

This book is dedicated to my proactivist sister
Darlene (Kidd) Leghart,
who is carrying her own torch
in Canton's inner city neighborhoods
through her two nonprofit organizations,
Summit United Neighbors, Inc.
and Hammer & Nails, Inc.

Acknowledgments

RARELY DOES A human life unfold toward enlightenment entirely from within itself. Rather, our evolution is the product of the combined guidance of those whose influences come to shape us throughout our lives, either in person or through writings and teachings. My favorite original metaphor is the explanation that we as humans are all climbing toward the same mountaintop; even while we may be using different trails, we are all inexplicably linked by indelible threads of a spiritual, cord-like material. As we advance, we gently pull others on with us; and all the while we too are being gently pulled onward by those ahead of us.

My life has been clearly and profoundly influenced by the inspirational writings and teachings of a few specific individuals whose advanced degree of consciousness and vision has pulled me onward to discover within myself a growing knowledge and awareness of my Self. This is something for which I will always be grateful. Those individuals, living and dead, not necessarily in order of importance, include: St. Francis of Assisi, Elle Collier Re, Ralph Waldo Emerson, Mahatma Gandhi, John Gray, John Hagelin, Jesus of Nazareth, Maharishi Mahesh Yogi, Jeremy Rifkin, Edith Shaw, Henry David Thoreau, Walt Whitman and Marianne Williamson.

My heartfelt thanks also goes out to each of the following individuals who assisted me in the research and writing of this book, and to those without whose assistance there would have been no story to tell: James Abernathy, Ron Abraham, Maribeth Abrams, Deborah Akel, George Barclay, Marshall and Diana Belden, Jr., Joseph Benner,

Paul Bingle, Earl Blauner, Margaret Capurso, Clyde Cleveland, John Dorka, Stephanie Kidd Dorwart, Greg Edmonds, David Ewing, Pam Feagler, Mark Gaynor, Deborah Gerber, Joseph Guenther, Brad Graef, Cheryl Hintz, Becky Huggins, Sara Kidd Hundertmark, Michael Kanakis, Annie Kidd, Douglas Kidd, Karen Kindel, Lisa King, Janet Kullman, Reverend Patricia Lee, M. Jack Leghart, Sr., Ricky Ly, Jenepher Lingelbach, Lauretta Lintner, Howard Lyman, Charles McClaugherty, Kathleen McKinney, Kathleen O'Connor, Linda Paul, Heidi Prescott, Dristina Quinn, Claire Robinson, Connie Rubin, Rita Schneider, Mike Schmidt, Kalman Stein, Drew Todd, Kristin Wellman, Bruce Williams and Fred Worrell.

To my publisher and editor, Martin Rowe at Lantern Books, a special thank you for encouraging me to try to put some of my experiences into written words for the first time and for keeping me on target.

Table of Contents

Being and Doing

On the path
retire within
and seek
to develop
perfect Silence.

However,
once realized,
do not hide
in the quiet
of Being.

For the test
of stability
of calmness
is found
in the midst
of dynamic
activity.

dkidd 1986

Introduction

IN THE 1780s, when pioneers first settled what was to become the state of Ohio, 96 percent of the territory was covered with massive hardwood trees. These forests were mostly vast expanses of mixed oak and hickory trees with American beeches and sugar maples in the northeast. The remaining 4 percent of the land was composed of prairie grasses and a large, black swamp in the northwest, upon which the city of Toledo now sits.

Ohio's trees were cleared to create trails and farmland, and to build log homes. Safe gun-firing zones, or "fields of fire," were established around settlements. Well into the late 1800s the settlers were still afraid of both the human and nonhuman native inhabitants of Ohio's woods. Incredibly, after the first 150 years of more "civilized stewardship" by the settlers, the total amount of forest cover had been reduced from 96 percent to just 12 percent. In a story typical of what has occurred in all of North America's heavily forested states east of the Mississippi River, increased settlement and more sophisticated tools finally "tamed" the wilderness and brought about the massive deforestation that has left so much of the United States denuded of trees.

No one in the nineteenth century seriously considered that there would be such an accumulative effect from individuals using a small amount of space and lumber to build their cabins and fence off their land. In those days, America seemed boundless and its resources unlimited. Nevertheless, forestry experts agree today that across these United States between the 1600s and year 2000 there was a net loss of over 50 percent of all of our native forest cover. In particular parts of the United States the loss was even greater. The virgin sequoia and redwood forests in California and the Pacific Northwest, with some of the largest and oldest trees in America, have been reduced by over 95 percent. The total effect has been a net loss of over 30 billion trees.

Given these figures, therefore, it is a demonstrable fact that every person has already made a cumulative difference in the loss of America's environmental resources. And a similar story to that of deforestation could be told about non-renewable resources during this period—such as coal, precious and industrial metals and oil and gas. We have been mining and plundering these resources recklessly throughout the history of the United States; and all this occurred during a time when the population of the United States has been relatively small in comparison with the surface area of the country.

In view of the undeniable fact that each person has already had a negative impact on the environment, it never ceases to amaze me when people say they cannot possibly make a positive difference to our environment. The fact is that, with our ever-dwindling resources being tapped by an ever-growing population, the impact of each individual is today more critical than ever before.

Growing America
The message of this book is that it is time for us to "Grow America." It is my belief that the job of creating our country is not finished. In this effort, every individual will once again make a difference. My premise is that we have, for the most part, built the infrastructure of our country. We have built hundreds of thousands of miles of roads and highways and hundreds of thousands of schools, churches, retail stores and offices, parking lots, and over one hundred and fifteen mil-

lion residences. But we haven't finished the job. In both a social and an environmental sense, it is time for us to complete the work of creating an ideal America.

Over the last decade, I have spoken with many people from Europe. These Europeans believe we Americans are ridiculous when we complain that our communities are completely "built up." In Europe, where civilizations have lived for over two millennia, every square foot of land is used to maximum advantage. My European friends find it amusing that we are so proud of our new neighborhoods with $300,000 homes that have virtually no trees around them. Where, they ask, are the hedgerows, the flower and vegetable gardens? Where are the fruit trees?

Over the last fifteen years, I have been attempting to teach students that "everywhere you see the sky there used to be a tree" (see Chapter Five). I have argued that we don't have to live in cities filled with roads, parking lots, houses, schools and businesses with only a few trees scattered among them. Rather, we can live in a vast forested area with roads and houses and buildings underneath. The projects that I have initiated, and which you will read about in this book, have given trees to hundreds of thousands of students and invited them to begin "regrowing" America in their own backyards. Our tree projects have empowered both young people and adults by tying them directly to the Earth through the planting of a tree.

I do not expect us to replace a majority of the trees that have been removed. However, we can certainly take a new and serious look at every twenty-foot square of unforested land in America and ask ourselves whether we can plant a tree there. We need to go back and re-examine the forgotten or polluted areas that exist around us and replant as many trees and bushes as possible. We need to look at empty lots and huge pieces of land that we are mowing and ask ourselves whether instead of cutting grass all day we can plant trees and let them work for us. We may find that most of our mowing is simply a bad habit we need to break.

It is not the government's job to plant trees on private property. To regrow America it will require a massive effort by private citizen activists using private money to buy and plant trees on private land. This book illustrates how one such community project grew within five years to involve over one million private citizen forestry volunteers in a network of over 1,500 schools and civic groups. My "free tree" idea could be easily used by your community with the help of just one inspired volunteer. You may know just the right person for the job. You may be that person. This book will provide you with some ideas for helping the environment and starting your own organization, as well as suggestions for creating a successful campaign and avoiding the burnout that happens to so many activists.

Community Activism
The "free tree" project I initiated represents the environmental half of the equation for growing America. But community forestry is only one small aspect of the completion of our unfinished nation. We need to address the social problems of the homeless, the hungry and undernourished, the infirm, the mentally ill, the emotionally disturbed and the illiterate. We need to preserve our historic structures while building the nation with new structures that use the best environmental technology. We Americans are so proud of our own country while being quick to find fault with other cultures around the globe. Isn't it time we undertook a greater effort to fix our own social problems at home before condemning others for their inadequacies?

This book highlights how one person has made a difference through one community environmental project. It proposes more environmental actions and issues a call for new activists in large numbers to take part in their own projects. Each of these environmental projects can also serve as models for any number of other community action efforts in every segment of society.

Private volunteer activists are going to be needed in every field in increasing numbers. This will be especially true as those of us born between 1946 and 1964—known as the "baby boomers"—become senior citizens. What I hope to show in *Growing America* is that every person can truly make a positive difference and how you can work within the system to help change it. I hope all of you who read this book will challenge yourselves to step forward and be the activist that is needed in your field of choice.

The word "activist" has been given an unfair label; it's about as popular as the word "politician." In my opinion, such a negative label has come about because the modern-day definition of activism is most associated by those in power with those who are perceived as being *against* something: whether it's against government, taxes, logging, pollution or any large organization and the insensitivity that often accompanies it. Some activists, both on the right and the left, have taken their "anti-something" practices to such lengths that they have created a whole philosophy of being against social order. They believe we should burn down the entire country and return to an agrarian society with no government.

There is a place in life for those who are against things. Someone needs to be brave enough to cry out when a great wrong is being committed. There may even be a time and place for anarchism, such as when society shifts too far to one extreme and fails to protect the most basic rights of citizens. Nazi Germany could have used a strong anarchist movement.

But whether you resist or agree with the idea of "activism," you should know that you already are an activist. If you are alive, you are an activist. If you do anything, you are an activist. If you do nothing but sit and breathe, you are still an activist. You were an activist before you took your first breath. Ask any mother and she will gladly tell you which of her children was the biggest activist while still in her womb!

I, for one, am not an anarchist. I don't see myself as against anything; instead, I am *for* things. My method of social activism is to be *pro*-active, not *re*-active. I believe that we are each by nature proactive. A proactivist is one who performs actions through peaceful means within the existing system in order to change it. A proactivist is one who ultimately aspires to peace, harmony and social order. A proactivist is a builder of unity. Being a proactivist is easy. To be a reactivist one has to struggle and work really hard, going against the grain. Proactivists empower others to grow and take on more responsibility; reactivists take power away from another.

This book aims to be an inspirational guide for all proactivists. Again, while it may appear to be about my specific community volunteer environmental projects, as well as some of the initiatives that I have supported or assisted in, the proactive ideas in *Growing America* will also serve as models for anyone in their community projects. My life to date has been mainly about fixing our environmental problems. Clearly, the same truths I have proactively applied to the environment could be applied to feeding the hungry, housing the homeless, educating the illiterate and caring for the infirm, the mentally ill and the emotionally disturbed. I hope that this book inspires you—whatever your age or whatever your issue—to pick your issue and pitch in.

Learning Young

During my childhood, with no particular effort on my part, I assimilated knowledge of our culture and its systems. I learned about poverty and riches, legal and illegal activities, responsibility and irresponsibility, maturity and immaturity in both the young and the old. Because I did not have many adults in my life who really cared for my opinion, I became a good listener.

While young, I practiced my methods of influencing those around me with mixed results. It was not until my three years in the military, two as a sergeant, that I had an opportunity to really practice and develop skills needed in the management of individuals and large institutions—in my case the United States Army. That experience stood me in good stead when I later on was hired to recruit and motivate a whole network of volunteers. It is surprising to me to observe how many of those military lessons learned when I was a young man have carried over to my civilian life. You will find throughout the book that my experiences in Viet Nam had an enormous influence on how I lived my life afterward.

When I returned to the U.S. after nineteen months in Viet Nam (about which you can read in Chapters Three and Nine), I was still only twenty years old. But I came away from the military and the war with several life-changing beliefs:

- A resolve to live every aspect of my life without violence. This was to include my personal life, my work and even my diet.
- The belief that the most lasting changes could be accomplished in society without hatred and violence.
- The understanding that life is not simply black and white—it almost always comes in shades of gray. Therefore, nearly everything is negotiable.
- The conviction that I had only survived two tours in Viet Nam because I had made a distinct change in my life. In the face of my imminent death, I had made a commitment to God that if I died, I would die willingly. But if I lived, I would spend every moment for the rest of my life dedicated to the re-establishment of an original personal relationship with Him and, in turn, to sharing that knowledge with others.

The result of this deep commitment has been the lifelong dedication of my every action to God. As part of this, I have practiced Transcendental Meditation for over thirty years as a way of cleaning out all remaining inner negativity and habituating my mind to operate on its deepest and most inspired levels of thinking. TM is the subject of Chapter Eleven. I have lived as a vegetarian for over thirty years, and have worked toward the creation of joy and fun in my life and in the lives of those around me through the empowerment of both the young and the old. You can read about my vegetarianism in Chapter Six. I have undertaken decades of research to gain a deeper understanding of what keeps humankind suffering and bound in ignorance of our Higher Self. Through all of this, I have gained some insight into how to assist humankind to move beyond these boundaries and to recognize their own worth, their highest good. I continue to gain more insight each year. The practical result for me has been that my most inspired ideas are also those that have been most successful.

Throughout my life, even though I have undergone what to others may seem like hardships, I feel I have been blessed. I have been blessed with the resilient joy of being alive and with a genuine lack of anger in almost every situation. I have also been blessed by being surrounded with countless friends who have willingly assisted me in my endeavors and have had fun with me in the process.

A Larger Accomplishment

On one level, *Growing America* is about some of my proactivist accomplishments. It details how to get things done without being negative or tearing down the system. It discusses how we can and need to "grow America" through the efforts of private individuals and groups. On a deeper level, however, my message is that every person without exception, young or old, has an opportunity to rise to a higher awareness and accomplishment. I believe that we all have the opportunity to break out of our boundaries, out of the mentally constructed boxes we are living in, and open ourselves to a greater sense of our own Being.

Twenty years ago, in *The Greening of America*, Charles Reich wrote that "Transcendence is America's greatest need." That truth remains valid today. I believe that it is the lack of direct human experience of transcendence that is the greatest epidemic on this planet. I believe that there is no lack of knowledge, power or possibilities once we have tapped into the transcendental level of Universal Intelligence. Once we are freed of our own ego-driven, self-imposed limitations and become more connected with the Universal Awareness within us, there is virtually nothing we cannot accomplish. Don't worry if this sounds complicated or vague, or even a little intimidating or "New Age-y" at the moment; I will talk about the subject at length and on a practical level in Chapter Eleven. All you need to do is open to the possibility that the self is more than the everyday ego that worries about mundane problems. It has been my experience that there is a transcendent self that can place everything in its proper perspective and provide us with a higher awareness—more wakefulness. In order for us to finish growing America, we will need tens of thousands of individuals with such higher awareness to mobilize and add their strength to those already leading the way in the nonprofit sector. If you understand this concept, you qualify for the job. We will need more volunteers, more skills, more time, more resources and more money.

When Social Security retirement was implemented in the United States, Americans were not living much past 65 or 75 years of age. Today, American men are living to an average of 75 years and women until they are 84. That means there are 13 to 22 years for retirement—and yet we are programmed to ignore our most sagacious years. What a waste of human brilliance! We need to rethink the whole idea of retiring; we need to pay back the system that has been so giving to us. A new worldview is needed that encourages every person to decide what they plan to work on in their retirement years as their avocation.

The government cannot regrow America for us. Beyond the initial creation and maintenance of our major infrastructure, our state and federal governments were never designed to help "complete" our society. Government was created to protect America from invasion and to protect individual rights. The completion of an ideal society has always been the responsibility of those private individuals who were awake enough to see our problems and needs and begin to fix them. We need to finish the growing of America to create an ideal society. For this we need your help—each and every one of you.

David A. Kidd
Canton, Ohio
January, 2003

Figure 1:1 The Stark Free Tree Program logo

1: Practical Grassroots Activism

EVERY SPRING THE United States celebrates Arbor Day. It's a day on which we're meant to honor trees, and perhaps plant a few by way of celebration. Arbor Day in April 1989 was a bit different for me. In fact, my Arbor Day wasn't limited to one day. With several friends as volunteers, I had decided to purchase and distribute for free not merely one or two trees, or even a hundred. I had decided to launch a project to distribute for free three million tree seedlings over the next eleven years. This chapter is about that week and how everything I planned finally came together.

That March, I declared the last week of April 1989 to be "Tree Week" in Stark County, Ohio, which is where I live. According to the foresters I had talked to, no one had ever done such a massive tree giveaway before. It was to be a community celebration of trees, and we were making history in the process.

Before our first "free tree" distribution, I issued a news release launching the Stark Free Tree Program and proclaiming our upcoming "Tree Week." The theme for the new community project was: "A responsible citizen is one who will plant one tree every year of their life." We wanted to give hundreds of thousands of trees away for free each year so that every local citizen could begin the habit of planting at least one tree each year.

In every one of the thirteen local daily and weekly newspapers I placed a notice inviting anyone living in Stark County to participate in the project by picking up a "free tree" order form at any branch of their local public library. Individuals, businesses, farms, churches and any civic groups who wanted a hundred or more trees could simply fill out the advance order form and mail it back. Schools, however, would be different. Special forms for every school were mailed directly to the principal of each building. A few of the papers took the liberty of also inviting people to call me at home to place their orders. That was a mistake, as I learned, resulting in more than a hundred calls to my home over the first two weeks, each taking a long time to process. The calls came at all hours, including several in the middle of the night. "Well, your line was busy all day," was the aggrieved response when I asked why the callers were contacting me so late. "So I thought I would call you while I was working the night shift."

The response to my notice and press release was overwhelming. I received over 371 written orders totaling 195,550 trees, a response that presented me with an immediate problem: I had only purchased 105,000 tree seedlings in advance for our first year. Scrambling for a solution, I carried the pile of tree orders with me and dropped them with a thump on the desks of a few potential donors. With the additional funds raised in just a few days from corporate and individual donors, we bought 50,000 more trees. To eliminate the rest of the deficiency, I personally cut back everyone's tree orders with a red pen as needed. I did it proportionately so that everyone would at least get something.

The orders that I finally whittled down proportionately included 62,000 trees for 134 separate school buildings in 20 districts; 35,000 trees for 67 businesses to hand out to their employees; 9,000 for 44 civic groups and churches and 34,000 for 126 individuals, including many farmers. Another 15,000 trees were reserved for public giveaways at 20 locations for individuals who didn't have students in schools or didn't need over a hundred trees (the minimum advance

Figure 1:2 Canton South Rotarian Don Ross picks up trees for his club's geographic area.

order I had allowed). Our project's first year results: 155,145 trees distributed.

If nothing else, the first year of "Tree Week" proved my belief that there was not only a need but also a huge pent-up demand for trees—and in a county with a population of only 364,000! Thus, as "Tree Week" approached, I had the orders and I had the trees coming: now the rest of the project was simply a matter of logistics.

On Wednesday morning of "Tree Week," three carloads carrying fourteen students from John Allen's Jackson High School horticulture department arrived at my house at 7:30 a.m. Several other adult volunteers were already there to help me sort and distribute trees to our Rotary International Tree Chairs for each of the thirteen geographic areas of the county. The trees would be picked up by Rotary in the afternoon, from three to six o'clock. Then the Tree Chairs would further sort and distribute the trees in their own communities.

But trees were only a part of the logistical problem. Each coordinator also needed bags and planting instructions to give out with the trees. Every geographic area had a different tree total, a different school total and different numbers of businesses and churches giving out the trees. Therefore, they all needed odd counts of bags and instructions. Volunteers were formed in teams and armed with clipboards with the exact totals of trees, bags and planting instruction forms needed in each pile.

First, the volunteers began to count out the 70,000 plastic bags that would be used in schools to keep the tree roots moist. The schools were to be delivered trees, bags and planting instructions (some assembly required). Student volunteers in each school would put the bare-rooted trees into bags with the instructions stapled around the trunk, holding the bag closed, and deliver them to every classroom.

The 140 boxes with 500 bags each went into thirteen piles next to stakes that had been put in the ground along both sides of 26th Street in front of my house. I had spoken to each of my three retired neighbors across the street from me in advance to make sure they didn't object to my running a charitable project on our respective front "tree lawns" for one day. While one neighbor expressed reservations, in the end everyone agreed to allow it. Each stake had the name of a Rotary community on it: Alliance, Canal Fulton, Canton, Canton South, East Canton, Hartville, Jackson Township, Louisville, Massillon, Minerva, North Canton, Perry Township and Plain Township.

In addition to the four-by-twelve-inch bags purchased for single trees, we had been given 5,000 bread bags from Nickles Bakery. These were extra bags from bread batches whose ingredients had been changed, making them unusable. We needed them for our public giveaways. They were ideal for 25 or 50 seedlings at a time. These bags were distributed to each pile.

As we apportioned the bags, a huge ten-ton dump truck rolled up carrying the first load of trees—about half of our 155,000 white pine trees (the first-year species chosen). The one-year-old seedlings were about twelve to fifteen inches tall, with long green needles, which would provide instant gratification for our recipients. (After a couple of years of distributing pines, we switched to hardwoods. They took more faith. A one-year-old hardwood looks like a dead incense stick.)

Counting the Trees

The 160 bags of 500 trees were each unloaded in my driveway. Our pine trees were sorted and graded and bundled by Smith Evergreen Nursery, about twenty miles away in Magnolia, Ohio. The nursery hand-checked every seedling and rejected the ones that were over- or under-sized, then machine-tied the seedlings with a light string into bundles of 25 seedlings each. Smith Evergreen, using an old-time nursery industry standard, actually put 26 trees into every bundle— their version of a "baker's two-dozen." The bundles helped immensely when we had to count out orders into quantities of 175 or 225. To help us handle our massive counting logistics, all of our advanced order forms required all orders to be rounded up or down to the nearest 25.

The truck and driver were donated by a local construction firm run by Jim Jeffries, a member of the Plain Township Rotary, and his brothers. Jim's truck delivered trees we purchased from Smith Evergreen, a delivery that saved us a considerable shipping cost each year. By the time the first load was carefully checked, counted, sorted and then re-counted, the second truckload arrived. The trees on that truck, too, were sorted into each station.

We started to count out planting instruction forms for each area. We had printed up 80,000 flyers. The instructions, which came 5,000 to a box, were packed by the printer with a colored sheet every 250 pages to help us count them more easily. The instructions were designed three-up on standard 8.5 x 11-inch recycled paper, then cut into thirds. The front gave simple written and illustrated planting instructions: the green part goes up, the brown part down. The back listed all the Rotary clubs and our other major donors.

The handout also featured our tree logo. Graphic artist Janet Kullman had created a design better than I had asked for. I wanted Stark Free Tree Program in a circle with a seedling in the center. She had added an open hand at the bottom that lent a nurturing quality to the symbol. It was perfect. Such wholesome advertising was one hook for our donors: "Dr. Smith, how much would it be worth to you

Figure 1:3 Unloading plastic bags containing 500 trees

to have your name attached to a living tree that will be carried home by 62,000 students and then handed to their mothers?"

After an early lunch of pizza and soda, the kids took off for school. Two or three of us continued checking the sorting until the trees were all ready to be picked up.

Shortly before three o'clock, the Rotary helpers began to arrive with every kind of rig imaginable. There were pick-up trucks, mini-vans, homemade trailers and company trucks. All the trees were gone by six o'clock. We were able to put about 5,000 seedlings in a passenger car, but it took a pick-up to carry 10,000.

The Rotary helpers pulled up on both sides of the road in front of their respective signs, loaded up trees, bags and planting instructions, and were off in a few minutes. Their evening was just beginning. The plan was for them to break down and lay out every order on Wednesday night, deliver to schools on Thursday morning before 11 a.m., give out all of their advance-ordered trees on Thursday and Friday and hold a final public giveaway on Saturday morning. Any advance orders not picked up were put into the public giveaway so they could be planted that weekend. They had a short shelf life.

Joe Benner, Tree Chair for Canton Rotary, carried his trees back to the Ewing Chevrolet maintenance garage, where his team sorted them down into individual sizes and labeled every order. Rotarian Bill Zirhut, manager of Warner Cable TV, volunteered several of his service trucks Thursday morning to deliver 12,300 trees to the 29 Canton City Schools participating.

Massillon Rotarian Ray Dickerson, owner of Nelson Industrial Supply, ran his branch of the "free tree" project with his wife Nancy out of their family garage. Ray had stepped forward to chair the new Rotary project, and stuck with it through its entire eleven years. The Dickersons delivered to schools on Thursday morning, and had their advance orders picked up from their home on Thursday evening and all day Friday. On Saturday at eight o'clock in the morning, as he pulled into the Massillon AAA parking lot with 1,500 trees for the public giveaway, Ray Dickerson was alarmed to find the lot full of cars. "Oh, no," he thought, "There's another event going on today." But it turned out that *he* was the event. More than forty cars were already there waiting for his free trees. His trees were gone in two hours.

Dr. Doug Birks, Principal of Minerva Local's Hazen Junior High School, had his students sort the trees for all the schools in his district, including the Catholic schools. They even sorted and labeled the other advance orders for pick-up. Doug, who became a school board member after his retirement, continued to handle the project for all eleven years.

Occasionally, throughout the years, someone would get confused and think the project was a government giveaway. It never was. The money was privately raised and the trees were privately distributed. We had complete discretion over who could or could not have our trees. But we did run tens of thousands of trees short of the written orders every year. Schools and churches never got cut. How could we give trees to only half of the students or congregations after getting them so excited over the prospect of having them?

In order to balance the numbers, I had to cut advance orders from individuals and businesses. While almost every recipient was very gracious and appreciative when they received their trees, greed sometimes set in. Some of the recipients were annoyed when I had to cut their orders down from 500 to 150. While I could have operated on a first-come, first-served basis, with half of the orders getting all of the trees they requested and the other half getting nothing, I thought this grossly unfair. Instead, everyone got cut a little (except for the churches and schools) and every order got something. I suggested to the Tree Chairs that when they called advance orders for pick-ups, they tell them of any cutbacks. If someone got upset, they could simply ask callers whether they would rather get part of their "free tree" order or none at all. When faced one year with an unreasonably annoyed client, Doug Birks looked the man straight in the eye and asked him a straightforward question: "What part of 'free' don't you understand?"

Pastor David Schoen of Trinity United Church of Christ developed his own eco-sermon to give on the Sunday after Arbor Day, just before his tree giveaway. He spoke about stewardship and nature, the value of trees, and how trees have played an integral role in Christianity. Father Tom Crum, the Priest at St. Anthony's, told me he liked to stand on the front steps after his service and personally hand out trees to each parishioner, young and old. Before he let go of the tree, he told me, he would pause and say to the congregant, "And I want you to promise me that you will plant this tree today."

Kids Crying

One lesson I learned in year one came after a frantic call I received on the Friday of "Tree Week." At about 2:15 p.m., a principal from one of the Canton South elementary schools called me on the phone.

"Is this David Kidd?" she asked, obviously annoyed.

I told her that it was.

"Listen," she continued, "I've got my kids standing in the hallway waiting to get on their buses, and about 300 of them are crying because they didn't get their free trees. We didn't have enough for everyone. Now what are you going to do about it?"

Ouch. Trouble in River City.

"Well," I said, thinking fast, "Why don't you go out in the hall and tell them to get on their buses and that we will bring them their free trees on Monday? Then come back in and talk to me some more so we can work it out."

Figure 1:4 Students bag trees for distribution.

When the principal returned to the phone, she was somewhat calmer. She told me they had followed the curriculum. Her students had planned all week who would get trees on Friday and where they would plant them in their yards on the weekend. Her order, she told me, had been shorted.

"Listen," I said. "The first thing you need to know is this: The Rotarian who counted out the trees and delivered them to your building is a volunteer. He grew up in your community, and went to your schools. So if he doesn't know how to count, that's your fault, not mine."

She started to laugh.

"Now, I don't know quite how," I continued, "but I'll buy 300 more trees and bring them to you by 11 a.m. Monday."

In the end, I needed to buy over 3,000 trees just to fix order mistakes. We were extra careful each year after that. I also held back a small inventory just for such emergencies. From those trees, I gave leftovers to people whose orders I had cut.

Stark County has a population of 364,000. We had 62,000 students and teachers each getting one tree. I conservatively calculated our actual tree-planting volunteers as one adult parent for every two students involved. That brought the school volunteer total to 93,000, and there were probably a lot more volunteers whom I didn't count. Sometimes whole families helped to plant one seedling. When I added the 9,000 volunteers who received trees through churches and groups, the estimated 1,000 volunteers from the 35,000 trees taken by businesses and the 2,000 volunteers from the 20 public giveaway locations, I calculated that our total volunteer involvement was at least 105,000, or nearly one-third of the population of Stark County. I thought that wasn't a bad start for a first-year grassroots project.

The total cost for the Stark Free Tree Program in our first year was $12,150. Over $9,000 came from the various International Rotary Clubs. The balance was from individual and corporate donors. Everyone involved was a volunteer. No one got paid, including me.

I believe our project was a wild success because it involved a winning combination: kids, nature and something free. And it was altruistic. I also hope you will have seen that people from all walks of life got involved, owned the project and felt invested in it. There were problems, as you saw. But, as you also have seen, the logistics, while complicated, ran remarkably smoothly once everybody knew what they had to do and how they could do it. More than anything else, though, I hope you have glimpsed some of the enthusiasm and commitment that this community (no different or more generous than any other community in the United States) expressed when they were given a plan they could *believe* in—a plan that helped them to learn that they, too, could make a difference. In the next chapter I talk about how I came up with the idea and how I got the community to rally around the project. In the process, I hope you'll learn a little bit about me, why I think large and how I learned the tenacity, and yes, perhaps the cunning, that you need to get people to want to do what you want.

2: The Seed of an Idea

THE SPRING AND summer of 1988 were particularly hot. There were several weeks of over 100-degree temperatures in much of the United States, followed by a drought. During that time I was on what I call "the canoe trip from hell." The trip, which could have been a sequel to John Boorman's movie *Deliverance*, was an almost-unmitigated disaster and taught me a lot about human nature. However, the trip profoundly affected the next fifteen years of my life, because out of it was born the "free tree" idea.

I had been invited to join a group from Ohio whose aim was to canoe down the entire Missouri River from Three Forks, Montana to St. Louis, Missouri, and then down the Mississippi to New Orleans. The goal of the 3,820-mile trip was to set a new Guinness World Record. The old record was about 135 days. The new goal was to be 75 to 90 days.

My friend Jim called me around the first of May to ask me to join the group. The expedition was set to leave at the end of the month, and one of the paddlers had just bailed out, so that the group needed an experienced replacement. I told him I was too busy. The next morning I took stock. I was still recovering from the aftermath of an emotional and costly divorce, the loss of custody of my children, a major business closure, more personal debts than I could pay for, no steady income and the hovering depression that goes with a very uncertain future. They were dark days. I decided I needed a real break. So I called Jim back and told him, "I'd like to meet with the group and see what they have planned."

After the first meeting, I had mixed feelings. The organizer of the project appeared to be a control freak—and I know one when I see one because I've been one. Damian (not his real name) was six feet plus, square-jawed, 240 pounds and strong as an ox. He was subject to quick mood changes and didn't like being questioned. When I asked how much he had canoed (which I thought a fair question), he told me that he knew what he was doing but that he had only canoed short distances on a few lakes. Summer camp, I thought.

To his credit, Damian had successfully pitched a PR firm in Chicago that represented a Canadian beer company to put up $15,000 to fund the trip. Our job was to get publicity for the company all the way down the river, then arrive in New Orleans with some fanfare and receive the keys to the city from the mayor. Again to his credit, Damian had bought some of the best gear available and had had two We-no-nah canoes donated for the venture.

I should have seen red flags, however, when I first learned that the paddler I replaced had bailed out for no good reason. Or when I learned that Damian, his brother Tom and his sister Carol (not their real names), all over thirty, still lived with their parents. Or when I learned that both the brother and sister refused to drive cross-country with him and planned instead to fly out and meet us in Montana.

Jim, a nature photographer with incredible strength and athleticism, was to go along for the first three weeks as one of the paddlers and shoot pictures along the way. Carol would then replace him. Damian, Tom, Jim and I would trade places daily so we would all get time with each other in the two canoes.

There was a woman, Mary (not her real name), who would drive a support vehicle. She was to pack up camp each morning and meet us down river with tents set up and a meal ready to facilitate our camping needs. I didn't like the way Damian and Mary interacted at the first meeting. After I expressed my doubts to Jim about Damian's personality, both Jim and I decided that I was being overly cautious. Jim suggested that I was being hypercritical because of my own tendency to like to organize everything. I confessed then, as I do now, that that might have been true. However, by then I had had three years in the Army plus fourteen years' experience working with every kind of person in my stress management classes, and I knew trouble when I saw it. In the end, I figured the worst that could happen was that we would see the west for a while and, if the trip broke up, we could all go home. So I committed myself to the trip.

Around the Lakes without a Paddle

The group left just before Memorial Day. The week before we left, the media came out for our practice paddle, which I had insisted on, at a local reservoir. In a shaky start, we nearly tipped over for the cameras. After the first two days of riding with Damian, both Jim and Mary refused to get in the car with him, so I had to travel alone with him.

On the drive, Damian tried to impress me with his knowledge of American history and told long, fantastic stories about his two tours of duty in Viet Nam. Having been there for two tours (nineteen months) for real, I rapidly came to the conclusion that Damian's tales were fantasies. I added "delusional" to my lengthening list of adjectives to describe the leader of the expedition.

Other problems discovered en route included the fact that Damian had spent nearly all the discretionary money for the trip on his kids at Christmas, and didn't have enough cash to pay for our food costs down the whole length of the river. "Not to worry," he replied. "My brother will be bringing some cash with him when he arrives next week." He told me that his sister would bring more money (from Dad, it seemed) at a later date when she joined us.

The river system had about thirty-eight dams or locks to portage. The *Guinness Book of Records* rules on this particular trip made allowances for us either to carry the canoes across the portages or to put the gear on top of the vans and drive around the man-made obstacles.

The paddle itself was fun. I was the most experienced, followed by Jim, and each day on the river we got stronger. Several long sections of the river were away from roads and man-made noise, and canoeing along these stretches was like slipping back into another century.

Serious problems arose when Damian decided to cheat. He started off one morning by driving us around Holter Lake. I questioned his decision, since it seemed he wanted to drive around all the lakes and skip them entirely, thus knocking hundreds of miles off the trip. Damian's rationale was that the maps clearly showed where the river ended and lakes began, and then where the river picked up again at the end. "See, it says 'Missouri River,' then 'Holter Lake,' then 'Missouri River' again," he helpfully informed us. We could therefore, according to him, simply drive to the other end of the lake and put in again without ever technically leaving the Missouri River. Damian had sincerely convinced himself that we could then honestly say that we had paddled the whole river. I refused to accept this. In fact, Jim and I together made Damian take us back to the start of the twenty-mile Holter Lake and paddle the whole thing. He was, as you might imagine, not happy. Apparently, I was not being a "team player." It didn't help that Holter was a miserable ten-hour paddle in high winds and white-capped waves.

Meanwhile, Mary, our support driver, was becoming increasingly frantic at being alone all day and uncertain about where exactly our party would end up each evening. We couldn't help her much, since these were the days before such high-tech communications as cellular phones or pagers. I remember that Mary and Damian had screaming matches each evening that nearly came to blows. She had already decided to abandon the expedition and take a bus home once we reached Great Falls, creating a potential logistics problem for the group.

One night, while camped about a week from Great Falls, Montana, it became clear that Damian was planning to drive around the entire 110-mile Fort Peck Reservoir that was on our itinerary in two weeks. In addition to the fact that he was deceiving the *Guinness Book of Records*, Jim and I had both been excitedly looking forward to the reservoir as one of the most pristine wildlife and nature areas on the whole trip. We liked the fact that we would be paddling for days without any human contact. The whole idea, however, seemed to terrify Damian. It was, after all, grizzly bear country.

One evening, I got on a pay phone at a riverside bar and called Marie, the publicity firm's agent for our expedition. I had memorized the number from watching Damian call in each night when we were near a phone. I felt really bad that Marie had already lined up most of the major TV networks to fly their camera crews into Great Falls to film us (footage that could be used later when we arrived in New Orleans). Not only, at our current rate, were we going to arrive at Great Falls several days later than Damian told her to have the crews there—if we got there at all—but it was also clear by then that the whole "expedition" had no chance at all of making it to New Orleans.

Jim and I were already comparing notes every evening as to whether we could tolerate another day with Damian and the crew. Marie was about to embarrass herself and her client in the national media and someone owed her some honesty. I told her about the cheating and the personnel problems and suggested she cut her losses by calling off the Great Falls event. She was disappointed but grateful. The result of my call was that Marie grilled Damian for some specific details when he next called in to give his report. He came back into camp with a full head of steam. "We have a traitor among us," he announced, "and I aim to find out who it is."

"That's not a problem," I said. "I'm the one who called and talked to the PR lady. It seems you've been lying to her. I don't want to have my name associated with such behavior. And I won't be part of a record that involves cheating."

After what seemed like an hour of ranting and raving, Damian declared melodramatically that, by God, this was a maritime expedition and he was captain of the trip. "And under maritime law," he continued, "I have the right to enforce all the rules. What you did is just like mutiny."

I laughed. Damian then threatened to go to his tent and get his rifle. "I know how to make you listen," he said. Although we all had survival knives, Damian had the only gun, which gave him something of an advantage. He was the only one scared enough of the wild animals (and perhaps his fellow travelers) to have brought a gun on the trip. I smiled in disbelief and said, "Don't even think about it." That was the end of the trip for me and Jim.

The next morning, Jim and I assembled every bit of the gear we had acquired for the trip and piled it up next to the campfire, took our personal stuff, said our goodbyes and walked out of the remote riverside camp. We hiked a few miles to the nearest highway and began a 200-mile hitchhike back to Three Forks, Montana, where Jim had left his van.

Jim and I were both very glad to be out of the trip. Incredibly, we had joined a group not only with a leader who was probably mentally ill or at least manic-depressive, but also with a support car driver who was emotionally disturbed. We howled with laughter regularly during the first few days as we relived most of the idiotic behaviors of the whole group. We agreed that in spite of the human foibles we had endured for a few weeks, both of us had relished the sights and sounds of the Missouri River. We thought it would be wonderful to do the whole trip properly, with a good group, and go all the way to New Orleans.

Since we had already cleared our schedules, Jim and I traveled for the next two weeks to various parks and nature preserves. Jim scouted them out for photo opportunities and then we returned to the chosen sites each morning and evening for the best light. Jim took some very professional shots of both flora and fauna, and we had a couple of "too close" grizzly encounters as well. We saw both Glacier National Park and Yellowstone, along with a couple of lesser-known bird sanctuaries. Using ice picks, we were the first ones that spring to climb Mount Reynolds in Glacier Park.

To our astonishment, at the end of two weeks of driving around and camping we saw Damian and his brother and sister driving into Yellowstone as we were leaving. We couldn't miss the two colorful We-no-nah canoes on the roof of the car with the beer logo emblazoned on them. They were playing hooky over 240 miles from where

Figure 2:1 Atop Mount Reynolds, Glacier Park, Montana, June 1988

they were supposed to be at that time—paddling across the 110-mile Peck Reservoir. They never finished their trip.

Global Warming and What to Do about It

My canoeing experience reinforced three important lessons that I have learned and re-learned throughout my life. The first was always to be informed about what you're getting yourself into. The second was to be prepared for the unexpected. And the third was that we live in an incredibly beautiful world. The beauty of the western forests, I found, provoked deep thought. Some time during our driving tour, I told Jim about a disturbing article that had been sent to me by a friend. It discussed the possibility of a phenomenon called "global warming" occurring from the accumulation of actions taken by human beings around the planet. (This must have been one of the earliest published articles about the subject. Of course, "global warming" was later to become a headline phrase all over the world.)

The article suggested that there were four primary gases that were the cause of the potential heating up of the planet. These included chlorofluorocarbons (CFCs), methane, nitrous oxide and carbon dioxide (CO_2). These gases have always existed, at least as long as life on the planet, and are responsible for the wonderful atmosphere that allows life to exist and thrive. But never in recorded history, the article said, had humans done so much to change the ratio of gases and actually harm the planet itself as we had done in the twentieth century.

CFCs had been used for decades in products like spray cans as a propellant gas. Being very light, they floated to the top of our atmosphere, where they were dissolving the fragile ozone layer. The thinning of the ozone layer in turn let more ultraviolet sunlight into the atmosphere, causing dangerous levels of radiation that could sicken and kill animal and plant life and lead to increased instances of skin cancer and other problems for human beings. The other three gases were known to create a thermal blanket in the atmosphere that trapped some of the radiant heat from the sun that normally bounced off into space. This was the "greenhouse" effect. This greenhouse cover had remained fairly constant throughout the ages, but a sudden increase in these emissions could be calamitous.

Nitrous oxide is released as a byproduct of the use of petrochemical fertilizers, a usage that has grown dramatically over the last 50 years. Nitrous oxide, however, accounts for only about 6 percent of the greenhouse problem. Methane, on the other hand, is responsible for about 18 percent of global warming. It is released from the rotting of vegetable matter either in the open air or in a human or animal's digestive tract. One of the biggest existing annual producers of methane on the planet is the combined flatulence of 1.3 billion cows and hundreds of millions of pigs, along with a shocking number of termites (the equivalent of 1,500 pounds per person!). Another potential cause of increasing levels of methane in the atmosphere, scientists speculate, might be the melting and thawing of the tundra. If the polar ice caps and glaciers began to melt as the atmosphere warms, and formerly frozen tundra began to thaw, billions of tons of methane would be released into the atmosphere. This is a problem because the planet has many times more quantities of greenhouse gases stored in biomass than in the atmosphere. Due to its ability to trap more heat than carbon dioxide, methane may have an impact on global warming twenty-five times that of carbon dioxide. Larger amounts of it might be catastrophic.

Carbon dioxide is created when any fossil fuel is burned. That includes the burning of rain forests, and oil and its derivatives, such as gasoline, as well as the natural rotting of biomass. The carbon released combines with two molecules of oxygen to create a more stable compound. One major source of increased CO_2 levels is the absence of the 30 billion carbon dioxide absorbers known as trees that have been removed from North America over the last 300 years. Just like the human skeleton, trees are formed of carbon. Thirty percent of the weight of a person or a tree is carbon. Trees are, therefore, a storehouse—like a safe deposit box—for carbon. It doesn't matter whether the tree is cut down and burned or if it dies naturally and rots. When it is broken down it releases the carbon as a gas into the atmosphere.

It occurred to me in the car with Jim that growing trees would be an easy way to recapture some of the carbon from the atmosphere. I knew that trees breathe in the carbon dioxide and use the carbon to grow, releasing much needed oxygen, a process called the carbon cycle.

A few months before the canoe trip I had been given a copy of the French author Jean Giono's book *The Man Who Planted Trees*. This was a fictional account of a World War I veteran who spent several decades after the war replanting trees in an isolated area of France that had been completely denuded in a battle in the war. As a result of his efforts, whole forests had sprung up, the rivers and creeks had begun to flow again and a multitude of birds and other wildlife had returned to the newly reforested hills. The award-winning book was so inspiring that it moved me to tears.

I pondered the tree-planting idea for several days. I remember thinking, "What if I were to return to Ohio and dedicate my life full-time to planting trees? I'm not committed to anything else at this time anyway." I thought that I could raise money each year to fund the trees and pay myself a salary, and then quietly go out and plant trees on land that had been strip-mined, or along highways, and in people's yards. I calculated that I could probably plant 30,000 tree seedlings per year. In thirty years, if I lasted that long (I was thirty-seven at the time), that would be nearly a million trees.

Quite frankly, even thinking about planting all those trees by myself made my back hurt. There had to be a better way I thought. I felt I had enough skills to recruit a host of volunteers instead, replacing myself a million times over. If I could get each of those individuals to plant one tree every year of their life, then my one million trees could easily be surpassed. This idea appealed to me: Could I do my part to help avert the possible global warming problem by launching a massive volunteer tree-planting project in my hometown? How would I begin?

I started a dialogue with Jim. How much do trees cost? Could I afford to plant ten-foot-tall ball-and-burlap-sized trees? Or should I only plant one- and two-year-old bare-rooted seedlings? Are trees available at wholesale prices in large quantities for such a project? How many trees did a human being use in a lifetime? How many should we try to replace? Who would plant them? Could I use students? Could I get farmers to plant them between their fields, where they had been systematically taking them out for the last fifty years? Did we have room for more trees? How many more? What about reclaimed and abandoned strip-mines or highway corridors or land along roads where they put up snow fences every year? Who could be the volunteers for my project? Who would contribute the money to pay for it?

As you can see, I had a lot of questions. I also knew I would need to get nearly everyone in the community involved and teach them to plant at least one tree every year of their life. I began at first to consider a tree project just in Canton, my hometown, with its population of about 90,000 people. But it wasn't much more effort to consider involving the whole county of 360,000 citizens. What if I distributed 100,000 trees? Or 300,000 trees? What if I did it for five years, or ten years?

By the time I returned to Canton, I had one of the best suntans of my life, some fond and not-so-fond memories of the aborted canoe trip and a few of the best pictures of me ever taken. I also had a pretty well-thought-out project idea and a detailed list of questions about running a community tree project. I now needed a forester to answer them.

Finding the Trees to Give

The first person I called about the tree project was a forester who worked for the state. He confirmed to me that trees were readily available at wholesale prices from both private growers and from the two Ohio state nurseries. Not only that, he said, but the seedlings were affordable. The costs that year were seven cents for pines and nine cents for most hardwoods in quantities over a thousand. That made me happy. I never expected them to be so cheap.

The news wasn't all good, however. First, there were no free trees available from any state agency to give away to anyone. Second, he was pessimistic about my project. "It's a complete waste of time and money to give tree seedlings to kids," he told me. Except for the potential educational value of such a distribution to schools, he felt that trees for school kids were unlikely to make it home and, if they did, were unlikely to be planted. Any trees that did get planted, he thought, were unlikely to be cared for enough to have a real chance for survival. He suggested that farmers would have the best chance because they were trained in agriculture, and that I should target my distribution to farmers or to people or groups trained in forestry or horticulture—or just use professional foresters.

Something about what the forester said didn't seem right to me. His comments flew in the face of my personal experiences. When I was about fourteen, after seeing the beautiful landscaping on golf courses while caddying for my father, I had gone to a field around the oil refinery near my house and had dug up two maples and an ash sapling. I had carried them bare-rooted back to the house and plant-ed them. The maples had taken off right away. The ash experienced a setback when my brother mowed the top of it off, but I fenced it in and soon it was growing as well. Within a few years, the trees were a beautiful addition to our front yard. I had no idea what I was doing, and no guidance, but it worked. I trusted students, with some guid-ance, to do as well.

I then asked the forester what he thought about my idea of run-ning a massive reforestation project in my county involving millions of trees.

"It isn't possible," he replied.

"Why not?"

"Because no one has ever done it before."

The next forester I consulted hated my use of the term "citizen forester" for all of my student and adult volunteers. He told me in no uncertain terms that a private citizen was *not* a forester. The term "forester," he insisted, should be reserved for those who are specifi-cally trained in the field. It should be held sacred. Those most trained and tested were "certified foresters." Using the term with untrained private citizens, he continued, would cause confusion with the public and somehow weaken the importance of and need for professional foresters.

I thought the distinction was ridiculous. In today's America we have accountants and certified public accountants, financial planners and certified financial planners. The public knows that there is obviously a difference. But I thought that inviting every citizen to be a volunteer forester and giving them some education around that activity might later lead some of them to become professional foresters. I just might be creating future foresters. The forester's professional jealousy struck me as misplaced.

If we hired professional foresters to do the project, the labor would become the largest project cost and we wouldn't have enough public land to plant massive numbers of trees on. I realized that giving away free trees to private citizens would eliminate both the labor cost and the problem of limited land. Every recipient would donate their own labor and yard space for the trees. I decided on the spot, therefore, that henceforth foresters would be used exclusively for their professional technical advice about trees. I decided to take all foresters' forestry advice, but not to listen to their other ideas or naysaying.

After talking with and visiting nurseries to get firm prices, I finally created a budget for my program. It was an eleven-year budget totaling about $270,000, a very manageable community project. My original thinking was that I would plant 300,000 trees every year for ten years, totaling three million trees. However, to make the transition smoother, I projected a start-up with 100,000 trees in year one, increasing to 200,000 in year two, then leveling off at 300,000 per year from years three to eleven.

Thinking Big and Preparing the Ground
Offering a massive tree planting was evidently only the first unique aspect of my environmental project.

In 1988, a large tree project was one that had planted 250 to 500 trees. Projects planting 500 to 1,000 large trees in urban areas were receiving national awards and recognition. Launching a project involving over 5,000 trees, not to mention 100,000 or three million trees, was, at that time, unthinkable, even with seedlings. Most of the people I spoke to couldn't quite wrap their minds around the number "three million." But it always got their attention.

The second unique aspect was that I had decided to give every tree away for free. Granted, the trees would not be free to me; I had to raise the money and buy them. After researching what was already being done to promote tree planting, I learned that there were already several tree programs in place. First, municipal tree commissions existed to plant large trees along streets and in parks in over 300 cities and villages in Ohio, most with fully developed written forestry plans. Ohio leads the nation in such urban forestry activities. However, Canton was not one of the Tree Cities.

Second, the landscape business thrived on planting large trees in yards, mostly the front and side yards. Third, seedlings were already being sold each spring by the state and through county agencies to farmers and other individuals. However, even with all these opportunities, there was no massive rush for whole populations to quickly reforest their land. In fact, in urban and suburban areas, there was an increasing net loss of trees occurring each year. Nationwide, only one out of every four trees removed in urban areas was being replaced.

What was missing was a program to offer backyard trees. I felt that giving away free trees was the optimal way to quickly involve the maximum number of people. I also liked the rhyming sound of "free trees." It was catchy and memorable, and I proceeded to put together the project on this basis, knowing full well that there were never any actual free trees. I had to buy them all, then give them away.

My next task was to write the project up and begin to attach to the proposal various necessary components, or "exhibits." The advisory committee list was to be Exhibit A.

My degree is in finance, not forestry. I needed to bring together tree experts to tell me what species of trees should be purchased for the project. As I soon discovered, however, foresters are like economists—if you get three or more together they will all disagree with each other. But I knew that if I somehow left out even one tree expert in our county, that individual would rear his or her head and publicly become my critic at a later date. I therefore set out to recruit every tree expert I could find to be on my first advisory committee.

I started with the park directors of every community. I did this because the public thinks that every park director is the local expert on trees; after all, they are in charge of the local parks. The truth is that they are not usually particularly knowledgeable about trees. Park directors have mostly become experts on mowing grass and managing people, and they, too, use professional foresters for their tough decisions on trees. Nevertheless, I knew I needed every one of them on my board. As it turned out, after the first two agreed to join, it was easy to sign up the rest. I then sought out professors from the area colleges and universities with degrees in botany or biology, and added two more members to the advisory committee. Then I added both the state urban forester and service (rural) forester for the area I was targeting.

One particular member was a real find. Dr. Charles McClaugherty, a professor of biology at Mt. Union College in Alliance, had his Ph.D. in forestry. He became a close friend and a supporter of my program, serving as Board Chair for our nonprofit organization for over fourteen years.

I asked the group to meet twice. At the first meeting, I deliberately didn't ask the group to decide whether I should buy and distribute trees. Instead, I told them that the project was decided upon already and the number of trees had been set at three million. The board, I said, had the critical task of choosing which species of trees and how many of each should be distributed. I told the board that their decisions would have an influence on the future of our county for both human beings and wildlife. My guidelines were that the trees should preferably be native to the area and needed to be available as one- or two-year-old seedlings at less than 25 cents apiece. By the second meeting the group had decided on about twenty species, with the breakdown being that 70 percent of the trees would be deciduous (leafy hardwoods) and 30 percent coniferous (pines and spruces). The advisory board list became my Exhibit A of the project outline.

Figure 2:2 Rotary Club logo

The eleven years of annual tree goals by quantity was Exhibit B, and the detailed list of each species with its totals was Exhibit C.

Meanwhile, I asked the mayor of every major city or village in the county and the county commissioners to write me a letter of support. Of course, the mayors usually asked me what the park director thought of the idea, and I was able to reassure them that their park director, and in fact every park director in the county, was on my advisory committee and had already chosen the trees to distribute. I got seven mayors and the commissioners to write letters. Those letters became my Exhibit D.

Next, I called every one of the twenty school districts in the county and spoke to either the superintendent or the assistant superintendent. I was able to get a promise either orally or in writing that the schools would participate if the project was funded. I had to promise to deliver the trees along with the packaging materials to every building, since they felt that there was not enough staff in each building to send someone out to pick up the trees. The list of participating school districts became Exhibit E.

In January 1989 I set about organizing the funding of the project. The overall budget was Exhibit F. I broke both the funding and the tree distribution down into smaller, more manageable projects, each with its own chairperson. Then I had a target for funding and manpower. As befitting a former Rotarian, my idea was to build a foundation for annual funding support by enlisting all thirteen International Rotary clubs in the county for the whole eleven years of the program.

Rotary is a community group comprised of owners and managers of businesses who meet weekly and run several civic projects every year. Some of the projects raise money and some of them always lose money, by design; the winners help to pay for the losers. The largest Rotary club in Stark County was the Canton Rotary. I knew that if I could enlist the support of its nearly 350 members, the other dozen groups would probably come on board with me as well.

The first person I talked to was Canton Rotarian Dave Ewing. Dave is a third-generation Chevrolet dealer with Ewing Chevrolet. He was a former Rotary Club President and was soon to be a Rotary District Governor. He liked the project but wasn't sure the clubs would work together. He referred me to Joe Ginther, the current Rotary District Governor. Joe and Dave helped me to get the contact names for all the clubs and to understand their relative sizes. Some were big enough for me to ask for and expect contributions of thousands of dollars; others could only be expected to give $100 or $500 per year. I developed a $10-per-member rule of thumb as a reasonable annual funding request. For some clubs, even that was a lot to ask. I used this information to create a budget for the relative contributions from each of the Rotary clubs based on their size and then calculated the balance of support I needed from individual and corporate donors.

Joe Ginther then had me meet with Joe Benner, a local insurance agency owner who was the Environmental Chair for Canton Rotary that year. I showed him the project and he liked it. Like most successful projects, it was a win-win situation. I would get my project funding, the community would get something free and Rotary would get credit for giving away the free trees.

I needed Canton Rotary to buy into the program first. I decided that the Massillon Rotary Club, the second largest in the county, would be my final request. Massillon was always extremely serious about competing with the Canton Club and was shaping up to be a hard sell. Being a smaller town than Canton (30,000 versus 90,000), Massillon was painfully aware of its place in the county. Canton and Massillon high schools have had the longest football rivalry (over a century) in the history of the sport. I was told that Massillon often came up short in district Rotary competitions against Canton and did-n't like it. They would look warily at any proposed partnership with Canton. I therefore figured that once every other club in the county was on board, Massillon would have a hard time saying no.

This is the secret of Rotary funding: The Rotary fiscal year runs from July 1 to June 30. Each Rotary Club's incoming president is elect-ed before the end of the calendar year. The president spends the first half of the year before taking office deciding exactly how she or he will run the club during his or her tenure. By the president's first day in office, the budget for the whole year is presented and approved. In a club the size of Canton's, it is not uncommon to have an annual budg-et of over $200,000. Smaller clubs may only have a $10,000 budget.

The problem I had was that it was already January and I was com-ing in during the middle of the fiscal year to request a donation. The Canton Environmental Committee did not have enough funds remaining in its budget to fully fund my request for $5,000. Therefore, Joe and Dave systematically approached other members of the board who chaired the various avenues of service and asked them each to consider how much they could cut loose to give to the envi-ronmental committee to run this project.

I was called to be present when the Canton Rotary Board voted on the project idea. My presentation was short and followed the proj-ect outline. The questions were predictable.

"Well, what does the park director think about this idea? He's our local tree expert." One would have thought that I had put that board member up to asking that question.

"Great question. If you look at Exhibit A," I said, "you will see that the park director is on the advisory committee I formed. In fact, every park director in the county agreed to serve on the committee. If you look at Exhibit B," I continued, "you will see our tree goals for the eleven-year period, and in Exhibit C the detailed list of tree species and quantities decided upon by the advisory committee."

"Well, what does our mayor think about distributing trees in the city?" asked another person.

"If you look at Exhibit D, you will find a letter from the mayor stating that he thinks it will be great for the community. And if you look at the rest of the letters, you will see that nearly every mayor in the county has written their support as well."

"Well, how do we know that if we fund the project the schools would even be willing to participate?"

I could have hugged him.

"If you turn to Exhibit E, you will find a list of the school districts that have agreed to participate. It basically includes every district in the county and some of the adjacent townships in neighboring counties. That's because the school districts don't honor county lines."

There was silence around the table. The president finally spoke. "Well, you clearly have answered all of our questions and doubts. Now the question is: Do we have enough funds available to support your request? Let's hear from the environmental chair."

Trouble. The environmental chair said that he had only $1,500 available for the rest of the fiscal year. What about the other stakeholders around the table? As the president systematically went around the circle, each chair of the various avenues of service, such as Club Service, Community Service, International Service (which handles the well-known student exchange programs) etc. offered to give up some of their department's budgeted money to help out.

I was stunned. This seemed to me an unprecedented action. Here were individuals actually giving up a part of their turf, their hard-bargained-for, carefully debated and budgeted dollars that they controlled. They were happily giving them over to the Environmental Chair to accomplish my project. I was deeply moved by the unselfishness on display. The $5,000 was raised. Canton Rotary agreed to support the program that spring, and, while they could not make a commitment for the future club administrations, they told me I was welcome to resubmit an updated proposal for consideration each year. I have nothing but gratitude to Dave Ewing and Joe Ginther for all their contacts that brought this miracle about.

After Canton said yes, it was fairly easy to walk the project through the eleven smaller clubs around the county. I signed them all

Figure 2:3 Canton Rotarians Dennis Saunier and Joe Benner celebrate their new "free tree" project in 1989.

up and got money from everyone. The next approach was to the Massillon Rotary Board of Directors. Not surprisingly they asked the same questions:

"What does the park director think about it?"

"What does the mayor think of the project?"

"How do we know the schools will participate?"

The results were the same. Massillon joined in. A new first! For the first time in their eighty-year history, the thirteen Rotary Clubs of Stark County had all agreed to work together on the same community project. The truth is that they never really had to work with each other; each of them just had to work with me. I then had the foundation of a project, most of the funding and a network of experienced volunteers to run a massive tree distribution and delivery.

After the first-year project ended, I went back to each of the thirteen local Rotary Clubs to speak and show them what we had accomplished. With the help of graphic artist Janet Kullman, we created a four-panel display of over fifty-seven media articles that ran on the program in just four months in our twelve daily and weekly papers. It was four feet tall and twelve feet wide on yellow foam board. The actual newspaper articles were copied on white paper and framed on a green background across the panels in chronological order. With a bright yellow marker I highlighted every headline and every paragraph that mentioned Rotary. It was clear at a glance that the Stark Free Tree Program was the best public relations conceivable for Rotary. No one could have afforded to buy all of the free press we had received.

Before one of my follow-up lectures, Alliance Rotary Tree Chair Paul Froman spoke briefly about my project, then introduced a fellow Rotarian whose job it was to introduce me as that week's luncheon speaker. That Rotarian, a veterinarian, began his introduction quietly and solemnly: "I cannot really say too much about the 'free tree' project and whether it will ultimately be of great benefit to our community. And I really cannot say too much about whether we have begun to make a difference in the potential problem of global warming. However, as a veterinarian, I can say this with certainty about David's tree project: We sure have made a lot of dogs happy!"

Figure 3:1 My twin Debbie (right) and me

Figure 3:2 Debbie and me at four years old, 1955

3: From Darkness into Light

EVEN TWO YEARS before joining the Army, I sincerely believed that I was meant to die in Viet Nam. Obviously I lived, but I was forever changed by that belief. Once you know this story about me, and its ramifications, then you will know everything there is to know about who I am, why I aspire to do what I do and why I am grateful for each new day. But let me start a bit further back in my life to put my story into perspective.

While I didn't know it until I was about fourteen, I grew up in a poor family. I found out how poor our family was when a kind science teacher, Mrs. Diamond, took my twin sister Debbie and me home for lunch at the end of our ninth grade school year. She liked the idea of twins. I had never been in an apartment before or seen wall-to-wall carpeting or a picture window with a view of a lake. That was my first inkling that everyone didn't live at the same economic level. I felt naive. Our big linoleum and bare-floored house on Bellflower seemed pretty stark after that. But we weren't among the poorest of the poor. Indeed, my father's father was poorer. A former railroader, for the last two decades of his life he was essentially confined to his couch with a bad heart, and for many years his family was destitute. In the first years of my parents' marriage, following my father's return from World War II, they moved back in with my father's parents several times to help pay bills for both families.

When my twin sister and I were conceived, my family lived on Gross Avenue NE in Canton. But after six months of a pregnancy fraught with problems, my mother was assigned to strict bed rest and told not to climb stairs or lift anything. She moved back into her parents' one-story home on Bellflower SW along with her second child, my brother Douglas. My father, meanwhile, moved back into Warner NE with his parents and my oldest sister, Darlene. After our births, my parents moved into a housing project on Seventh Street SW off West Tuscarawas. Today those old project homes are the site of Canton Center Mall.

My twin, Deborah, was born forty-eight minutes before me. We slept in dresser drawers the first few months of our lives. My brother Douglas was only eleven months older than we were, so my parents had three sets of diapers to take care of all at the same time. Three years after Debbie and I were born came my youngest sister, Denise. The five D's.

I am convinced that my soul was not entirely fixed in my child's body in this world until I was about fifteen. I feel that I was only about half here in my early years, since, although I have a few memories of early childhood that are crystal clear, there are large gaps of time where I seemed to have run on auto-pilot. I remember as a child feeling a clear sense of a big space inside me some of the time. It must take some of us longer to settle in on this planet than it does others. However, the childhood that I do remember was mainly happy and active. I enjoyed baseball and wrestling, and took up judo and karate at the Canton Police Boys Club as I entered my teens. I was perhaps a typical boy, fishing, playing baseball, getting into a few fights and narrowly avoiding others. I got my nose broken twice, and it leans to the right to this day. It used to go the other way.

Our family may have been poor, but our neighborhood was close-knit. Unlike today, when we seldom know our neighbors, everyone knew each other. We sometimes fought, but we also helped each other out. We knew who could be depended on in the event of a crisis. Bags of homegrown vegetables arrived regularly in return for favors my dad did for others.

Preparation for Viet Nam

One thing that has stood me in good stead in my life has been my awareness of danger and my ability to cope with stressful and physically distressing situations. I learned the importance of this firsthand when I was about thirteen.

It was an ordinary summer day in 1964, with nothing much going on. Suddenly, I heard the loud crash of what sounded like cars smashing into each other. Along with several other neighborhood boys, my brother and I ran several blocks to the crash site on Navarre Road and 21st Street SW. The sheriff and ambulances were just arriving. Apparently a convertible with teens in it had run head on into a heavy truck from a local crane company. The shaken truck driver had a bloody head and was walking around in a daze. The convertible, if it was a convertible, was severely damaged. There were two boys dead in the front seats, one without his head. A third boy in the back had been pinned under the driver's seat, his dead body mangled by the force of the crash. Beer cans were all over the place. I was told the car had sideswiped people for several miles before going under the front of the truck. Looking at the young men, I wondered who they were and what their parents would feel. I felt the utter waste of their lives, taken in a careless moment.

The two ambulance attendants put the kids from the front onto their gurneys and rolled them to their vans. An attendant brought out a stretcher for the third, and I offered to help. The attendant picked up his end first, however, and a large puddle of blood and brain rolled off the stretcher between my feet. I gagged, nearly throwing up on the dead body. My brother stepped in and carried our end of the stretcher. Welcome to the real world, David, I thought.

Ever since then, I have often been the first on the scene of car wrecks and other messy incidents: rear-end collisions, railroad suicides, a kid on a bike pinned under a car, the smell of burned bodies. It was around that time that my mother asked me to clean up for a neighbor who had been rushed to the hospital with a bleeding ulcer. His wife was with him and he had vomited blood all over his porch. My twin sister babysat the kids while I cleaned up the mess. These experiences provided me with a vivid introduction to the fragility and preciousness of life, and instilled in me a sense that it was worth protecting and confronting, even if you were exposed to some very unpleasant scenes. You never get used to the violent loss of human life, but you learn how to handle it.

Without a doubt, the most influential activity I engaged in during my high school years was not at school but in an extra-curricular activity—Junior Achievement (JA). JA teaches students how to start and run their own business. Guided by real business leaders, the students actually incorporate, sell stock, create and sell a product, then liquidate by the end of their school year, showing either a profit or loss. For me, JA was both educational and a great social outlet.

While the program was officially available only to juniors and seniors, I joined JA my sophomore year and stayed with it for three years. I served as my company president for the last two years and was a delegate to the JA national conference twice. JA taught me how to speak in a group, how to lead a business meeting, how to manage fellow workers in both an office and a manufacturing section, and the ins and outs of the structure of corporate America. I have used the skills learned in that activity hundreds of times since.

Today JA volunteers actually go into schools and offer practical business curricula to grades K to 12. In the upper grades, students still have a chance to run a business. I recommend JA to every student activist. You have to understand the system in order to change it, and JA offers a hands-on way to understand capitalism.

Starting in my sophomore year in high school, I became keenly aware of the war in Viet Nam. By 1966, the war had become a vivid nightly news drama—Walter Cronkite in living (and dying) color. After years of obeying early-to-bed orders from my parents, I felt empowered to ask for permission to stay up to watch the graphic news of the war at 11 p.m. Before I began watching the news, I had never paid attention to anything but my own small circle of events in Canton. Watching the evening news, however, broadened my awareness not only of the war but also of our country and the world. Suddenly, I wanted to understand everything.

Unless the war ended suddenly, I knew that I would be going to see action. My family has a short but strong and patriotic history of military service and discipline. My father went through five Pacific invasions in the Navy in World War II, while my favorite uncle, Lynn, spent a career in the Army, including service in WWII, Korea and Viet Nam, rising through every enlisted rank, receiving a field promotion in Korea to Lieutenant, then retiring as a Colonel. My brother, six first cousins and I obediently went into the military. Six of us were sent to Viet Nam.

I was brought up on lessons and anecdotes from military service and I enjoyed them. I love this country and fully believed then (as I do today) that it is not unreasonable to ask every able-bodied man and woman to give up two years to serve the needs of the nation. I do, however, think there should be well-respected alternatives for a nonviolent means of fulfilling that service for those who do not want to face the possibility of hurting someone or being hurt. However, back then I never considered becoming a conscientious objector as a viable possibility for me, and I didn't want to flee to Canada to avoid the draft. Instead, I saw military service as my duty and its subsequent financial reward (as written in the GI Bill) as my only means to get to college. No one else had offered to pay for my education, and I was determined to be the first one in my immediate family to get through college, whatever the cost—even if it meant risking my life.

My only remaining choice was to decide which branch of the military to enter. Making no choice would result in being drafted, which in the mid-1960s meant you entered either the Army or the Marines, usually directly into the infantry, for two years. As an alterative you could join the Navy or Air Force for four years or enlist in the Army for three years. By enlisting, you got to sit with a recruiter and try to make a choice of which job specialty you would train in. The recruiters didn't always tell the truth, but draftees had to take what they were assigned.

When I graduated high school in 1969, the lottery for the draft drew my birth-date as number forty-three. Since the Selective Service System was expected to draft over two hundred birthdays into the service that year, I was going into the military one way or another. I therefore opted for the Army, thinking that four years in the Navy or Air Force seemed too long a commitment, even if they were safer. I figured that I would be killed for sure in the Marines. With the Army, if I could pick my job and possibly stay out of the infantry, I might at least have a chance to make it through alive. Viet Nam was inevitable, and I knew it might be bad. My brother, Doug, one year ahead of me, had already joined the Marines and was sent to Viet Nam immediately after infantry training, before I graduated from high school. I joined the Army in November of the year I graduated, having worked through the summer in a forging shop.

I'm not sure exactly when I began to feel like I might die in Viet Nam, although I believe it was sometime in my junior year of high school. The more I learned about Viet Nam, the more I felt a low-level dread build up in me. When I was about sixteen, the fear suddenly crystallized in me one night. I woke up in the middle of the night with a start. All I could understand in that moment was the sense that my fate was coming to meet me head on, and I would not be able to control it in any way. The more I had learned about our role in Viet Nam, the more I knew that it would be hard to stay out of any fighting. First, there was no real front line. Second, I knew I couldn't keep my self-respect if I hid out in a relatively safe job on a large base somewhere. Knowing that about myself, it seemed that my chances at seeing action were going to be somewhat higher than most.

Looking back, it's clear to me that this nagging awareness of the possibility of death affected all of my personal relationships. It colored my entire dating life in high school. The only girl I really adored and had actually wooed for two years in high school developed cancer and died suddenly when I was a senior and she was a junior. First she lost a leg, then her life. I had been hopeful of developing a more

Figure 3:3 High school graduation photo, 1969

Figure 3:5 Basic Recruit, 1969

meaningful relationship with her after I got out of the military. Stunned, I became more emotionally aloof. I watched other guys my age getting very passionately involved in relationships and professing their undying love to their girlfriends, all the while knowing they, too, would be going off to war. I swore that I would not let myself get into that same predicament. I reasoned that it would be harder for me to do my duty with the additional worry of a wife or fiancée at home. Besides, leaving for war would be a cruel fate to offer someone you loved. While I dated casually, I resolved to make no commitments until I returned—if I did. It cost me a couple of potential loves, who went on to marry friends, but I feel even today that it was the best thing to do.

I graduated from high school in 1969. In November, I went to Army basic training in Kentucky. While I was training, the last girl I dated before joining the service sent me a "Dear John" letter. It hurt, but I figured it was all for the best. I sheepishly tacked it on a bulletin board with all the other, similar letters received by guys in my unit. We all let go of our close ties together.

While my recruiter promised I would get to fly on helicopters, my advanced training was as an aviation hydraulics repairman in Virginia and Oklahoma. I assumed I would probably end up in a helicopter unit. During my training I had a rather intense encounter with a sour-faced, mule-headed National Guard trainee from Missouri. He had about fifty pounds on me, and had obviously not heard about the wrestling reputation I had built up through high school. Our tense relationship added some entertainment for the others in my unit during the last few weeks of training. I ended up with a sore jaw and a greater appreciation for large fists connected to small minds. It was again clear to me that fisticuffs did not resolve differences; winning or losing a fistfight did not make one side suddenly agree with the other.

Having gained some very good test scores and demonstrated proven leadership ability, I was put into an accelerated program for advancement. (It seemed that sergeants were dying too fast in Viet Nam.) I went to a special leadership school and became a Specialist

Fifth Class (a Spec-5 was a buck-sergeant equivalent) just eight and a half months into my Army service. It usually took four to six years to get promoted to E-5.

The training was blunt. We learned to fire every weapon, including the enemy's, and to lead squads in combat. The trainers told us we were likely to be cannon (actually rocket and mortar) fodder. The training helped to further insulate our emotions from both killing and being killed. What I learned in leadership school offered nothing to dissuade me from my fatalistic attitude. Therefore, I trained intensely, as if my life depended on it, which indeed it did. Even so, I had a fairly sunny disposition, certainly sunnier than most of the draftees around me. I was considered RA, regular army, which means that I was an enlistee. Most men whom I served with were called US, meaning they were ordered to serve. It may not have seemed like much of a difference, but it had a tremendous psychological impact on the soldiers. As an enlistee, I had taken an active role in deciding my fate; I had volunteered, and was therefore more content with my time in the service. Others who had been drafted had very negative attitudes.

In spite of my sense of dread, I wasn't really afraid to go to Viet Nam. I didn't even bear a grudge about being chosen. In a strange way, I thought the whole exercise of going to war was "interesting." My greatest worry was that I would not be able to handle my job under fire when the time came. Viet Nam in particular interested me, and I looked forward to experiencing an Asian culture. I had resigned myself to being offered up to what I came to call the "God of the Statistics of Mortality." It seemed that about five percent of American soldiers were likely to become casualties, and sergeants and lieutenants were one of the highest-risk categories. I decided to do my part but keep my head down. Beyond that, I reasoned, my fate was entirely out of my hands.

During my first year in the Army, I was recruited for Army Security Agency and investigated for and given top-secret crypto-security clearance. I heard back from my family that quite a few of our neighbors and family friends asked my father what I was up to because the FBI had visited them to ask questions about my background. Evidently the unit I was headed for was highly classified. Its passive, secondary electronic mission involved flying aircrafts daily to listen to enemy radio transmissions, record them and send them back to the National Security Agency in the United States for decryption. Our government knew a lot about what was going on in Viet Nam. The active, primary electronic mission of that unit was so secret that it was never used in Viet Nam.

Settling in "The Nam"
On arriving in Viet Nam in December 1970, I was assigned to the First Radio Research Group on the peninsula at Cam Ranh Bay. During my first night in-country, just hours after I arrived at a receiving center, sappers attacked the army unit. The front gate guard was killed by a rocket-propelled grenade, and all three infiltrators were killed after blowing up a few things. I spent the night in a bunker with the other new arrivals, without even a weapon having been issued to me. I swore that I would never again be caught empty-handed in such a situation.

Our unit flew old post–Korean War Navy submarine surveillance planes called RP-2E Neptunes. A squadron of P-2s had already been used in Viet Nam in the mid-sixties to interdict the huge supply line of small boats being used to ship supplies from North Viet Nam to the south down the coast. These interdictions forced the North to develop the complex Ho Chi Minh trail in the jungles of Laos and Cambodia as a supply route instead.

Technically, our P-2s had already been retired into storage in Arizona, replaced by the newer P-3s. The old Navy planes, however, had been taken out of mothballs and refitted with radio gear because the Army didn't have a big enough plane to fit the eleven men required for this special mission.

After a short walkabout on my first day on the flight line, I discovered that we had too many hydraulics repairmen and a shortage of plane captains. That was the Navy's equivalent of an Army crew chief. Thinking the war would be over sooner, the Army had stopped training replacements. I asked the company First Sergeant to let me

Figure 3:4 Cam Ranh Bay Air Force Base, Viet Nam

Figure 3:5 A RP-2E Neptune used by Army Security Agency

and another recent arrival and friend, Jim Dudley, train on the job to be plane captains. Since it took one year of study in California to learn that job, we were both laughed out of the office. The next day, however, we were called back in and given permission to train ourselves for one month and then be tested. We studied together, literally memorizing a thick flight manual. Within the month, we were given our new job titles and began flying missions right away. We later ended up training several others to work at the same job as they were needed. Eventually, we received our flight status and extra pay.

By my records, I flew over 1,500 hours of both training flights and combat intelligence missions in fourteen months with that unit. We were shot at on most of the missions, usually with anti-aircraft fire. In spite of what the anti-aircraft fire could do to us, the tracers it made were beautiful to watch in the night sky. Tracers came up in three red lines, went dark for an instant, then burst in huge orange-red balls of fire. In addition to regular missions, we flew in-country pilot training flights and maintenance trips to Japan, the Philippines, Okinawa and Taiwan. During my first year, I also went to both Thailand and Australia for a week of rest and relaxation. Every day out-of-country was cherished.

The first time I was shot at by incoming rockets on the ground I was extremely scared. No one had ever explained how phenomenally loud the explosions would be, nor had anyone ever told me how the air would literally split from a rocket explosion, and how a shock wave hit you like a sledgehammer, shaking you to the very core. When the shock wave hit me the first time, I hugged the ground and tried to recover from the sensory overload.

The second time I came under fire, I became angry. I remember thinking, "These people are actually trying to kill me." I wanted to shoot back at someone, anyone. But you can't shoot back at rockets; we had artillery and mortar crews and gunships for that.

By my third rocket attack, I had it figured out; there was no need to panic. By the time you heard the rocket going overhead (a *shh shh shh* sound), you knew that one wasn't going to hit you but was after someone else farther away. It was the rockets you didn't hear that would hurt you; they were coming in right on your head. If *that* was going to happen, I thought, what good would worrying do? I knew I simply had to hit the dirt at the first sound of the rocket coming in and hope for the best.

I reasoned also that there was no need for anger. I had concluded that the enemy fire was not personal, even though it felt that way. An enemy soldier was simply shooting at another enemy soldier: country against country, uniform against uniform, number against number. Special forces excepted, war for us regular soldiers was very impersonal—even if we saw the enemy. It was a comforting realization for me to know that no one was out to get David Kidd. This critical knowledge that most attacks aren't personal has served me well in every individual and community activist confrontation.

Within months of my arrival in Viet Nam, I developed a kind of "serenity under fire" that I had seen in more senior veterans. Nevertheless, the thought of dying still made me afraid.

Situational Awareness

One interesting effect of being in a war zone is that you develop a heightened sense of awareness. Well before I finished my first year in Viet Nam, I had developed a very keen sense of my personal safety. I call it "situational awareness."

I used my situational awareness to keep myself out of trouble. I also used it to keep track of my men when I was with a group for whom I had been assigned responsibility. It was most clearly needed when our base was upgraded from green to red alert. A few months after my arrival, I had volunteered to be in charge of our reaction squad. Having learned from my first day in Viet Nam, I didn't ever want to be without a weapon when the action started.

Even in moments that seemed calm, being in Viet Nam made us acutely aware of minutely small movements that could make a difference between life and death. You could bend down to tie a shoelace and be missed by a piece of shrapnel that would have killed you had you been standing up straight. It always mattered when you moved around and where you went, twenty-four hours a day. Whether on duty or off, awake or asleep, it paid to be alert.

Even off duty, when I was able to visit a bar or restaurant off-base in a village or town, I would automatically sit away from the front entrance with my back against a wall and a clear view of the front door. I preferred to be near a rear exit. One of the ways Americans got into the worst situations off-base was to be so self-engrossed as to forget where they were. My other rule was to never get so drunk or stoned that I wouldn't be able to react swiftly. Trouble usually came in the front door and came in fast; those with heightened awareness were the ones who stayed alive. This sense has never left me. I still sit with my back to a wall and with my eyes on the crowd.

In the 1990s, twenty years after returning from the war, I went with my girlfriend Kelly to a local restaurant in Jackson Township, Ohio. The restaurant was in an upscale area and trouble was practically unheard of. I looked around as we sat down and turned to Kelly.

"There's going to be a fight in here tonight," I said.

"That's ridiculous. There's never a fight in here," responded a woman sitting next to me.

We ordered drinks. Within five minutes a fight erupted at the left end of the bar. I watched as two bartenders climbed over the bar to try to break it up while another went to the phone. I stood up and said to both women, "Excuse me for a few minutes, but I think I need to help." The stranger warned me to stay out of it, lest I get hurt.

I went around the bar and saw that a short but rough-looking biker was standing at the bottom of some steps, holding a chair over his head, yelling and threatening. He wore a T-shirt and his jeans were tucked inside his leather riding boots. His larger but more sober buddy was behind him. I figured that they both had weapons handy in their boots. In front of the short biker were the two bartenders with open hands raised to stop him, something neither of them manifestly knew how to do, since neither fighting nor bouncing were in their job descriptions. Behind them, up the steps was a tall, lanky man who seemed to be the object of the attack. He looked lost.

I walked over to the lanky man and gently pulled him back up against the bar. He was the son of a local builder.

"Stay right here," I said. "This fight is over for you."

"I lost my glasses," he replied.

I picked the man's glasses off the steps and returned them to him. The smaller man had evidently thrown some coins at him, hitting him in the head, deliberately picking a fight. He had then turned and jumped on his attacker. They had both fallen down three steps to the dining area.

The biker then dropped his chair and pushed through the bartenders. I could tell that he was blind drunk and would remember nothing about this the next day. I turned my back to the biker and stood in front of his victim. He reached over my back and tried to punch the tall man over my left shoulder several times, missing. Another lefty, I thought. I backed against him then turned around and gave him a gentle bear hug. He started to resist me, so I spoke into his ear: "I'm your friend. You can't do this anymore. This is Jackson Township. You can't fight here. The police are on the way. We have about two minutes to get you out of here or you're going to jail tonight."

I turned to his friend, who was starting to move toward me, and asked him to help me take the guy outside before the cops arrived. He looked relieved. Both of us put our arms around the biker's shoulders and walked him briskly toward the door, even though he was yelling and gesturing and still wanted to fight someone. Once outside, we loaded him face down into the back of their car. By this time, the biker was co-operating. As they drove out the side exit, the cops arrived at the front of the restaurant.

When I returned to the bar and sat down the woman next to us turned to Kelly. "Does he do this all the time?" she asked. She nodded that, yes, indeed, I did.

That was situational awareness; and it earned me a free drink from the tall guy's brother.

Figure 3:7 Photographer

Figure 3:8 Photographed, Saigon, 1971

Gifu, Japan

In September 1971, I was sent on a trip from Nam to Japan to pick up an aircraft that had been repaired. Gifu was an exotic rural community where the ancient emperors had traditionally gone duck hunting. While roaming the streets of Gifu at night with several other enlisted men looking for our next entertainment hot spot (and finding few), we passed a gray-haired, grizzly older man leaning casually against a wall. He had a long, wispy chin-beard and spoke softly to us as we passed: "Tell fortune, ten dollars." No one else paid him any attention. It was as if they hadn't even seen him.

I, however, stopped in my tracks. I immediately hollered to the others that I would meet them later and turned to the old man. "I will be happy to have you tell me my fortune," I said. He was my first fortune-teller, and I was curious.

The old man smiled and took my hand. After a half a minute or so, he looked up at me and stepped back half a step, straightening.

"You go to Viet Nam?" That required no great genius, I thought. My colleagues and I were in uniform.

"I am stationed there now," I replied, "and I am going back tomorrow."

"Hmm," continued the old man. "You have a very unusual hand. It says you have two choices. If you go back to the war, maybe you will die soon." Immediately I was sober and he had my attention. This was my wake-up call number one. "But," he continued, "if you decide to live, you will have the chance to reach Nirvana in this lifetime. This is very unusual. You understand?" His eyes were compassionate.

I told him I got it. I knew that Nirvana was some kind of Eastern enlightened state. He told me about some other less important things, which I've forgotten. The reading was only a few minutes, but it was very provocative for me. It was ten dollars well spent. I didn't join the others later as I had promised, but went back to my hotel room and thought deeply about what was said. I had a choice, he said. What kind of choice? I prayed silently, trying to understand.

Cholon, Saigon, Viet Nam

By October 1971, two years into the service, I had learned that with a clipboard and an attitude you can just about get away with anything in the Army. After all, it had already worked for me many times. On a couple of occasions while in Cam Ranh I had sneaked a C-130 flight to Saigon, where I took my own three-day in-country break. For that I typed my own orders, simply deleting the third copy that would end up returning to my company. Friends covered for me in my absence. The senior NCOs (Non-Commissioned Officers) thought I was being noble for volunteering to be CQ (Charge of Quarters) and sitting in the company headquarters all night monitoring the radio and holding down the fort! They didn't know I could type.

It was during this time that I received another wake-up call. I was visiting Mark, an old school-friend from Canton, at Ton Son Nutt, the Air Force base in Saigon. He took me to visit a local bar downtown. While I was drinking, I befriended a local woman called Mai, who decided to give me a Tarot card reading using a regular deck. I cut the deck and the first card I cut to was the Ace of Spades. Mai started to cry, loudly. One of her friends told me that Mai had had an Army boyfriend who had drawn the Ace of Spades, which is the card of death. He had died the following week on a mission. Mai was fearful I would die soon as well.

I was instantly sober. Wake-up call number two. I could sense the fibers of my fate stretching across the sky like a boundless spider's web, waiting for the right moment to ensnare me. Mai was very attentive to me for a couple of days, and cried when I left. On learning that I would be going home on leave for a month before coming back to Viet Nam for a second tour, she suggested in all seriousness that I go AWOL and not come back at all. However, I knew that my tour at Cam Ranh, although vigorous (I worked full time and flew fourteen-hour missions about every third day), was not bad duty. It was certainly beautiful, since there was a spectacular beach to frequent on the ocean side of the peninsula. The bay side was heavily mined.

The main risk of enemy attack my first year was getting shot at with Anti-Aircraft Artillery (AAA) on most of our missions. We flew

in circles for hours over a radio target area near the Demilitarized
Zone (DMZ) and would usually simply move our circle over a bit to
get away from any AAA guns. We also got sniped at with machine-
gun fire on the approaches to some of the airports, especially on the
approach over water going into Da Nang, which we did every night
about midnight to refuel. On the ground, Cam Ranh was shelled
about once a month with a few 130-millimeter rockets. Mortar
attacks were less frequent. Although Cam Ranh was a large air base
with a two-mile-long runway, our company and intelligence-gather-
ing planes in particular were usually the target.

Other than my first night in Nam, ground attacks were rare at the
airfield, although some occurred further south on the peninsula. Our
section did have the Air Force ammunition dump blown up one night
by sappers who penetrated every layer of security, set charges and
then escaped. The woman who cooked for the Air Force dog teams
and brought them heroin (known as the "hooch maid") turned out to
be a colonel for the Viet Cong, and knew all their routes. It was she
who set up the attack. Nevertheless, I felt pretty safe compared to
smaller compounds in more remote areas of Viet Nam. Although I
was certainly alert to my "fate" coming at me, I was not terribly afraid
of facing it. I knew I would be doing another tour in Cam Ranh, and
I prayed to understand what I needed to change in order to survive.

The end of my first year in Viet Nam arrived. I had survived, but
had volunteered for another tour. The alternative was to come home,
take a thirty-day leave and then have eleven months left to serve
somewhere in the United States, probably painting rocks or supervis-
ing other people painting rocks. I would then get out in November
1972, three years after I went in.

However, if I stayed another six months in Viet Nam, I would
return home with only five months left in the service. The Army at
the time had a special policy that anyone who came back to the U.S.
from Viet Nam with fewer than five months remaining to serve would
be immediately released. That would get me out in July 1972, and I
could start college in September on the GI Bill instead of January of

the next year. At least in Viet Nam, I reasoned, my work would amount to something.

The Presence of God

While home on leave, I met a woman named Kandy, a friend of my cousin Mike. She was divorced with teenaged boys and was what one might have called at that time in our society a free spirit. We had a lot of fun listening to music and hanging out with some of Kandy's hippie friends. It was nurturing to be back in a normal, peaceful environment, and Kandy and I had an instant and profound connection, even though I was twenty and she was thirty-two. Kandy was very compassionate toward and understanding of what I had been going through and we got into some deep conversations. I never told her of my "prophetic" experiences of dying in Viet Nam.

One night near the end of my ten-day visit home, Kandy and I were partying late in her living room with about six or seven people. There were drugs present and drinks were flowing. Kandy and I had smoked some reefer. The stateside stuff was weak compared to Asian weed and I thought that it had had little effect on me. Suddenly, however, while sitting on the living room floor, Kandy and I both felt as if we were in a room apart from everyone else. While the others were only ten feet away and the music was loud, we had become enveloped by a profound silence. It was like a glass dome over us. The music and voices faded to a distant murmur.

What we both went through for about two hours was, I believe, the living, vibratory, and blissful presence of God. The drugs we had taken had not created the experience but, I believe, opened us up to the possibility of it. We shared our experience and the joy was rapturous, almost unbearable. It shook me to the core. Energy raced up and down my spine.

It took some time for me to adjust to this Presence. It was as if there was someone else in the room with us and my sense of my body was completely gone. At first I felt bigger than my body, then I realized that I was bigger than the room. My awareness expanded up into the heavens. There was a black void that at first became grayer and then vanished in a shimmering light. It was as if I was observing the fabric of the universe. I was aware of distant stars floating everywhere, but they were all in a celestial light that far exceeded anything I had ever imagined the heavens could look like.

Kandy began to hear a voice, but I didn't hear anything; I simply had a profound sense of space and peace. Waves of bliss moved between us as we continued to talk. Kandy was being given a lot of knowledge and insight. She was told that the voice was God's voice. She was being given large amounts of information, while I was only able to get smaller amounts of that knowledge—the parts that were permitted to pass to me. Some of it she was not permitted to tell me.

The parts for me were very specific, while the rest was for her. The simple version of my message as she received it was: "When you return to Viet Nam, you are going to die." It was pre-ordained. My time on this planet was complete. I realized that this was my third wake-up call.

"However," the voice continued, "since no future fate is entirely fixed, you still have the free will to change your fate."

"What do I have to do to live?" I asked.

The answer was to make a major change in my life. For one, I would need to clean up my life 100 percent; purity was a prerequisite to survival. I also needed to change my worldview. If I succeeded in making enough personal changes, reported the voice, I would be allowed to live. Otherwise I would die. It was entirely up to me. "What on earth is a worldview?" I wondered.

I stayed up all night. The next morning I was sitting at the bottom of the steps at home when my mother came downstairs. I was still pretty airy from the cosmic awareness that lingered. I told her what had happened in brief and that I was not afraid to go back to Viet Nam. I also told her that I had decided overnight to become committed to nonviolence and that I was not able to eat meat anymore. I didn't want to kill anything or have anything killed for me. I was beginning to clean up my act. My mother was a little alarmed by my decision but said that she respected it.

Belo Horizonte, Brazil

When someone signed up for an additional tour in Viet Nam, he or she was offered a break—a paid thirty-day leave to go anywhere in the free world. I thought about going to Europe, but decided I could afford to go there later in my life at my own expense. I chose instead to let the Army pay for me to see South America for a couple of weeks, a much more expensive trip. After a few days in Rio de Janeiro, on the Copacabana Beach, I left for Belo Horizonte. Belo was a cooler mountain city on a plateau in the mining district. Uncannily, although I never had studied Portuguese, within a few days I could understand almost everything spoken. I had studied Spanish, which is a similar language, but I attributed my ability to some aftermath of my spiritual experience. In fact, one night at a party in Belo, a college student heard that I could understand Portuguese but not speak it and had never studied it. He argued that that was impossible, and decided, mockingly, to test me in front of everyone.

"I'm going to dictate a long paragraph of information," he said in Portuguese. "Then I want you to translate it back to us in English. My friend will translate it back to me in Portuguese. Understand?"

"Yes," I said, repeating what he had said. "I will try."

The student then went off on a long diatribe about how he was studying at the university for a master's degree. His thesis was research on a rare and specific tropical plant that was believed to have great medicinal properties. I got most of what he said. He was so impressed that he invited me with him the next day on an hours-long drive into the rain forest of Brazil on a field trip in search of the specific plant he wanted to find. I was truly enthralled by the jungle.

On that trip, I befriended a young woman who was, like me, a twin. One morning, she told me in tears of a dream she had had the night before. "I dreamed that you went back to Viet Nam and were suddenly killed," she said. "It was so real. I woke up screaming." Another wake-up call, I thought—my fourth. Enough already!

She could not be dissuaded from believing in her prophecy. She was terrified for me, and argued for a long time that I should stay in Brazil and not return to America or the war. I told her I had to face my destiny, whatever it was. Besides, I told her, the place I was stationed was not that unsafe. I was amazed at how many warnings I was getting, and how insistent they were, telling me I would die if I went back to Viet Nam. It was getting ridiculous as well as scary.

In Belo, I was interviewed by a local newspaper. When I was asked when America would win the war, I said that I didn't think we would. The interviewer didn't believe me and was stunned into silence. The interviewer knew the U.S. had never been defeated. "We will not really lose the war either," I continued. "It seems that we are simply going to quit fighting and go home. We've already started. When we are gone, I don't believe the South Vietnamese will survive on their own for very long." I never saw the newspaper article that followed, but hoped in earnest that our American Embassy didn't pick it up. My security clearance was at risk.

Back in Cam Ranh Bay

After my leave was over, I spent about a week in Ft. Lewis, Washington waiting for a flight back to Viet Nam via Japan. When our flight left Japan, there were only three of us who had been to Viet Nam before, something you could tell mostly from the fact that our uniforms were old and faded. I knew some of the TWA stewardesses by name. The rest of the plane was filled with about 300 fresh recruits. As we lifted off, there was dead silence. I knew that every one of them was thinking: "The next stop is Viet Nam. Will I be coming back?"

I knew this because I was thinking the same thing, just as I had a year before. With all the premonitions, this time the trip hit me harder. To make the moment even more poignant for me and memorable for all of us, and because by then I had developed a bit of a morbid sense of humor, I took out my harmonica and played a perfect rendition of "taps" that could be heard clear to the back of the plane. I thought someone might attack me. But no one said a word, although you could hear a few muffled sobs among the passengers. It was a delicious and provocative moment, however macabre. Maybe they should be facing their Maker and getting their heads on straight, I

Figure 3:9 South Vietnamese troops fleeing the Easter Offensive, May 1972

thought. It's now or never. It was near the end of a meaningless war and no one wanted to be the last one to die.

Upon my return to Cam Ranh Bay I was promoted from leading the plane captain shop to maintenance line-chief. That meant I was put in charge of the maintenance on all of our multi-million dollar aircraft, the personnel and shops, and the schedule of missions and training flights. I still flew missions myself. I was an E-5 holding down an E-7 slot. I was still only twenty.

The Americans were withdrawing, mostly by attrition. When people went home, they were not replaced. Our company started to shut down twice in the next two months, but was stood back up due to the critical need for enemy intelligence. Evidently, the South Vietnamese Army (ARVN) was not doing well on its own.

By March 1972 our company finally closed down and I was transferred to another army intelligence company north in Phu Bai, the Valley of the Dead. I had traded in a white sand peninsula for the red dirt and mud of this inland valley. An ancient burial ground, the rolling red countryside hills of Phu Bai were filled with thousands of mounds of white mausoleums. The beauty of death, I thought on the flight in. Our company in Phu Bai did essentially the same radio intercept mission but in smaller planes. It could also triangulate the intercepted radio operators and order air strikes on them. I was made sergeant of the guard on the Army portion of the air base. We worked from dusk to dawn, or "dark to dark" as we called it.

The North Vietnamese were becoming more aggressive as the Americans withdrew, and no one knew how long the South would hold out. From my four years of studying the war by then, I knew that the first major nationwide attack against the Americans had been the Tet Offensive of January 1968, conducted by thousands of Viet Cong troops supported by the North Vietnamese Army (NVA) regulars on suicide missions in every part of the country. Even though the Communists lost every local battle, and were almost all killed, they won the more important public relations battle. Americans at home were shocked, for they had been told we were winning the war overwhelmingly.

When I arrived in 1970, it was at the end of the subsequent build-up of 400,000 troops in Viet Nam. But by March 1972, when I arrived in Phu Bai, we had only 40,000 troops remaining in-country. The NVA, which had been waiting for years for such a moment, thought it was time to roll over us and continue south into Saigon.

The NVA and Viet Cong's second major invasion of the war was the Easter Offensive of 1972. It involved North Vietnamese Regulars, artillery and armor in a major set piece battle. Twenty thousand troops in 2,000 trucks with 200 tanks came south across the DMZ and, within a few days, captured all of the northern fifth of Viet Nam. Surprisingly, the army stopped at the ancient moated citadel of Hue and laid siege to the fort and citizens with artillery, mortars and rockets.

Phu Bai, then the Army's northernmost air base, was seven miles south of Hue down Highway One. The NVA shelled us with rockets and 130-millimeter artillery to disrupt reinforcements who were landing every few minutes on our airstrip. Because I was the one in charge of part of the base defense, and I knew our weaknesses, I am certain the NVA could easily have rolled over us and right into Da Nang had they wanted to.

I was worried about our situation in Phu Bai. It amazed and occasionally terrified me to learn that we were so defenseless. I used to assume that, because I was only a small cog in the Army machine, there was always someone above me in rank who really knew what was going on and was watching out for all of us. As it turns out, although at times there was someone there, most often there wasn't. In Cam Ranh, every professional soldier who should have been counted on to be responsible was stone drunk by 10 p.m., something that scared me more than the enemy did. That's why I often took charge of our common defense: so I would be safer, and to take care of my men.

In Phu Bai, we had officers who didn't even speak to the NCOs, let alone the lower-ranking enlisted men. Many of them went across the road every night into a more secure compound. Our standing orders were that if ever we were overrun, we should blow up our planes and run across the highway to the fenced-in compound. There was, of course, not a chance of that happening. Instead, we dug in deeper; I had guys filling sandbags during the daytime.

Among the members of my company, we had about six men who shot up a lot of heroin and couldn't be depended on to do anything in a crisis. They were mostly left alone by the career soldiers, who were afraid of them. I was usually the point of communication between both groups. Since all of us assumed that the addicts would, like us, be going home soon, we didn't bother them. They lived in a trashed, anything-goes hooch about fifty yards out of the company area.

The one thing that bothered me about the addicts was that they lived on the edge of our perimeter and I couldn't protect them properly at night. I felt they were unsafe, and resolved to do something about it. After getting the support of our First Sergeant, I made that group all move back into one of the central Quonset huts. They gave me a very hard time for it. The night after their move, an incoming rocket hit halfway up a pole next to their old hooch. The blast not only virtually demolished the hooch but sent shrapnel through their building like a giant shotgun. That got the addicts' attention. I felt I was no hero, however; I had simply followed my intuition. In truth, I could have just as easily moved them and then gotten them all hit

Figure 3:10 Lifer

in their new location, but the God of Statistics and Probabilities had struck again.

The battle of the 1972 Easter Offensive saw the South Vietnamese Army soundly defeated. I have photographs of South Viet Nam's elite ranger battalion troops riding on top of tanks, looking terrified, in their retreat south past us en route to Da Nang (see photo on page 66). Imagine how good that made us feel! Almost none of the soldiers on the tanks had their personal weapons. These were the same troops who had landed in Phu Bai the week before and bravely headed north. We were issued the new shoulder-fired, wire-guided TOW missiles for anti-tank defense. The air was tense.

There was one event that made for some pleasure amid all the stress. When one of my front gate guards, Rusty, was shot in the groin, we stopped the bleeding and put him on a stretcher in a truck to head off to the dispensary. I told him I would round up his things to be shipped home. The last thing he said, and all he cared about as he was evacuated, was to ask me to promise to take care of his dog for him. I did. Rusty had inherited a beautiful German shepherd named Lifer from another GI and had cared for him for ten months.

Lifer was also already partially bonded to me. While he was well fed, Lifer was poorly groomed. Having agreed to take care of Lifer, after some advice from our dog team handlers, I spent every evening before guard duty for several weeks grooming him. He had ticks as big as my little fingernail, and he would bite at me while removing them, then lick my fingers in appreciation. He stayed by my side while I worked and slept. That dog was as good a companion to me as any soldier I had befriended while in Phu Bai. It was understood that he would be put down when the last Americans in Phu Bai left the area. Otherwise, he'd end up in someone's soup, which was still unthinkable to most Americans.

Getting Right with God

In March 1972, I got down to the business of making peace with myself. It happened one very memorable night after I walked my rounds from bunker to bunker with Lifer. I usually had long portions of every night to sit on top of my bunker and think. I concluded that I had seriously miscalculated how safe I would be on my second tour. I was now a prime target, with an enemy only seven miles away more numerous than our unit could handle. It was time to make my most serious commitment to change whatever remained that I needed to change within me. It could have been my last chance if the enemy advanced. I figured I was at that moment when I had to make my last act of contrition.

I took stock of the changes I had already made in my thinking and beliefs in the last three months. I was a participant in a war I questioned deeply, and I had absolutely no anger toward the enemy. By that time, I believed that the United States was a foreign invader interrupting a civil war for the reunification of Viet Nam. I had learned by then that Ho Chi Minh, the enemy leader, had been an American ally during World War II, fighting fiercely against the Japanese. It was not he who abandoned us by turning to the Communists but rather we who abandoned him after World War II, forcing him to turn to the Soviet Union and China for help, some facts they hadn't taught us in basic training. Knowing all this, I had become more sympathetic with, interested in and appreciative of Asian peoples and cultures.

I had already become nonviolent in my thinking and actions, and I was in a quandary as to what I would do in a ground attack. I valued my life a lot, and the lives of my men even more; I was committed to helping my men at the least. But, if pressed, I would fight with regret, not anger. I had become a vegetarian and had completely stopped taking all drugs and drinking alcohol since returning to Viet Nam.

Drugs and drink were omnipresent in Viet Nam. In my first three months in the country, I had started getting bored and had begun to join many of the other troops in drinking heavily every night. However, it had only taken about three weeks of bingeing in this way to cure me of drinking. One morning after a lot of vodka I had woken up with stomach cramps. I remember my first thought being "Man, do I need a drink." I was shocked to hear myself think like this. I remember my next thought even better. "Like hell, I do!" I wondered whether I was an alcoholic, and immediately swore not to drink for a while. I was not about to let my body tell my mind what to do. That very night, I watched soberly as several of my friends got roaring drunk and fought senselessly, beating each other to a bloody pulp. I made a vow to never drink again. Looking around, it was clear that almost every Army lifer was an alcoholic; the only sober ones were the few devout Christians.

During those months, I had decided I would have better luck hanging out with the "heads." These were the guys who shunned alcohol in favor of the sweetly enticing marijuana that was so readily available. I made some contacts and smoked with the boys for most of the rest of my time in Viet Nam. Being in charge of a group, however, I rarely let myself get too wasted. Heroin, which was also easily available, was not part of my scene. (I remained a teetotaler for eleven years. What finally got me loosened up about drinking again was the single life after my divorce, where I allowed myself to drink socially, but sparingly. I was aware of the cost of abusing drugs of whatever kind, since nearly every adult male in my immediate family was or had been a substance abuser.)

Incredibly, I observed to myself, the most noticeable and surprising thing that had happened to me during my second tour in Viet Nam was the realization that I was clearly no longer in control of my life. Throughout my life, my mind had always been able to provide for my every need, and had helped get me out of virtually every predicament. This situation, however, was different. I felt that events were coming at me faster than I could handle them. My mind wasn't big enough for the job at hand.

I can remember that March night on top of the bunker as if it were yesterday. The sky was filled with stars. The fields of stars in Nam had a depth to them and looked very three-dimensional. For nearly the entire night, I sat on a lawn chair looking up instead of out. I had an M-16 with a grenade launcher on my lap and an M-60 machine gun at my feet. Two of my men were alert below me with a starlight scope. After a long time, I began to feel the same way I had the night I was with Kandy. I felt like I was floating, and I couldn't feel my body very well. I remember looking at a particular constellation and feeling my full awareness being, as it were, "sucked up" into space. I reached an expanded state, much bigger than my body. There was no "me" at that moment, just a warm vibratory presence. And this was without drugs!

In that exalted state, I prayed the most fervent prayer of my life. In it I spoke precisely: "I hereby unconditionally surrender myself to you, my God. I acknowledge my human inadequacies and offer myself completely into Your hands. I hereby accept whatever my fate is meant to be from this moment forward. Thy will be done.

"If I am to die," I continued, "I will die in faith, not cowering in a corner. But, if I am to live," I concluded, "I vow right now that I will spend every moment of the rest of my life trying to understand the relationship that exists between humans and You, God—so that I can live my life as a God-realized man. If I am successful in this effort, I will devote the rest of my life to sharing that information with others."

That was it. I cried cleansing tears and felt a release, a lightening in my body. I had made my deal with God. A load was lifted from me. I felt certain that I had a clean slate and was ready for what was to come next. After all the times I had laughed in my life at my own feeble attempts at prayer, or the efforts of others to draw me into one organized religion or another; after all the ridicule I had heaped on foxhole conversions, and after feeling left out when others expressed religious zeal, here I was completely humbled, on my knees and utterly unembarrassed about it. In fact, I felt better than I had for months.

The lingering black shadow of low-level dread that had been with me since first coming to Nam had intensified since I had been moved up to Phu Bai. Now it was completely gone. After experiencing all those preposterously clear omens about my death, the nagging sense of my fate mysteriously coming to get me had completely vanished. I really didn't worry anymore. I knew I was no longer in charge. I no longer dreaded the future. In its place was a heightened sense of being more alive in each moment.

I didn't become arrogant about my newfound faith. In fact, I didn't even tell anyone about it. Instead, I gently enjoyed it. When the next artillery attack began, I found that I was no longer afraid. In fact, some of my best photographs were taken after that night. During incoming rocket or artillery rounds, I would make sure all my guys were hunkered down in a bunker, then cautiously go outside or on top and take some pictures. Maybe it was crazy, but it was fun not to be afraid.

In the end, the American Army rounded up dozens of helicopters mounted with the new wired-guided TOW missiles and flew up north and destroyed most of the enemy tanks. The NVA fled back across the border, not to return for another year and a half. At that time, in 1975, their third major offensive, they would go all the way to Saigon.

Home

Suddenly, my nineteen-month tour was at an end. Five days out of Phu Bai, I went through Saigon and San Diego, and was home in Canton. On my first night, I was sitting at the dinner table with my parents, my brother Doug and my youngest sister Denise, when a truck out front conveniently backfired loudly. Instantly I hit the floor, knocking over my chair in the process. Yet, even as I was falling to the floor, my mind told me that it wasn't necessary.

Sheepishly, I stood up right away. My mother looked confused, but my father, a vet, grinned at me. He understood. My brother, recently back from Viet Nam himself, laughed outright. My little sister Denise cried. In Viet Nam, you hit the ground at the sound of gunfire, and sorted out what was happening from there. It was my welcome home. Time to reprogram the nervous system, I reasoned.

In the last thirty years, not a day has passed during which I have ever forgotten that I am grateful and blessed to be alive, and I usually wake up to that realization. I still believe that I was meant to die in Viet Nam, and that I changed just enough to be allowed to live. Each day reinforces my belief that my life has a purpose that must be fulfilled. It is that purpose and the spark of Divine Light that cannot be extinguished that has been the constant thread through my life of community activism. That Inner Light has guided me and created thousands of tiny miracles that have added to my successes. That brightness leads my way; it is the light that makes my work shine.

4: Volunteers Reforesting America

MOST AMERICANS DON'T consider George Bush Sr. to be a particularly strong environmental president. He's perhaps better known for telling the world at the UN Conference on Environment and Development (UNCED) in Rio de Janeiro, Brazil in 1992 (more popularly known as the "Earth Summit") that the United States' lifestyle was non-negotiable. Nevertheless, in 1991, after I had had discussions with our U.S. Congressman, Ralph Regula, I learned that President Bush had launched a special initiative to reforest the country. He requested the U.S. Forest Service to implement through its Urban and Community Forestry department a new program to plant ten billion new trees as part of his "America the Beautiful" initiative.

Congressman Regula, the head of the Appropriations Committee for the Department of Agriculture, was already very familiar with my "free tree" community volunteer project in his home district. In fact, he had twice come to our group-planting projects, bringing his own dibble bar to help plant trees with student volunteers. A moderate Republican who had been a representative for more than twenty years, Regula openly proclaimed himself a "tree hug-

Figure 4:1 Congressman Ralph Regula at St. Michael's School for the planting of a symbolic tree, October 22, 1998

ger." He had personally planted (with his family) several tens of thousands of trees on his farm near Navarre, Ohio.

Regula's finance committee funded the Department of Agriculture, the U.S. Forest Service, the Interior Department and the Bureau of Land Management. Mr. Regula had earmarked monies to go to each state that would be used specifically to promote the President's new community volunteer forestry activities. Naturally, he made sure that Ohio got more than its fair share of the funding and for that I am forever grateful, since some of that money was destined to come to my nonprofit organization, the American Free Tree Program, after we applied for a grant to get it, of course. Ralph encouraged me to apply, and nine months later I received a call from the Deputy Chief of Ohio's Department of Natural Resources (ODNR) Division of Forestry to tell me that he had received the federal funding to expand the America the Beautiful program to the state.

Ohio's Governor was suddenly anxious to get started and wanted a project proposal on his desk almost immediately. The Deputy Chief asked how soon I could come down to Columbus to discuss the situation and whether I might like to go to work for the state (two hours away in Columbus) to head their statewide volunteer tree project. We agreed to meet a few days later.

This offer required some thought. The first thing I decided was that I did not want to work for the state as an employee. I didn't want to move to Columbus, and I didn't want to work at the ODNR office complex, where I would be micro-managed and scrutinized daily. I'm too much of a free spirit to be productive in that venue. Instead, I decided to propose to them that I would work as an independent contractor and stay in Canton, where all my best contacts and supporters were.

The second thing I did was to stay up long hours for three days writing a formal proposal to the Division of Forestry on how to use the American Free Tree Program (AFTP) as the key nonprofit organization to implement their statewide volunteer forestry project. In my proposal, I addressed one major issue I saw coming with most of the new forestry projects. Most states planned to dole out the money to various tree-planting groups that existed in their larger municipal areas. This approach had two problems. First, being centered primarily in municipalities, it would leave huge geographic gaps not addressed in community forestry activities in those states. Second, it left each state forest agency dealing with several, or in many cases, scores of local groups. Additionally, if a "free tree" giveaway was to happen in every community across the state, the forestry agency would likely get thousands of calls from people who simply wanted to know how to get free trees. The State Forestry departments had no person or mechanism for dealing with thousands of calls and making efficient referrals. I felt AFTP could efficiently coordinate that job for Ohio.

I typed my proposal on an ancient Swiss typewriter without a correcting ribbon that was left over from an office I had closed a few years earlier. In the end, I had to edit and retype it three times, working day and night. The final proposal was about forty pages of text and about sixty pages of financial and tree-planting goals with copies

Figure 4:2 American Free Tree Program logo

of local media articles from the first three years of my local project. It was about half an inch thick, bound with a clip in the corner. I made five sets and put them in a briefcase.

I was living as a grassroots activist pretty much hand-to-mouth at that point. I could hardly afford the ream of paper needed for the proposal. Since my old car had blown a piston through the hood a few weeks earlier, I was without wheels, and temporarily stuck with walking to the grocery store and local restaurants. Still cleaning up paperwork from the 1980s' closing of several business ventures and still without a lucrative job, I was not in a position to buy a new car anytime soon. However, I found a ride to Columbus on the day of my meeting. I would have to hitchhike back.

I met with the Chief, Deputy Chief and two other fellows in the Division of Forestry office. Because I was running the most successful volunteer tree project in the state, I was asked how I thought a massive volunteer effort could be implemented across the state. I explained my idea and rationale, which they loved. They then said, "We are under a lot of pressure to come up with a written project to present to Governor Voinovich. How long would it take you to put your project idea on paper?"

I finally opened my briefcase and brought out the five copies of my statewide proposal, passing them around. "Is this what you're looking for?" I asked. They each lifted the hefty package and smiled. "This is just what we need," they said. I found a ride halfway home and happily hitchhiked the rest of the way, still wearing my suit and carrying my briefcase. The Division of Forestry, just like my local Rotary clubs, never knew how difficult my financial situation was in those early years. I had run my local tree project for its first three years as a volunteer, nearly starving in the process. A basic rule in sales is: Never let them know that you are desperate.

A few weeks later, I ended up receiving a unique two-year special services contract with Ohio Department of Natural Resources' Division of Forestry. It ended up running for over four years. My title was to be State Volunteer Coordinator for what was to be called the Ohio's TreeSource Project. I received a nice salary for those four years.

Ohio Project Overview

My original proposal to the State of Ohio ODNR Division of Forestry requested first-year funding of $225,000 for a contract to organize and administer massive community volunteer reforestation projects in 20 Ohio counties in 1992 and 44 counties by April 1993, with the goal of distributing and planting over two million trees. Subject to Division of Forestry review and continued funding from the U.S. Forest Service, second-year funding of another $225,000 would be used to initiate projects in the other 44 Ohio counties, bringing the statewide tree planting under this plan to four million trees. The state conservatively cut my tree and volunteer goals in half, then accepted my proposal.

The project would establish a state headquarters office with a director, an assistant and a secretary, and three regional directors who would work out of their homes. The goal was to initiate projects within two years that could plant two million trees per year after the first two years and would aspire to plant trees each year until April 2001, a total of 20 million trees. The regional directors would work for two years to organize the startup of local projects in their assigned territories, which would then be funded and run by newly recruited local volunteers and community service organizations. The statewide network of groups and their county directors would then be overseen by a scaled-down staff from years three to ten.

In addition to my efforts with TreeSource volunteers, the state would continue to sell trees and promote other forestry programs, bringing the projected total tree planting over the next four years to fifty million trees.

The establishment of local community volunteer projects was, to my mind, a labor-intensive effort that necessitated someone actually visiting each local area for some time and working through the community until the proper codirectors could be identified, trained and helped to form, find local funding for and then run each local project. This activity could not be done by mail or telephone, or by state or local media exposure. In fact, it was my experience that too much pre-project publicity is detrimental to the formation of projects and securing of funding from individuals, groups and corporate donors. However, once organized, each project could indeed continue to exist on its own for years to come and be available to implement various other state tree and environmental initiatives. Even after ten years, several of these projects continue to operate today.

The best and quickest method of organizing projects modeled after the Stark County project was, I felt, to have a central office that trained, coordinated and administered three regional directors. Each director and the state office (me) would have 22 assigned counties to organize within specific time periods.

Since my "free tree" program had already shown its ability to work nicely with other pre-existing tree distribution and planting groups, I thought it would not be necessary to have a separate organized effort to identify and work with these groups around the state from within the Division of Forestry. Each local county codirector would seek to identify and utilize already existing groups during the formation stage of their project.

The state director's office would establish a toll-free telephone number for receipt of all leads from private citizens, groups, schools, businesses, churches and others who wanted to participate in any capacity in supporting tree-planting efforts. All such leads would be channeled back to established county codirectors who would integrate them into their respective local tree-planting activities. This infrastructure would greatly increase the efficient use of these leads. This was critical because the state office was already receiving calls frequently from interested parties and groups but had no specific local project to refer them to. The state office would also endeavor to help promote other state tree programs such as the rural stewardship projects and urban forestry programs through efficient use of our county codirectors and extensive community educational and media opportunities.

Once projects were underway in all counties, it was projected that well over one million private citizens would be directly involved in the distribution and planting of the two million tree seedlings each year. It was estimated that one million hours of free volunteer labor at a value of ten million dollars per year would be used to accomplish project goals. Obviously, the state could not have afforded to accomplish this project if it had had to pay labor costs to plant the trees.

The educational value of the ten years of school lessons on the value of trees and the annual hands-on experience of tree planting by every student would, I believed, provide a further benefit by creating a whole generation of citizens who knew the value of planting and maintaining trees. The future value of these students alone to the public and private nurseries and the environmental health of the state was, as it remains to this day, inestimable.

None of the federal money was to be used to buy trees. It would be allocated for staff necessary to organize new volunteer-run tree projects and non-tree project costs. Our contract was accounted for in detail and audited by the state.

In order to accomplish the goal of buying and planting two million trees per year, the local county projects would have to raise over one million dollars statewide each year—all of it donated by individ-

Figure 4:3 Group planting project along the highway

Figure 4:4 Planting ball-and-burlap-sized trees

Figure 4:5 Anyone can plant trees...

Figure 4:6 ...young and old.

uals, businesses, churches, community service groups and private foundations. These private monies, along with the value of the volunteer labor provided on the projects, would qualify as matching dollars required to offset the money received from the U.S. Forest Service. The total four-year administrative cost to set up the infrastructure for county-based private tree projects under this plan would come to approximately three cents ($.0325) per tree at the ten-year 20-million-trees planted level.

It would be determined by the Division of Forestry at the end of the two year start-up period whether to continue the project as an independent contract with AFTP, Inc. for administration from years three to ten, or to take the program in-house and administer it within the Division. This decision would be made based on the accomplishments of AFTP at that date, the continued funding from the federal government and the cost-effectiveness of the decision as determined at that date. As it turned out, the state decided to continue to fund my program for four years, on a scaled-back basis.

Our First Local Project: Stark Free Tree Program
Chapter One describes my first efforts at putting together the Stark Free Tree Program in April 1989. For that project, I had announced a goal of buying and giving away "free" three million tree seedlings by the year 2000 in a county with a population of 364,000 people. By 1991, that project had already succeeded in distributing 542,988 trees. An estimated 110,000 local citizen volunteers were directly involved each year in the distribution and planting of these seedlings during our first three "Tree Weeks" in Stark County. In addition, project costs for this entirely volunteer run program had been kept at a nominal level, with total costs of $12,150 for the first year and $16,100 for the second year.

In its first three years, the Stark Free Tree Program was featured in over 265 newspaper articles in the twelve county daily and weekly papers, along with segments on numerous radio and TV shows. I believe that the media cooperated so fully in describing and promoting the project and educating the public about it because the program was, and remains, truly altruistic and has a winning combination of factors: it involved kids, the environment, and something free.

The Stark Free Tree Program served as a model project for how to bridge the gap between state and federal foresters and the private sector. Ironically, while my Stark County community project was taking off and consuming a lot of my time all year round, I was personally experiencing a great deal of hardship. I lost my house and a car. In 1992, I could barely make my new land contract house payment. However, taking the program statewide provided me with an opportunity to generate funding to pay not only for me but a whole staff to start tree projects in every county of Ohio. Originally, I hadn't expected my tree project to turn into an actual paying job for me personally; I have George Bush and Ralph Regula to thank for that.

AFTP Sets National Goals

As I indicated above, the first goal of the American Free Tree Program was to establish "free tree" projects throughout North America to buy, distribute, plant and maintain one billion trees. Once organized, these local county and city projects would need to be locally funded and administered by volunteers. Launching the Ohio project was a big step toward that goal.

Another AFTP goal was to instruct the public in the theme of individual responsibility. Our motto was: "A responsible citizen is one who will plant one tree every year of his life," or, in a shorter version, "Plant a Tree a Year for Life." Our projects proposed to give every citizen one tree free of charge each year for ten years to help to establish a pattern of tree planting. In determining the commitment for a decade, our plan emphasized individual long-term responsibility for and pride in the trees planted.

In addition to the tree planting itself, each local project entailed a major educational program. The objective was to teach about the intimate relationship that exists between humankind and the planet, with a special focus on trees. Continuous public speaking engagements, educational seminars and symposia, lesson plans for schools and maximum media exposure through print and broadcast media were to be a part of each program. That said, each local project was to define its own goals and objectives, and local forestry and environmental experts were invited to serve as advisors to every local project to decide what the goals should be and what trees should be distributed.

In this way, we began spreading statewide. After the first-year success of our Stark Free Tree Program, I spoke with members of Rotary clubs in five other counties who had heard of our project and knew that projects were underway or about to be started in those counties. These new projects were modeled exactly after my Stark County program. That's another great thing about clubs like Rotary. Their members meet weekly, and need to visit other clubs to make up meetings they miss, creating a phenomenal business network and quickly spreading the best ideas from group to group.

The Stark Free Tree Program, which became the first local chapter of the American Free Tree Program, established a model that could be used throughout the world. It was based on the widespread understanding that trees represented a benefit to the community, and on the intrinsic pleasure derived from the activity of tree planting.

AFTP ended up hiring several "regional coordinators" who were each responsible for recruiting and training volunteers to run local projects in 22 counties. I set up a simple outline that could be followed by our regional coordinators and county codirectors around the state. The general program, which needed to be flexible enough to evolve into variations for each community as the need arose, consisted of the following steps for organization and implementation. We have found these steps to be essential in creating a successful program.

Step One: Recruit and Train Directors
The "free tree" project ran best with three codirectors to share the real responsibilities of administration. The three principle areas of the project were 1) overseeing the project and local fundraising; 2) keeping track of the financial and tree numbers; and 3) buying trees and taking orders from schools, businesses, churches and private citizens and distributing the trees through public giveaways and to those who placed orders in advance.

Each codirector would be involved in activities at different times of the year. The codirectors would first select a name for the program that was broad enough to include every geographic area they wished to cover. One well-coordinated countywide project was easier to promote through local media than ten citywide programs that were all competing for the same space in the newspaper. **Lesson**: Make sure you have the right people for the right job, and don't give someone (especially a volunteer) too much to do.

Step Two: Form an Environmental Advisory Group
Every local area already contains enough experts in forestry to draw upon to make all of the technical decisions about the program. Park directors, city, county, state and federal foresters, extension agents, Civilian Conservation Corps agents, soil and water conservation agents, botany and forestry educators at nearby colleges, master gardeners and members of other conservation civic clubs or tree projects can be brought together to serve on what will be, for most of them, the largest tree-planting initiative of their life. Our experience in Stark County was that the local experts were thrilled to be involved in such a bold endeavor. They automatically started to talk up the project with friends and associates in the county.

Once given our predetermined tree goals, the initial task of these professionals was to select the species of trees and totals for each species to be given out. Later, their expertise was needed to determine planting and maintenance instructions for the project, handle special problems and develop follow-up research on the success of the planting. We also learned that the experts liked to be on hand during public giveaways to answer questions from private citizens. They often attended in their work uniforms. **Lesson**: Make sure all your experts are supportive and that all of them are aware of what you are doing.

Step Three: Endorsement Letters
As we learned in the Stark Free Tree Program, political leaders of each city, town or village, township and county, as well as leading educators or environmentalists, needed to be approached up front so that

they knew they were being included in this program. This has not changed. These individuals' support up front will insure that they will not later feel threatened by the project. If they have advance knowledge of a project, then they automatically get the bragging rights on it as well. Requesting letters of endorsement and proclamations is a good way to educate leaders and get their support, and you'll need those letters for your written proposal. **Lesson**: Make sure all your political leaders are informed of what you're planning to do and that they are part of a win-win situation.

Step Four: Contact School Districts to Participate
Each local and city school board will probably have a designated science curriculum director. Ask this person for tentative approval on the idea of giving trees to each school to distribute free to the faculty and students. Otherwise, you can approach the assistant superintendent or the superintendent. Seek permission to at least give one tree to every student. You should emphasize that the trees are free, and that bags and instructions will be delivered with each tree to each building. In this way, no one needs to leave the buildings. You should make clear that trees are to be assembled into the bags with instructions stapled to them by student volunteers (a very good educational activity for students or all ages). In Stark County, each building principal was mailed an order form with a cover letter each February with a short deadline (use a brightly colored paper so it doesn't get lost), and participation was voluntary on a building-by-building basis. What was important for us to make clear was that the "free tree" project was not a mandated project being forced on each building by the superintendent's office. **Lesson**: Make the project free and fun, voluntary and easy to achieve.

Step Five: Approach Funding Sources
What was good about the "free tree" project was that most of the money already existed in every county to fund the giveaway—and that money still exists. Service clubs such as Rotary, Lions, Kiwanis,

Figure 4:7 National Arbor Day Foundation Award—planting a tree with my daughters at the ceremony in Nebraska City, Nebraska, April 1989

Knights of Columbus, Elks, Eagles, Masons, Ruritans, Garden Clubs, Women's Clubs, American Association of Retired People, etc., and some business and civic committees, all have money that they have earned on other projects that they must spend on new community service activities. Many of these organizations are looking seriously for a quality environmental program to apply some of their budget toward. Or they should be, and don't yet know it. In addition, most of them are happy to help with a high-profile, high-impact environmental and educational project that, as I have said, involves kids, nature and something free. All that is needed is for someone to present the project to them in a professional manner and show them in writing that all of the local tree experts are already on the advisory board, that the schools have already agreed to participate (subject to funding by them) and that the local civic leaders have all endorsed the idea.

Our other sources of funding could include corporate, foundation and individual donations. It is important that all local programs are self-funded; my nonprofit groups do not have money to give away. However, when the national AFTP office has received restricted donations for tree planting, it has used that money to help buy trees for local projects.

In this project, the trees needed to be purchased quietly and given away "for free" loudly, and that remains true today. The largest cost of any massive tree-planting initiative is always the labor cost, and free trees have resulted in free labor. While the trees themselves are cheap (trees that are two to three years old still only cost 10 cents to 20 cents in bulk quantities), to pay planters would add millions of dollars to each local program budget. As it turned out with our project, by highlighting the fact that the trees were free, our program brought out volunteers by the hundreds and thousands—volunteers who wouldn't have come or schools who wouldn't have participated even if the trees had been only 10 cents. In addition, the media in Stark County devoted so many articles to the project *because* it was free. All twelve local papers told me that if the project had cost any money at all, it would have been looked at as just another "fundraiser" for someone, and would have received little, if any, space. **Lesson**: Making something free encourages volunteers and media.

Step Six: Announce the Project to the Public
It is very important to wait until the project is substantially funded before announcing it to the public. The initial articles in the media will tend to be the largest and most detailed due to the broad vision of the project, and the whole project generates more excitement when the funding is in place and the project is considered a "done" deal. Funding sources need to be given all the credit whenever possible in the media. The worst situation is to announce a bold project and then end by saying that donors are needed to pay for it.

It is also good to have the first trees ordered before going public so the initial article can direct people on how to make their individual orders. Additional media articles will occur as a result of the distribution to students and the public during "Tree Week." These distributions and any special planting project in the community generate great photo opportunities. Another summary article tailored to each local newspaper area can follow within the week after the program. **Lesson**: Embargo the story. Don't launch it until you have the money.

Step Seven: Tree Week Activities
Ideally, our "Tree Week" would begin with participating schools teaching specially prepared lesson plans to every student for ten to fifteen minutes each day for five days. These lessons teach the value of trees and their relation to the greenhouse gas problem, specifics about the tree species being distributed that year, and planting and maintaining instructions.

In our first project, in Stark County, as detailed in Chapter One, trees were picked up by truck on Wednesday and delivered to a central site, sorted and distributed to coordinators from thirteen geographic areas of the county that evening. On Thursday morning, trees, bags and instructions were delivered to 134 schools, where they were stored in the school walk-in coolers overnight. That afternoon and evening, all advance orders were called and told to pick up their trees on Friday. Friday morning, student volunteers in each building bagged the trees and delivered them to every classroom, where they were distributed during the last period to those students who wanted trees and had a location identified to plant one or more.

On Saturday, trees set aside for the public and any left over from advance orders that had not been picked up were given out in twenty locations around the county that had been announced by radio, TV and newspapers throughout the week. Individuals and park directors were on standby to take any trees left over from the Saturday giveaway each year. So far, there have rarely been any trees to take. **Lesson**: Make sure there's a written and well-thought-out educational component.

Figure 4:8 Planting trees all over America...

Figure 4:9 ...to make a difference

Step Eight: Media Follow-Up
Our news releases tailored the results of the program to meet the
· needs and interest of each local paper. A small local paper that serves
one town doesn't care about countywide results. They need the local
names and numbers. Recognition was given, when wanted, to those
groups who funded the local giveaway and to those who handled the
distribution. Newspapers were notified in advance of photo opportunities (i.e., schools, group planting projects and public distributions).
Lesson: Tailor your project to the media you want.

Regional Volunteer Coordinators
I found my regional coordinators fairly easily. I already had some people in mind for those positions when the state contract was signed
The regional coordinators each entered into a contract with AFTP. My
worst fear was that I would hire someone to accomplish certain steps
of the project only to discover, after much of the money was paid out,
that they had not done the work. Then I would not have the money
to get the work done. In order to avoid this, I made my contracts with
them performance-driven. We broke each county project down into
manageable pieces and paid our regional coordinators for each step
they completed. As envisioned in my proposal, the coordinators
worked out of their homes as independent contractors. Each of them
was given extensive training to do what I had done, and they all did
very well. I was only called in to solve problems or offer new ideas
when the coordinators met obstacles they couldn't surmount.

County Codirectors
It was fun for me to help identify key volunteers to run our projects.
Imagine driving into a new county where you know no one and finding someone who not only would help to distribute free trees but also
was capable of raising money, keeping track of orders and distributions, and reporting results to my office each year. In some areas, it
was easy. My initial point of contact was to talk with every district
governor for Rotary in Ohio (each covering a multi-county area). I
asked them to give me the most current list of their club presidents.

OHIO'S TREES NEED YOUR HELP!

Ohio's TreeSource Program is looking for experienced business and community leaders to organize and co-direct countywide projects to buy and distribute millions of "free trees" to volunteers who will plant them in every urban and rural area of Ohio.

To learn more about this exciting new reforestation project write or call:

American Free Tree Program,, Inc.
PO Box 9079
Canton, OH 44711
1-800-686-1886

This is a cooperative project sponsored by the Ohio Department of Natural Resources, Division of Forestry

O H I O ' S

TREESOURCE
GREENPRINT FOR THE FUTURE

OHIO'S TREES NEED YOUR HELP!

Ohio's TreeSource Program is looking for experienced business and community leaders to organize and co-direct countywide projects to buy and distribute millions of "free trees" to volunteers who will plant them in every urban and rural area of Ohio.

To learn more about this exciting new reforestation project write or call:

American Free Tree Program, Inc.
P.O. Box 9079
Canton, OH 44711
1-800-686-1886

This is a cooperative sponsored by the Ohio Department of Natural Resources, Division of Forestry

Figure 4:10 Advertisements for AFTP's TreeSource Program

TreeSource

GREENPRINT FOR THE FUTURE

Figure 4:11 AFTP's TreeSource logo

Figure 4:12 Ohio Department of Natural Resources Annual Report, 1994 (photo reprinted with permission from artist Richard Lillash)

This was a valuable commodity, since the presidents changed every July 1.

AFTP systematically approached the Rotary club presidents and got names of their community service vice-president or their environmental chair, if they had one. When we met with these people to pitch the "free tree" idea, we would pick their brains for additional community leaders to assist them in the effort. In this way, we usually had a list of three to five community leaders to interview. We also kept a database of everyone who ever called my office to find out about my "free tree" program. I sorted the names by county and gave them out as possible leads for my regional helpers. Often someone who started out wanting trees for themselves was converted into a volunteer running a program for the whole county. These methods were almost always successful. However, I remember trying several times to find someone in one county, and failing miserably. On that occasion, I recall that in desperation I walked unannounced into the town's biggest Catholic church and asked to see the priest. He saw me right away.

"Father, I have a problem," I said.

His response was immediate. Leaning forward, he asked gently, "How can I help you my son?"

I explained my dilemma. "Don't you have a group within your church that performs community service?" I asked. "I need the name of the person who chairs that group." We found our leader, and got some financial support from the church and several of its members to staff the project. If in doubt, turn to God!

As I indicated in the outline to my proposal, we rapidly learned that it was usually necessary to divide the tasks into three distinct areas and find three different people to do them. We developed three titles: Organizational Codirector, Financial Codirector and Distribution Codirector. Organizational codirectors needed to have the broadest vision. They needed to handle fundraising, solicit letters of support from schools and mayors, work with the advisory board and oversee the other codirectors. They would recruit and train volunteers. The financial codirectors needed to be people who, while they might not have the right personality to run the tree distribution, raise money or work with volunteers, could balance a checkbook and keep the books tidy. We always tried to find a person with impeccable credentials for that job—usually a local CPA whose name would give confidence to donors. Or a banker, or the head of a foundation. For the job of distribution codirector, we found the person who first wanted to handle the trees, or get some for themselves. They were always enthusiastic and great with students, and, correspondingly, not usually the person able to grasp the concepts necessary to write up the project, raise the money or keep track of the checking account. These three roles carried out by different personalities enabled us to make sure the task of volunteer codirector was never too overwhelming. By dividing the tasks by personality, we also broke an overwhelmingly big project into smaller parts. We only asked the volunteers to commit to head the part of the project they were qualified to run. Then we went off in pursuit of the other helpers.

I recall that in one lightly populated southern county along the Ohio River, we had an enthusiastic young man who worked in community action who wanted to help us distribute our trees. However, although the project was not large and the amount of money required was only about $1,500 for the first year, the young man was simply unable either to set up or raise the money to fund the project. He didn't know how to start. After repeated attempts by phone to try to assist him to recruit his help, I had to drive three hours to show him how to find them. I had no clue what I was going to do.

When I arrived, just after lunch, the young man and I drove in a circle around town for ten minutes. Finally, I turned to him and asked him who had the biggest real estate office in town. He named a couple just down the road and I called and asked to be able to drop in immediately. A few minutes later, we arrived at the realty office.

"We want to start a new community project," I said, "and we want your help. Yes, we're going to ask you for money. But let's just set that aside for the moment. We'll get back to that later, and you can decide then what amount you will want to give. But first, we need to talk to you about actually helping us run our project."

"Wait a minute," the man said, "I'm going to need my wife in here." After his wife had arrived, we explained the project idea to them and the positions open. The realtor agreed to be the organizational codirector and his wife agreed to be the financial codirector. The young man would handle the tree distributions. We then talked money. The realtor told me that he had spent nearly all his budget for annual charitable giving. I told him "That's really great. Since we don't want to make it too painful for any one person or organization to fund the project, we want to divide the cost among several contributors. Do you have anything left in your advertising budget for this year?" I asked. He did. I explained the advertising spot for sponsors on the back of the instruction form attached to every tree. I asked him to give $250, and then to go to his board of realtors' meeting and ask the board to match his contribution. He brightened and told me that he felt certain that the board would agree to that, especially if he gave first. He was the biggest broker in the county. Both would have their names on the 25,000 planting instruction forms. That was $500 raised.

Then I asked him who else he thought would benefit by having every student in every grade in every school take a live tree home and hand it to their mother with the name of the donors on it. He mentioned that both his general practitioner and his wife's gynecologist were likely targets to each give another $250. The real estate broker said he would ask them, and expected an easy yes. He agreed to then ask them to go together to the board of directors of their local hospital and tell them that they had given $500 and ask the hospital board to match their contribution. In ten minutes we had figured out a fundraising plan for the whole $1,500 and it worked out exactly the way we planned. My young friend was amazed. He later got so much notoriety that he ran for village council and won.

In one Rotary club, they became reluctant to put up all the money I requested after a few years. One key volunteer, who had worked on the tree project, stood up and said, "I want this project to continue. I will match every dollar that the club or any other individual or business puts up." Another done deal. **Lesson**: Always use leverage. You can leverage one enthusiastic volunteer into several by asking them to recruit their friends. You need to always look for opportunities to obtain matching dollars so you can turn each dollar raised into two. **Lesson:** Break big problems into smaller problems that are manageable. When I divided my countywide project into thirteen smaller districts, I didn't say to donors that I needed $20,000. What I said was that their area needed to raise $1,500. That was more palatable. The overall cost was my problem, not theirs.

Other Community Support

In 1992, Dave Ewing walked into my new Ohio's TreeSource State Volunteer Coordinator's office, located in a commercially zoned house that had been rented to us at a discount by Rotarian Masid Shaheen, Jr., a local orthodontist. The house, as you might imagine, was surrounded by trees. Dave was a former Canton Rotary President and outspoken supporter for my tree project.

He sat down and looked me straight in the eye. "I think you need a new car," he said.

I thought a moment. "Cool," I replied. "What color?"

"I was thinking about red," replied Dave.

It turned out that he had just received a new red Chevy Geo Tracker convertible and had decided that our "free tree" project needed to be seen in that car. The Geo Tracker had just won an environmental award because it was rated at 43 miles per gallon. Dave had some special promotional dollars that helped him to offer me the car. We signed a simple lease and Dave handed me the keys and told me to bring it back in two years. I warned him that I might need to put a large amount of miles on it since I was traveling all over Ohio to start new tree projects. He helped to fix us up with nice magnetic door signs and a silk-screened cover for the spare tire, all with our AFTP tree logo on them. Two years later I returned the car with 94,000 miles on it. Dave grimaced, then took it in stride, and we were able to work out a deal to buy the car (cheaply) and use it for another two years. We eventually sold it when it had nearly 200,000 miles on it, mostly from the roadways of Ohio. Dave's kindness was indica-

tive of the generous community support we were to receive again and
again locally and in our "free tree" projects across Ohio.

Project Evaluation
There were many direct and indirect benefits from the "free tree" programs that I could point to. These included:

- the value of the educational experience of each individual
  planting a tree per year for several years;
- the lessons taught about the intimate relationship that
  humans have with the planet;
- the instillation of a sense of "individual responsibility" for
  the environment and how one person can make a difference;
- the total media exposure and its educational value;
- improved habitat created for birds and other wildlife;
- the aesthetic beauty and reduction of auto pollution and
  noise pollution;
- lower costs from snow plowing, soil erosion, ditch work,
  mowing, etc. for city, township, county and state maintenance crews;
- the successful establishment of other similar tree projects
  around Ohio and across the nation as a direct result of the
  Stark County model. Each new project launched would
  also serve as a model in its area to inspire other programs
  in adjacent counties as well.

Nevertheless, I knew that the state and federal government would be
interested in seeing the two principle criteria for a proper evaluation
of the success of each local tree project: 1) total trees distributed; and
2) survival rate. The project codirectors were responsible for keeping
accurate records of the total number of trees distributed over the life
of the project. Each of them gave us a written summary after closing
their project each April.

In Stark County our goal was to distribute three million trees
before the year 2000. In the end, by 1999, we actually distributed 3.3

million. Records were also kept of the actual numbers of trees distributed into each of the thirteen geographic territories of the county and the types of trees given out.

How many trees survived or would survive was more difficult to calculate, since many factors affected and continue to affect the survival rate of the two-year-old tree seedlings. These included soil quality, heat, drought, rainfall, handling, proper planting, accidental mowing, wildlife browsing, vandalism, weed encroachment and the quality of the seedlings purchased in a given year. Most state foresters consider a survival rate of 25 percent for trees planted and not supported to be possible and acceptable. This rate is based on farmers who are reforesting land and on highway plantings. However, we discovered that, with some weeding during the first two years and application of water during prolonged dry periods, the survival rate could easily be increased to over 50 percent. We also found out that, to our surprise, the trees planted by the students had the highest survival rate. I remember how skeptical the forester I had approached before the first "free tree" project had been about students. It turned out, however, that far from being indifferent, not only did students like planting their trees, but the younger students enjoyed paying attention to their trees and watching them grow (and it helped that they only had one tree to care for each year).

A survey taken at 89 of the 134 schools that participated in the first year of the Stark Free Tree Program showed that over 90 percent of the trees that were actually planted were still alive a year later. However, it turned out that not all the trees distributed to students were planted. There was a 20 percent loss in rural schools, and nearly a 40 percent loss in city schools. Some of the trees never made it home, and some that did just never got planted. The largest cited reason for this failure was that the parents did not help the children plant their trees, even though the project had been cleared with them in advance. The school survival rate overall was still higher than that of farmers. That said, school trees represented only 70,000 of the 300,000 trees that were distributed each year in Stark County. It is anticipated that each year the numbers of successful plantings will improve, as the students become more involved in the program. I believe today that our overall survival rate was about 50 percent.

The Environmental Advisory Committee in each county project is responsible for the formulation of procedures for the proper evaluation of the survivability rates of the trees distributed. I believe continued random checks of trees given to schools, churches, businesses and special groups, along with individuals who take quantities of trees, will provide a good assessment of the rates of survival. The committee will also be responsible for issuing as needed news releases about proper tree trimming, maintenance and emergency watering instructions when appropriate to improve the success of the project. It should be borne in mind that fourteen years is a short time in the life of a tree, and we may not know for decades how successful the overall aim to reforest America has been. What we can know is that we have tried our best, and had fun in the process. Whether 60 or 40 percent of the three million trees live, I defy anyone to come up after twenty years and tell me that what we did was harmful to the community or the natural world.

Volunteers Reforesting America
After fourteen years, the American Free Tree Program has been responsible for the distribution of nine million trees across Ohio. Projects started in other states have added another three million trees to our tree-planting totals, and some of these projects are still operating. That's just what we know of. In addition, we have sent out packets of information to hundreds of communities across the U.S. and abroad. We will never know what was accomplished in those programs.

At the peak of our projects in the 1990s, we had over 1.5 million student and adult volunteers involved in our effort. We had created a new network of over 1,500 schools, churches, civic groups and government agencies statewide, all focused on the same project each spring during our Tree Week. As of the end of 2002, many of those projects have run their course, but many others are still active, buying and distributing trees in their communities each April. Even though the bulk of the project has come to an end, there is no reason why anyone with even a modest amount of organizational skills cannot start a similar project in his or her school, church or hometown. This book has highlighted some of the opportunities and methods available to everyone who wishes to make a difference in their community by planting trees. As I hope I have shown, there are vast numbers of people of goodwill who are willing to help. All it takes is a vision and planning. And that one person who has learned that they can make a difference by becoming a community proactivist.

Figure 5:1 Addressing a school assembly

5: Mobilizing the Next Generation

PUBLIC SPEAKING, AND speaking effectively, is an essential component in organizing and motivating people to change—especially those groups that may be hard to reach. Learning how to speak in public requires dedication and work, but it can be done. In this chapter I will highlight my lecture style and the actual content that eventually evolved out of my presentations, along with some of the do's and don'ts. I have developed a style of speaking that may be useful to anyone wishing to offer similar short presentations on any subject to an elementary age group.

In the last thirty years, I have given over two thousand public lectures, mostly related to my career as a teacher of the Transcendental Meditation (TM) technique. Most of those meetings were held in places like libraries, YMCAs and TM Centers and were promoted as free public lectures. I have also taught over thirty weekend in-residence seminars, and have even led training groups on the international level for some months.

Of all the fun things in my life, it is giving talks that I have enjoyed the most. Speaking energizes me; I feel better after I've given a speech. It's as if the energy, creativity, intelligence and usually the right words flow through me and out to the audience. Even when I give the same speech week after week, no two lectures are ever alike. The talks automatically get adapted to the needs of those attending.

Sometimes when I am lecturing, I get inspired, too. I often find myself sitting on the edge of my seat waiting with the audience to hear what I am about to say next. When I get goose bumps from what has come out of my mouth, then I know that I'm on a roll and have reached the point where I have inspired my audience as well. At that point I feel I am a pure instrument of service. This kind of "spiritual speaking," where I trust the right words to be delivered to me and through me in each moment, is one of my most intimate, ongoing mystical experiences. When it happens, there is no ego in the experience.

At the beginning of my career as a speaker, I was probably too proud of my ability to give good lectures. However, as always, nature seems to have a way of correcting any imbalance in life. I got my correction regarding vanity early on, and to this day I have never forgotten it.

In the fall of 1974, my wife Karen and I started the Canton Transcendental Meditation Center, a local community service nonprofit organization. A major part of my job was to travel regionally in Ohio to give free introductory lectures about the TM program for stress management and invite people to take the course. By age 25 I had unbounded confidence in my ability to teach.

In the winter of 1976, we received a call from a sweet-sounding older lady who lived about forty minutes south of Canton. She led a group of about a dozen sorority sisters who were all retired schoolteachers. They had maintained their connections through the decades as a literary club that met monthly. I was invited to speak about TM to follow up their recent review of a book on the subject.

It snowed heavily the day of the talk. I arrived a bit late after getting lost in the rural area. It was already dark at six o'clock. Most of the roads were icy and the street signs were covered in snow. I actually had to get out and scrape snow off a couple of signs to find my way to the residence!

My lecture was received with a mixture of politeness and some mild enthusiasm. It seemed the retired schoolteachers enjoyed having a live speaker for a change. I thought I had done a good job and had kept everyone's attention fairly well. After finishing the lecture, the group's treasurer thanked me in front of the club members and presented me with a check for $25. I returned her thanks, but declined to keep the check. I had, after all, offered to speak for free.

She became flustered. "But I already made out the check," she said. "This will mess up my bookkeeping. Besides," she added, "we're really just giving you some gas money for your effort."

Inspiration came to me. I took back the check and thanked the group for the money. I then signed the back of it and said, "I have accepted your gift and now want to donate this money back to your club. You must have some special project that you are raising money for, and I want to give to that cause."

The club treasurer perked up. "Gee, that's really kind of you," she said, smiling. "We have just the right project to put this in to."

After I had donned my coat and gloves, I turned to the group and asked, "Oh, by the way, what project did I just donate to?" I expected to hear about some grand civic action.

The blue-haired treasurer, still beaming, stated with complete innocence: "Well, we've gotten so many complaints from the girls lately that we decided to start a special fund so we can afford to get better speakers."

It was a thoughtful drive home. While it was a humorous encounter, I never lost my sense of humility about public speaking after that night.

Thirteen years later, my adult-oriented public speaking ability helped me launch the "free tree" program. This in turn led me into a whole new arena where I had to present my environmental ideas in public: I suddenly needed to start all over again and learn to speak to students.

Newton Falls, Ohio, Earth Day 2001

The fog lay heavy on the Mahoning River. The waterfall was barely visible through the mist outside the window of the downtown restaurant. It was too early for me. At just past seven o'clock a.m., our new Executive Director for the American Free Tree Program, Pam Feagler, and I had already driven nearly an hour to get to Newton Falls. I hoped to wake up somewhat over breakfast before going over to the Catholic elementary school for an all-school assembly. I hadn't done this early routine for a couple of years, and it showed.

I started giving speeches at school assemblies in 1989. Initially, it had not been my idea. However, in response to my first year of "free tree" distributions, I had received scores of requests to give classroom presentations in Stark County's twenty school districts. I quickly figured out that the only efficient way to use my speaking time was to skip all of the single classroom presentations and limit my lectures to only those schools where I could speak to an entire building of students, or at least to a few grades at a time. So, in January 1989, I began to promise to give school assemblies that March and April. It then occurred to me that I had never done that before. While I had rather extensive public speaking experiences and good ability, it was almost entirely with adults.

To be honest, I did have a secret motivation. My ex-wife and three daughters lived in Overland Park, Kansas, a suburb of Kansas City. I thought it would be a great idea for me to practice giving school assemblies in Ohio until I got really good, and then to offer to speak at my kids' elementary school as a surprise for them. So I was highly motivated to learn how to be good. There was no way I was going to bomb in front of my kids and their friends.

You will remember that my early critics had told me that I was wasting my time with elementary students. Some of the foresters had said that I needed to teach high school students about trees because using younger students was useless. I was told that young students would not be able to plant their tree seedlings as well. I strongly disagreed. My personal experience has been that from about their sophomore year on, high school students are pretty well set in their beliefs, whereas younger students are still teachable. That's why Junior Achievement teaches its Project Business program to ninth graders. I was in that program for a couple of years in high school. Ninth grade is about the oldest group you can teach without encountering a lot of cynicism.

I believe that from about ages sixteen to eighteen, depending on maturity and gender, most young adults are fairly convinced that their parents (and virtually everyone over twenty-one for that matter) are not as smart as they are. This is probably a necessary evil that we all face as parents and teachers. I'm sure that it's a combination of our own karma coming back to us from the way we treated our parents when we were teens, along with the natural and crucial weaning process that is necessary for our kids so that they don't continue to cling to their mother's apron strings when they are thirty. Ironically, after their teen years, and after our children have moved out of our houses and away from us, often painfully, we praise our kids for that same independence that we previously couldn't tolerate.

In the end, our tree project did do well with those few high school students who were already committed to environmentalism. But the majority didn't want to be considered "uncool" by being seen carrying a baby tree home. However, our research showed that these same "cool" students often happily helped their younger brothers and sisters plant their tree seedlings.

My primary focus for speaking, therefore, was elementary and middle schools, of which we had about 5,000 in Ohio. I knew for a fact that elementary students could remember special events like school assemblies, sometimes for a lifetime, because I did. I still remember several of my early childhood school assemblies. Maybe fewer took place then, and therefore they were more memorable. But reaching back over forty years ago to 1958, I can clearly remember one in particular, when I was in the second grade at Prairie College Elementary School in the Canton Local School District.

We were gathered to an assembly to see a man in Native American headdress who gave a special archery demonstration that was, at least to this seven-year-old, "unbelievable." Our presenter made every kind of trick shot land right in the center of each target. After establishing his dead eye, to our collective horror he stood a student volunteer (whom we all knew and admired) in front of a target and fired directly at him. (Don't try this at home!) Twice he shot a bow with a special twisted string that turned the arrow off to the side to hit another target in the bull's eye. I remember my emotions during his show: first awe, then fear for my friend, and then elation as he lived through the ordeal. This is still a vivid memory to this day. So I knew that even young students could be reached with a compelling enough message.

In speaking at an assembly I knew I had a unique opportunity to teach thousands of students whatever message I chose. I knew I would have only one chance to make a presentation that each student could remember for a lifetime. It needed to be as awe-inspiring as the Native American archer had been to me. My speech had to be honest, simple, and yet lively enough to keep their attention for the full 25 minutes I promised for elementary schools and 35 minutes for the middle schools. It had to contain enough knowledge to keep fifth and sixth graders from being bored, yet be easy enough for kindergarten and first graders to comprehend. In Catholic schools, where there was no middle school, I usually had seventh and eighth graders in the group as well. To sum it up, I needed to do everything except sing and dance (and I would have done even that if only I had had the talent).

From 1989 to 1999 I gave over a hundred assemblies. They were usually followed by a "free tree" giveaway, either that day or during that week. After a rough start on the first two or three assemblies, they turned out great and were always fun to give. The 2001 Newton Falls lecture was actually just a refresher course for me. Since most of our "free tree" school distributions were over, I hadn't given that talk for two years. My goal that day was to have some fun while giving our new executive director a look at what I had learned so she could eventually develop her own presentation style for schools.

We were met in the principal's office by Dristina Quinn, a math teacher at Saints Mary and Joseph School. She was her school's Earth Day project coordinator for that year. I gave her my one-page, typed, double-spaced, size-14-font, 45-second introduction to look over. I wasn't trying needlessly and conceitedly to impress elementary students, but I had learned my lesson after experiencing both extremes of poor introductions. Some introductions had been so brief as to be non-existent ("Here's our speaker today. He'll explain to you who he is and what he does"), while others had been well meaning but so long and tedious that the kids were bored and restless before I ever began. The other result of the overlong introduction was that my speaking time was sometimes cut in half—something that forced me to edit on the spot and left me potentially looking foolish.

The public address system called the students to the assembly, which was held in the cafeteria. The dining tables were neatly stacked at one end in the corner, while the kids sat on the carpet, which, I took time to notice, was surprisingly clean. The youngest students sat in long rows at the front, while the oldest sat in neat rows at the rear. The eighth graders stood at the back. Teachers were either sitting with their students or leaning up against the wall, three with their arms folded. Every student and most of the teachers had on specially designed green T-shirts commemorating their Earth Day events.

Frankly, I love speaking at Catholic schools. While there may no longer be a nun running around smacking students on the hands with a ruler as there was in the old days, there just seems to be a discipline that is often lacking in public schools (I attended public school). Catholic students are not only quieter, but they are usually the most polite and attentive students I get to speak to each year. It's more fun to talk when you really know that the students are listening. Contrast that with an outdoor assembly I once gave to public school students on a grassy hillside. Throughout my talk teachers chased across the field after kids who had just jumped up and started running. In that lecture I saw several teachers discreetly sitting with their legs draped over their worst students' legs to hold them down. It was during that talk that I learned to walk all the way to the left and right ends of the 100-foot rows to fully engage the audience and keep everybody's attention.

No such need for wandering here, though. Dristina introduced me. My introduction was designed to teach a few key points while impressing the students with the success of the tree program. If the introduction was done correctly, I wouldn't have to spend valuable time bragging about it to establish my credentials.

"And now, please welcome Mr. Kidd, the Tree Man," Dristina concluded. There was a round of applause.

"Good morning," I said. I was sure it would be.

"Good morning," came the subdued reply, as the students wondered what they were getting into.

"Thank you for inviting me to speak to you this morning. I need to ask each of you to pay really close attention to what I say to you this morning. I'm only going to talk for a few minutes, but what I say today could change your whole life."

I looked around to make sure they got it. Two teachers still had their arms crossed.

"This morning I'm going to be really honest with you and tell you something that you might never hear again from another grown-up. And that is this: 'We have really screwed up the planet. Our planet Earth is sick. It has some serious problems.'

"Now who has done this? We, my generation, did it. Me, and my friends. And your parents and your grandparents. And all of the people who lived before us. Everyone who is living in this country and around the world. We have been causing problems on this planet for many years. And we are continuing to make some old problems worse and even creating new ones every year. That's the truth.

"Now, there's some good news and some bad news about this. First, the good news. We didn't do it on purpose. Well, maybe a few people did. But most of the people in the world didn't know that we were helping to make the Earth sick. We didn't know that driving so many cars would pollute the air or cutting down so many trees would hurt the world's animals and make the rivers dirty. But now we do know. So the good news is—that we didn't try to hurt the planet on purpose.

"Now here's the bad news: You get to fix the problems!"

Uniformly, mouths opened, eyebrows went up in dismay, and a slight recoil swept across the crowd of students.

"That's right. So you need to pay very close attention to what I have to say this morning. Because some of you will need to study what all of these environmental problems are about. And some of you will need to go to college and learn how to fix the problems. Then you will need to go out, like I am doing today, and help to solve these problems and make the whole world better. Got it?" There were a few nods. "Great. Now let's get started.

"Today I am going to teach you just three things. I want every one of you to remember the three things so that you will be able to say them when we are done. Think of it as a test. Then you will be able to go home and teach these three things to your parents. That's your job this morning. Can you all do that?" There were only a few enthusiastic nods, but I felt a great deal of interest.

"Great. Here we go. Ohio used to belong to the American Indians. Then the first pioneers came here to live over two hundred years ago. They came in covered wagons, on foot and on horses. Back then, the whole state was full of trees. Big trees. One pioneer woman wrote that they traveled for many days in the dark woods and never saw the sun because there were so many trees.

"The pioneer settlers had to cut down a lot of our trees. Why do you think they did that?"

Fifty hands went up. I gestured to a kid in the front.

"To build log houses."

"Right." I pointed to another kid.

"To make farms," he said.

"Right again. So the pioneers needed to clear the land of trees to make their homes, to grow food, to have firewood for heat, and for safety. They were afraid of the wild animals and Indians in the forests.

"What this means to us today is that everywhere you see sky, there used to be a tree. Now, this is the first point I am going to ask you to remember. This is point number one. I want you to repeat after me: 'Everywhere you see sky, there used to be a tree.' Together."

"Everywhere you see sky, there used to be a tree."

"Now say it again: 'Everywhere you see sky, there used to be a tree.' "

"Everywhere you see sky, there used to be a tree."

"Very good. Now who has it memorized? How about you in the red shirt?"

"Everywhere you see sky, there used to be a tree."

"Great. Now someone younger? In the front row."

"Everywhere you see sky, there used to be a tree."

"That's it. That's point number one. Everybody have it memorized?" A widespread nod in unison told me they did.

"Ohio is a great state. Everywhere you go now you can see that we have huge cities. Across Ohio we have big highways and many smaller roads. We have millions of houses and thousands of schools with playgrounds and lots of churches. We have stores and businesses where our parents work, and lots of parking lots. There are now eleven million settlers in Ohio. If you pay attention, you will see that some of the land still has trees on it. We still have about one third of our trees in Ohio.

"What I want you to remember every time you go outside is that wherever you can see the sun or the clouds, there used to be a giant tree planted right there in that space. We have built Ohio by cutting down most of the trees. Now we can never put all of those trees back in the ground. But my job is to ask people to put some of the trees back. As many as we can. In their backyards. On their school grounds. On their church land. Why do we want to do this?"

Another fifty hands went up. Kids were bouncing up and down. Now only one teacher still had his arms crossed.

"How about you answering?" I asked a young boy. "Why do we need trees?"

"Because...I don't remember..."

"How about you over here?" A girl.

"We need trees for the animals."

"That's right. Animals need trees to live in and for food. How about you in the back?" I asked, pointing to an older student.

"We need trees for wood to make houses."

Figure 5:2 Kids proudly show off their trees.

"Great. And what about you?"

"We need trees for paper and books."

"That's right. And what about the rest of the environment? How do trees affect the air and rivers and lakes?"

"Trees reduce pollution in the air and water."

"OK. So we need trees. Trees even make the air we breathe. Sometimes we forget all these things. Especially when we have to rake up the leaves and put them in bags. Sometimes our parents and especially our grandparents get tired of bagging the leaves and wish they could cut down their trees. They forget that trees don't just sit there doing nothing. Trees are always working to help make the world better.

"Now let's do an exercise that will teach us the second point we need to remember. Have you ever done a visualization? A visualization is what you call it when you close your eyes and try to see something in you mind. What I want everyone to do is to close their eyes right now and carefully listen to me while we do a visualization."

The kids sat mostly with chins up and grinning in anticipation.

"OK, what we are going to visualize is a tree. First I want you to see the trunk of the tree. You all know what a telephone pole is? I want you to picture a big tall empty trunk that looks like a telephone pole. Do you see it? OK, that's the tree trunk. Now let's get rid of all those wires. We don't need them here. Now we need some branches. Branches are smaller than the trunk, and they are sticking out of the tree in every direction. If you can't make the branches very well, then picture a hundred broom handles sticking out of the tree in every direction. Some are big. Some are small. Got it?"

There were some giggles and a lot of grins.

"Finally, we need to put leaves on the tree. Thousands of leaves. But our leaves are going to be special. I want you to pretend to see your tree covered with leaves that are made from the little attachments that your family uses on their vacuum cleaner. Picture every kind of attachment on your tree: The little ones with all the fuzzy hair on them; the long skinny ones; the big fat ones for vacuuming the floor. Can you see them? Now put thousands of them on all the branches. These are the leaves. Now your tree is like one giant vacuum cleaner. Every leaf is breathing in the dirty air and breathing out clean air. Trees vacuum the whole world.

"Now repeat this with me: 'Trees vacuum the whole world.' Together."

"Trees vacuum the whole world."

"Again. Together."

"Trees vacuum the whole world."

"Now at home your vacuum makes a lot of noise. I want you to turn on your imaginary vacuum cleaner tree right now and make some noise!"

"Errrrmmmm."

"It's OK. You can make it louder."

"ERRRRRMMMMM."

"OK everyone. Now stop. Let's open our eyes."

Silence. More giggles.

"That's point number two. 'Trees vacuum the whole world.' Can you say it one more time? Together."

"Trees vacuum the whole world."

"Now who can say it by themselves? You want to try?"

"Trees vacuum the whole world."

"And over here on this side, who has it?"

"Trees vacuum the whole world."

"Now who can say point one and two together?" There were only a few hands. "How about you?"

"Everywhere you see sky there used to be a tree. Trees vacuum the whole world."

"Excellent. Let's all do that together. Point number one, Everywhere..."

"...you see sky there used to be a tree."

"And point number two? Trees..."

"...vacuum the whole world."

"Now how about a teacher? Who wants to try?"

Kids always love that, seeing their teacher becoming a student, just like them. There was one female volunteer.

"Everywhere you see sky there used to be a tree. Trees vacuum the whole world."

"Very good. Now we know who's paying attention." There was laughter, and the teacher blushed and gave a slight smile. "So, we've learned two things. Now we need to learn the third point. First let's talk some more about trees. Trees are good for life. But whose life is helped the most by planting trees?"

"Animals."

"People."

"The planet."

"That's right. Trees are good for animals. They help people, too, by giving us wood and cleaning the air we breathe. Planting trees is good for the planet as well because trees might make the whole world cooler and prevent global warming. Planting trees is good for the trees also. Don't forget that one. We use trees every day of our lives. We breathe every day. We sit on wooden chairs. We read books made out of paper, which comes from wood.

"So we need to put back some of the trees we use. How can we do that? That's our third point to remember. I want you to repeat after me: 'Plant a tree a year for life.' Let's say that together."

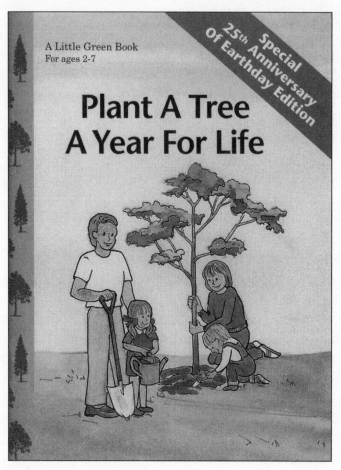

Figure 5:3 American Free Tree Program's Plant a Tree for Life booklet for kids

"Plant a tree a year for life."

"Again, together."

"Plant a tree a year for life."

"This is my third point. We need to plant a tree every year of our life. We need to do this for the trees, for the animals, for all the people, and even for the planet itself. Now, who can say it alone? How about you this time?"

"Plant a tree a year for life."

"Someone else?"

"Plant a tree a year for life."

"Now who can remember all three points? OK, you try it."

An older student goes for it: "1. Everywhere you see sky there used to be a tree. 2. Trees vacuum the whole world. 3. Plant a tree a year for life."

"How about someone younger? You try it."

"1. Everywhere you see sky there used to be a tree. 2. Trees vacuum the whole world. 3. Plant a tree a year for life."

"Now how about a teacher?"

I hit up the man who had had his arms crossed earlier. He got it right, too.

"I want you to promise to plant one tree every year of your life. Later today, you will be given a free tree to take home and plant. Your tree will make a difference in the world." Some nodded in agreement.

"Many people think that because they are just one person, they cannot make a big difference. So I have one more exercise that I want to do that will help you to understand that everyone does make a difference. First, I need two volunteers. I want volunteers who can yell really loud."

Several students offered to help. I picked one young girl and an older boy.

"Why don't you two come up here with me? What is your name?"

"Alexis Ginter," said the girl. "I'm in the fifth grade."

"Well, Alexis, I want you to do something you don't usually get to do in school. I want you to yell as loud as you can for me. But I want you to watch me, and when I go like this (I slashed my open hand across my throat), then I want you to stop. Ready?" She nodded, pulling herself together. "Go ahead."

"Eeeeeeeeee." It was more of a scream than a yell, but it was plenty loud, and I rapidly did the slash. Within seconds, the principal and school secretary looked in from across the hall to make sure no one was being hurt. I nodded to them.

"That's great, Alexis. That was pretty loud, right everyone?"

There was scattered laughter. It had been more than pretty loud.

"Thank you. You can sit down now."

I turned to the older boy. "How about you?"

"My name is Justin Chepke. I'm in the eighth grade."

"Justin, why did everyone point and say to pick you?"

"Because everyone knows that I have the biggest mouth in school!" he quipped.

"Well that's great Justin, because right now I want you to yell as loud as you can too. And I want you to watch me for the signal to stop. Go ahead."

"Ahhhhhhhhhhhhh!" I slashed and Justin stopped, red-faced. Justin's reputation was justified. He did have a loud voice. Everyone cheered.

"Way to go Justin. That was great. Your mother probably heard you at home. Let's give both of these guys a big hand." There were more cheers.

"Now you're probably wondering what the point of this is? This is what happens when you do something by yourself. It's pretty loud right? Well, what do you think it will sound like if we have everyone in the room yell all together?" There was a murmur of anticipation. "Everyone watch my hand for the signal to stop," I cautioned. "OK? Let's all yell together. Go."

"Ahhhhhhhhhhhhhhhhhhhhhh." Slash.

It took a few seconds for everyone to stop, but everyone seemed pleased with themselves, although they looked sheepishly around as if unable to believe they could make such a loud noise without getting in trouble.

"That wasn't loud enough," I said. Half the kids looked at me in disbelief, while the others began to gear themselves up for another yell. "I want you to do it one more time. This time, remember that you will probably never get another chance to yell like this in school for the rest of your life. So give it your best shot. OK, go!"

"AAAAAAAAAAAAAAAHHHHHHHHHHHHHHHHH!" Slash. Complete silence. The kids were breathless, and in awe of the noise they had made. The teachers looked somewhat wide-eyed, but relieved.

"Now that was awesome. Did you see what a difference that made? Whew. I think I felt the roof shake. When we all yell together, it makes a noise as loud as thunder. We did it together, as a team. This is what will happen when every one of you takes your trees home and plants them in your yard. By yourself, it's just one tree. But acting together, we will be planting a whole forest of trees. Got it? In this way, every person will be helping every other person to make a bigger difference.

"When you go back to your classrooms, I'd like you each to write down the three points so you can continue to memorize them all day. Maybe you can even write them on the blackboard. Later today, when you get your white pine tree, your teacher will explain to you everything you need to know about planting it. Just remember, the green part goes up and the brown part goes down! Thank you for your time, and have fun today. Happy Earth Day." Applause. The teachers were smiling.

The Lesson

Now the reason why I told that story at length and in such detail is this: There were several times over several years when parents came up to me in public and asked, "Are you the Tree Man?" When I said I was, they would then go on (often in enormous detail) to describe how their kids came home and instructed them on exactly why, where and how they needed to plant their free tree. One dad actually told me that his five-year-old son had heard my assembly in kindergarten. That night at dinner the dad had made the mistake of asking, "Well, son, what did you learn at school today?" His son replied "Well dad, I learned three things: First, everywhere you see sky there used to be a tree. Second, trees vacuum the whole world. And third, plant a tree a year for life." He then went on to explain to his family something about each point.

There were several lessons learned by me from being forced to give school assemblies. First, make it fun. If you as the speaker are obviously having a good time, then all the students will have a good time. If you are too serious or nervous, no one else will enjoy themselves either. Second, audience participation is critical when speaking to young people. Watch them for feedback. Are they still with you?

They are not yet physically equipped to sit and listen to a long lecture. Break it up with interactive exercises. Third, knowledge is always empowering, so teaching facts to students is empowering to them. It is not enough to say things once and expect them to learn them. We need to use all the senses. Have them repeat it, say it aloud, sing it, dance it, shake to it, clap to it, write it down, read it, and draw it. Fourth, repetition is also critical. How many times do you need to hear something before you own it? I broke my talks down into three main points. I wanted every kid and teacher to have the three points embodied before the lecture was over. When the children realize that you are not going to be content to let them just listen, they get invested in their own performance and ability to learn, and a bit of competitiveness creeps in. The children watch around them to see who else gets it and who sees that they have gotten it. I give lots of praise.

Finally, don't be afraid to make some noise. Bend the rules. If you plan anything too unusual, it's better to review it with the principal first. In my case, it was critical to maintain control. Teach the kids how to stop making a noise before telling them how to start to make a noise. It's just like teaching skiing. First learn how to stop, then learn how to go. That way you maintain full control, and everyone knows it.

Overland Park, Kansas, Shawnee Mission Schools

After a weekend spring visit with my kids in March 1990, I said my goodbyes on a Sunday evening as usual. The kids figured I was off to drive back to Ohio—all except my oldest, Sara, who was in eighth grade and in on the secret. I had already gotten permission for her to skip her morning class at the middle school and to walk over instead to Apache Elementary, which she had attended since second grade. Her sisters, Stephanie, fourth grade, and Annie, third grade, had no idea what was up. I had talked to the principal some weeks before and arranged to give a whole-school assembly about Earth Day.

Stephanie's teacher came into the office (where I was waiting out of sight) to whisper to me that she had barely managed to keep the secret, but hadn't been able to resist giving a couple of hints. Most of

Figure 5:4 My contribution to the next generation: from left, Stephanie, Sara and Annie

the faculty was in on the surprise and were watching my daughters with some kind of glee. I was moved down to the auditorium before the morning announcements.

Peeking out from the backstage door, I could see Stephanie in line, walking down the hall with her class to the assembly. She was pondering her teacher's hints and the PA announcement about the special science assembly with an out-of-town guest. I got to watch her bring it all together coming down the hall. "I got it!" she cried out and leaped lightly into the air, shaking her finger at her teacher. "I just figured it out," she mouthed. Annie, however, came in clueless with her classmates. All the students sat in rows on the gym floor. The principal gave one of those longish introductions.

At the point where I was introduced, Sara walked in and stood in the back. I came out from behind the curtain and watched my kids' faces. Annie was beaming, as were all of her friends. Stephanie started off beaming as well. Then a sudden look of horror swept over her face and she looked around her. I could read her mind. "What if he screws up and I get totally embarrassed? I'll never live it down!" She always had a strong sense of her social position. They both survived the lecture and enjoyed the notoriety for a few days. And I had a delightful 800-mile drive home to Ohio.

It's a truism, but kids represent the future. They were a crucial component of my "free tree" program and it would be worthwhile including them in your civic efforts, whatever they may be. While the presentation I gave to the children may be inappropriate in style for your presentations, certain truths still apply. Be straightforward, make your points simply and directly, and make them memorable. Be entertaining and provide facts. Don't be afraid to engage your audience and bring them into the lecture. If you can do that, you might even be invited to speak to those sorority sisters. I hear they're looking for good speakers!

6: Practicing Nonviolence on the Dinner Plate

FOR OVER THIRTY years I have been a vegetarian. My vegetarianism extends out of my belief in the need for a diet that is true to the principles of nonviolence that I adopted while serving in Viet Nam. I felt then, as I do today, that my commitment to nonviolence was a critical component of my spiritual growth, and, in fact, of my continuing ability to survive as a human being. I have practiced nonviolence in my life and taught nonviolent action over these many years. In this chapter I talk about my vegetarian diet; in the next I will talk about my animal advocacy. Both of these aspects of nonviolence stem from my continued attempts to live as much as possible without causing pain and suffering and to increase my circle of compassion to other beings who, in terms of their ability to feel pain and suffering, are just like me.

Please let me explain. As I related in Chapter Three, in December 1971, while on leave from my first full year in Viet Nam, I visited my parents in Ohio for ten days. Toward the end of my stay, I made a conscious decision to become a vegetarian. I didn't really know or use the "V" word back then or know that I was actually a vegetarian. I just felt that I didn't want to ever kill anything again, and decided not to—for the rest of my life. Once I had made the commitment to act with non-violence toward all humans, it became clear to me that I also couldn't kill any animals or allow them to be killed for me by proxy. I understood that all of the violence in my life had to end for me to survive my next tour in Viet Nam, even the violence that was encapsulated in the meat on my dinner plate. Eventually, I realized that I had become an "ethical vegetarian." Later on, I found that there were considerable health, mental and environmental benefits to the vegetarian diet as well, although that hadn't been my original motive.

After making a commitment to clean up my physical actions, I was immediately confronted with the sharp contrast between my commitment to internal peace and the violent and negative thoughts that I still had. I was truly programmed to kill, and was quite insensitive about it. I began working on those thoughts before I left Canton to return to Viet Nam, and I will discuss how I did this in Chapter Ten.

Meanwhile, that December, my short-term goal was to make it out of the Army alive. After returning for my second tour in Viet Nam, I found that it was impossible to maintain a healthy vegetarian diet just by eating Army food. This was because nearly everything the Army cooked had meat in it. Plus, Army food in Nam was not always healthful and there were many cases of food poisoning. (I remember the meat was sometimes green when it arrived at the units.) And I won't even talk about the rats!

Heat was the main culprit for spoiled food. In Viet Nam, it was often 95 to 105 degrees Fahrenheit by midday, with the humidity nearly always over 95 percent. Furthermore, the temperatures were much higher inside our corrugated metal hooches and the mess hall. Before the end of a meal, a fresh stick of butter just set out would melt off the saucer and run across the table. That was neither appetizing nor safe.

One alternative I took up was to eat rations that had been packed in preservatives back in the 1940s. We still had some of the old "C-rations" available to us then. In addition to the preservatives in these rations, a lot of foods contained formaldehyde to try to keep them free of bacteria—even all of the favorite beers from the U.S. tasted strongly of it. I remember the running jokes about how the Army wanted to pre-embalm as many soldiers as possible through the food and beer to save some work when we ended up in the morgue.

Two months after returning from my leave, I was transferred from the coastal air base on the peninsula at Cam Ranh Bay to Phu Bai, seven miles north of Da Nang. While there, I twice became severely ill. The first instance was probably from food poisoning. On the second occasion, however, my severe intestinal trauma was shared with about one-third of the 6,000 soldiers in Phu Bai. The whole base actually ran out of toilet paper for a couple of days and letters from home that week suddenly became more meaningful. Some of the men were so weak that they simply lay down in the shade between the showers and the latrines, where they could be close to both. We were told the epidemic was more food poisoning, and the meat was blamed. The problem with this argument was that there were separate food and water sources serving all the men on the spread-out air base. Furthermore, I wasn't eating any meat at that point. I therefore quizzed my medic, a man of the same rank as me, while he was giving me a check-up. He quietly agreed that I had to be right and that it couldn't possibly be the food.

"I just had food poisoning a few weeks ago," I told him. "This feels different. It feels like dysentery to me. I suspect the water supply has been sabotaged."

"I've been ordered not to say," he replied. "But your reasoning is logical."

At that time, Viet Nam was undergoing the second major invasion of the American portion of the war—the Easter Offensive of March 1972. The whole northern part of the country was already lost. As the nearest resupply air base, Phu Bai was critical to the outcome of that battle. I believe to this day that enemy agents had poisoned our several water sources with dysentery in a biological attack designed to weaken our support base at the onset of that offensive.

I lost 30 pounds in that two-week period. I had entered the military weighing 135, had been fattened up to 165 on Army food, then was released again weighing 135. I wouldn't recommend dysentery as a weight-loss diet. The only nice thing about it all was the opium-based drugs we received for the cramps.

After recovering from the second illness, I started paying to have one good meal brought to me each evening by a local woman who worked as a base employee cleaning our hooches. It was mostly stir-fried vegetables and rice. In this way, I was able to eat a great vegetarian meal each evening before going on guard duty all night from dark to dawn. From the Army, I only trusted eating fruit or toast during my last few months. No one really cared about or even noticed my diet in Viet Nam, and being a vegetarian didn't impede my social life in the way it sometimes does in the United States. However, once I returned home, I clearly became to many some kind of freak. This was true even in my own family, who for a long time didn't understand why I had become a vegetarian or how absolutely committed I was to become to that cause.

Eating Healthfully

For my first ten years as a vegetarian, I didn't concern myself much with whether I was getting a healthful or balanced diet. When you first become a vegetarian, you usually spend more time thinking about what *not* to eat than what *to* eat. This is because after cutting out meat, almost everything that is left is a lot better than the standard fat-centered diet. I was happily married most of that time in any event, and my wife obliged my culinary ignorance by cooking all the food. I simply ate what was put in front of me and thought all of it was good.

Once I became single again in 1982, however, I was faced head-on with my glaring inability to cook. I ended up eating out in restaurants a lot, and the vegetarian choices in Canton were frustratingly limited. I remember asking one restaurant in 1973 if they could go out of their way just a little and, instead of a tossed salad, make any kind of special dish for me as a vegetarian. "Sure," they said, and proceeded to cut a head of lettuce in half and serve it to me round side up on a plate with a bowl of dressing on the side. I'm going to have to do something about this someday, I thought.

Back then, most restaurants in my part of Ohio, as I'm sure elsewhere, cooked with lard—something they still do in Ohio's rural areas, especially desserts. At one local steak house, the waiter, annoyed with my attempt to bend his menu so I could eat something, actually sneered at me and said, "The menu is the menu!" I left. I had already discovered the importance of always voting with your dollars. They went under a couple of years later.

In the first four years after my divorce, I had to cook and shop for myself for virtually the first time in my life. I didn't have much success in finding healthy vegetarian meals in restaurants. This forced me to take a whole new look at my dinner plate. I knew that I wasn't eating a violent diet, but I began to ask myself whether I was getting what I needed nutritionally to sustain a long and healthy life. I became concerned. What if I was accidentally being negligent and was somehow missing even one essential nutrient or mineral over a lifetime? Would I face some incurable disease later on in life as a result? It seemed important to find out. I needed some facts, and soon. I also needed some better places to eat.

While there were books on vegetarian nutrition and cooking available (although only a fraction of the number there are now), I knew that the best way for me to learn about nutrition was to ask some really pointed questions of the best and most learned vegetarian minds in the country. One way I thought I could do that would be to attend one of the national vegetarian conferences. That, however, wasn't a priority in my budget when I had alimony and child support to pay. A better solution was to bring those speakers to Canton and get the answers delivered to me firsthand. It occurred to me that I ought to be able to set up a group that would do both things our area needed: 1) Bring in knowledgeable speakers who could address the major concerns for vegetarians; and 2) somehow finesse that lecture program into an organization that would entice our local restaurants to offer some good vegetarian food.

Therefore, I zealously began to gather the names and addresses of every vegetarian I had ever heard about. Most people I met told me that they had heard of vegetarians but that I was the first one they'd ever met. However, if someone told me, "My daughter is a vegetarian," I took her name and address for later. If someone even said, "I used to know a vegetarian," I pursued the topic until I got another name and address. Within a couple of years, I had over fifty names.

Vegetarian Club of Canton

Through compiling name after name, the Vegetarian Club of Canton came into being. In the fall of 1986, I asked some friends to help me plan the menu for a dinner meeting for a new club. We announced our first meeting to the media, and it was given good coverage in several local papers, one with a large photo. Then I sent a letter to my special list. The first meeting had 114 attendees. The catered food was fair, but the speaker was great. He spoke in a very compelling manner of how he believed he had put his cancer into remission after going on a vegan (strict vegetarian) diet. There was clearly enough interest in continuing to form a group, and those interested met to set up the organization. The duties were divided so that no one person would get too burned out with all the work.

When working with volunteers, I have discovered that titles are valuable, especially when no money is being offered. Titles give volunteers confidence to carry out their duties. Consequently, we created several roles. First, there were the positions that were absolutely required for a nonprofit organization: president, secretary and treasurer. Then we created a vice president of operations, a vice president of education and an editor for the newsletter-to-be. The VP of operations would help with restaurant coordination. The VP of education would deal with speakers and oversee the newsletter editor's activities. We had a contest and named our newsletter the *Veggie Digest*, a delightful play on words.

I explained my ideas to the group. I didn't want us to just become a regular vegetarian club. By then I had learned that most vegetarian clubs are social groups that get together about once a month, espe-

VEGETARIAN CLUB OF CANTON

Figure 6:1 Vegetarian Club of Canton logo

cially around holidays, to enjoy vegetarian potluck meals. Everyone has to cook something to attend. This is usually a great outlet for folks socially; the kids all play with each other and everyone gets to hang out with some friends of like mind. For a whole evening, there's no hassle over diet as there might be at a family gathering or in a restaurant.

I didn't feel that was enough for us. I already went out to eat with my friends, and, from a community activist's standpoint, having a potluck meeting was like preaching to the choir. In addition, vegetarian potlucks had been going on forever around America, and no evidence I knew of told me that they were the best way to build a larger community of vegetarians. Even in Pittsburgh, Boston or Kansas City, whose groups I had visited back then, and in many other major cities, vegetarian potlucks only rounded up thirty to fifty people at a time. What further predisposed me against potlucks were that they were sometimes intimidating for new vegetarians, even committed ones. In fact, by design, you have to already know how to cook something vegetarian to attend. I was concerned about the people who, like me, wanted to learn the basics of vegetarianism before jumping in and laying their culinary skills on the table in front of all the local experts.

Instead of a potluck I proposed an upscale vegetarian meeting. "Let's go to a different restaurant every month and have a quality four-course vegan meal and a speaker," I suggested. In this way, we would in effect be paying for all the best area restaurants to train their staffs about vegetarianism. I wanted to make our meeting a "Veggie Date Night." "Our members will be those who probably would have spent money to go out to eat anyway," I argued. "Now we can offer them a quality meal and lecture as a social event once each month."

It worked. Curiously enough, some of those same restaurants who often rudely couldn't find any way to serve me as a lone vegetarian suddenly became very accommodating when we dangled $1,000 to $1,500 in front of them. The prospect of 60 to 100 people at $15 a head visiting their restaurant was a necessary incentive for change. While individually we couldn't break through, our collective dollars meant something.

I caught some heat the first two years from locals who were not able to afford our gourmet meal and lecture programs, which usually cost $15 to $18. I was sympathetic; I usually couldn't afford to go myself. What we did, therefore, was to use our profits to pay for a lot of free meals for the impoverished in the first few years so they could come and hear the speakers. I encouraged the critics to set up their own potluck dinners, which I would help to promote. No one did. Later, when we added potlucks to our regular schedule, those early critics never attended anyway. I guess they were just interested in the concept of social justice and not the practice.

In this way, our new team set up the entire first year's program all at once, something of a rarity among vegetarian clubs. We planned and booked restaurants, menus, speakers and travel, and put out a beautiful calendar for 1987 with the whole year's program on one sheet. Thus we had the year at a glance. We found this was the only way both to guarantee the restaurants and to get the speakers since the latter typically plan as much as a year in advance with other groups. Most grassroots vegetarian clubs only look one to two months ahead in their planning. I believe this creates unnecessary

stress for all involved, including the members, speakers and restaurants, and eventually leads to activist burnout.

I wanted to bring in at least two national speakers each year. We
decided to hold ten dinners, omitting August and December. Two
months would have national speakers, two or three would have
regional speakers from around Ohio and the remaining speakers
would be local. We tried from the start to include in each year's agenda at least one speaker who was a medical doctor or osteopath, a chi-
ropractor or a registered dietician. This was because, according to a
law passed in Ohio (and other states) to protect registered dieticians,
only these professionals are licensed to give nutritional advice. As a
result of this law, people with Ph.D.s in nutrition and decades of
dietary counseling have been ordered to cease their illegal practices
and threatened with indictment. In our efforts to comply with this
law, we tried to include some licensed speakers in our events every
year.

Since no one can really learn all there is to know in one meeting,
from the beginning our club tried to cover all the bases each year over
a one-year period. Basic vegetarian topics include health issues and
the nutritional sciences, as well as cleansing and healing, emotional
and spiritual issues, moral and ethical issues such as animal rights
and environmental concerns. At the outset, our plan was to make
available a complete picture of vegetarianism if you attended every
meeting for one year. One month we would hear a lecture entitled
"Dispelling the Myths about Vegetarianism," which would cover how
to get enough protein, calcium, vitamins etc. Then we would have a
speaker on how to use soy products. Or someone would talk about
the environmental benefits of vegetarianism. Once each year we
would be sure to include, usually at my request, someone to speak on
the ethical and moral side of vegetarianism. For this we would hear
from either a vegetarian religious or spiritual speaker or an animal
rights advocate. Our goal was to offer the best information available
and encourage our members to make up their minds themselves as to
what they chose to believe. We never once told anyone, "This is the
way you have to eat." Often, we would have a speaker argue one view

one month and another argue the opposite position the next. Our goal was to bring the knowledge to the area, but we didn't want to sway people one way or the other regarding the details. We are all, after all, responsible for ourselves.

In fact, we were very clear that you didn't even have to be a vegetarian to attend the Vegetarian Club. We wanted to be a resource group for brand new people who even remotely wanted to look into the idea of vegetarianism, and then to be gracious to everyone who joined us. We taught by both knowledge and experience, and praised everyone who took even a little step in a healthier direction.

That was the theory, at least; it didn't always work that way. Ironically, a few of the more intense members whom I helped to convince to become vegetarians eventually attacked me for my dietary lapses. While I have not eaten meat (including chicken or fish) in the last thirty years, I have not always been a vegan. Having to eat out twice a day, my vegetarian diet often included dairy products in some years. The same critics occasionally railed at someone in the meetings for their carelessness. When this happened, I quietly took the member out in the hall and explained to them our rules and guidelines. One fanatical member, who had previously blasted me, took some new people to task at their first meeting for eating dairy products. I invited him into the hall and told him that we as a group had decided that there was to be no judging of people. He was furious that I would question him and his dietary intelligence. As I feared, the new people never returned. Being unconditionally accepting, however, we put up with his behavior for years, always gently trying to correct it. It is my sincere belief that attacking others is not the way to get them to change their viewpoint. Violence wins temporary victories. Love and acceptance open the way for permanent change.

Another mistake occurred one year in a meeting when I offered a brief prayer before the meal. My original club format included a prayer, or, at the least, a time of silence as a blessing before we ate. There is an ancient teaching that we digest our food better if we get quiet before and settled before and during the meal, which may be one of the reasons why most religious traditions recommend a blessing and an "attitude of gratitude" before and after meals.

VCC has always been a diverse group. Most of us are used to each other. My error that day was to open my prayer with my church's traditional address of "Father-Mother God." The Unity Christian Church recognizes that the Divine contains both the feminine and the masculine principles. I offended a somewhat fundamentalist couple who were attending for the first time and who were so bothered that they took me out in the hall to find out what kind of heathen group they had joined. I assured them that the group did not offer or endorse any specific religious beliefs. I then suggested that they were welcome to offer the prayer in the next meeting in any fashion they were comfortable with if they wished. And I then told them that another part of the guidelines of the vegetarian club was that everyone was to welcome everyone else, without bigotry. We had Jews, Buddhists, Hindus, Catholics and a full range of Protestants, from liberal to conservative, in our group, along with a few agnostics and a couple of Wiccans. If they were not comfortable with that, I told them, I would immediately give them their money back, and they were welcome to leave. They left. "Love thy neighbor, unless they are different from you" is not the scripture as I remember it.

Our speaker program in combination with the practical experience of eating good vegan food offered a complete vegetarian experience. We brought some of the best names in the vegetarian movement to Canton. Dr. Michael Klaper from Florida, the embodiment of a compassionate medical advisor, came several times to help us get started. So did Howard Lyman from Virginia, a fourth-generation Montana cattle farmer and feedlot operator turned vegan and author of the book *Mad Cowboy*, which talks about the environmental devastation and human health problems caused by factory farms and a meat-intensive diet. There was cookbook author Victoria Moran of Kansas, nationally recognized dieticians Reed Mangels and Suzanne Havala. Ingrid Newkirk, cofounder of People for the Ethical Treatment of Animals (PETA), came, and Heidi Prescott and Michael Markarian from the Fund for Animals also visited.

We brought in John Robbins from California after his book *Diet for a New America* came out on video, and 600 people attended. The brilliant consumer advocate and author of *Beyond Beef*, Jeremy Rifkin, who heads the Greenhouse Crisis Foundation and the Foundation on Economic Trends in Washington, D.C., spoke. As a community vegetarian event, I arranged for our 350-member Canton Rotary Club to hear a talk on population and world hunger by Dr. Werner Fornos, a consultant to world leaders and the United Nations and head of the World Population Institute. At the time of writing, we have had over 30 national speakers out of nearly 150 lectures held in Canton. I believe the VCC to be a community organization to be proud of. We have changed people's health and their lives, and, as an additional benefit, it is no longer socially weird to be a vegetarian in Canton.

Reaching Out to Restaurants and the Community

In the beginning, the Vegetarian Club sent our newsletter to every major restaurant and newspaper in our area. Even if the restaurants were not cooperative and just threw it in the trash each month, I wanted them to know that we were still out there. Within a couple of years I began to be recognized by most of the restaurant managers and owners, something that helped me personally when eating out, as well as helping our group to influence them.

We also sent the newsletter to every high school library. I heard later through my "free tree" program from some of the librarians who said that they began to keep copies of *Veggie Digest* in a three-ring notebook as reference material for all the students who wanted to write papers about vegetarianism and the environment.

Before John Robbins's visit, we bought 43 of his *Diet for a New America* videos and sent them to every high school, college and public library in the county. We heard from students who had teachers who had played the tape for every class all day long. We hope to do the same with a recent documentary titled *The Witness*. It is a compelling story of a New York businessman named Eddie Lama who woke up to suffering and became involved in the animal rights movement.

Four Key Reasons for Environmentalists to be Vegetarian

Animal rights activists are always dumbfounded by people who love and protect dogs and cats and wouldn't think of eating them, but who continue to eat chickens, pigs and cows. I recently read about a family who spent a fortune lovingly taking their dog to show at the national level. The owner attended the show in New York wearing a raccoon coat. This is called "speciesism." Speciesism is the idea that human beings have the right of domination over every other species. This goes back to the religious teachings of "dominion" over other animals that is noted in the book of Genesis in the Bible. The meaning for "dominion" that has most often been used is "domination" instead of "stewardship." Animal activists are equally critical of those who have become vegetarians for health reasons and never quite understand or become active fighting issues of cruelty. Both vegetarians and animal activists are equally amazed by devoted environmentalists who have not made the connection between the destruction of the planet and a meat-centered diet. Our vegetarian club has tried to address these issues.

Although I love public speaking, I have been the featured speaker at our club only twice in fifteen years. I once gave a much-overdue talk on proper colon maintenance, a delicate subject to offer at a dinner meeting. No one else would dare to do it. As the resident environmental activist, I also offered one talk about the environmental reasons for vegetarianism. I told the audience, "The problem with reading books about vegetarianism is that no one who isn't making a career about some aspect of vegetarianism could ever remember all the specific details. Consequently, when engaged in an argument, we have to fall back on generalities. In arguments, the one with the most detailed facts usually wins."

Thus, in my lecture, I presented four facts. Each represented a compelling environmental reason for becoming or remaining a vegetarian. To make it easy to memorize them, I reduced them to simple formulas and passed out index cards and asked everyone to first write the formulas down. The following section represents my attempt in this book to persuade you to become a vegetarian, to provide you with a more persuasive technique to help other people become vege-tarian, and to give you an example of how to be persuasive in turn-ing people on to any concern you may be promoting.

Although there are many reasons for an environmentalist to be a vegetarian, here are the four reasons most interesting to me, taken from John Robbins's powerful and inspirational book *Diet for a New America* and condensed by me:

1. 1M = 25 V
2. 300Y = -1/2T
3. 1/4# = 55 sq ft
4. 1#W = 25 G and 1#B = 5200 G

Confused? Well, so were my listeners! However, before I went over the points, I had the audience repeat the math formulas aloud as a group several times, then pair up and prove to the other member of the pair that they had them memorized perfectly. Sound familiar? I had used the same method of repetition with my "free tree" students. Next I explained each point.

1. 1M = 25 V
On the land that it takes to grow food for one person with a meat-cen-tered diet (1M), you can feed twenty-five vegetarians (25V). This is largely because of the additional land required for grazing or growing grain to feed the cattle, pigs, sheep and poultry. So 25 vegetarians can eat on the same land that is needed for one meat eater. Said differ-ently, each vegetarian uses one twenty-fifth of the land resources needed for each meat eater.

2. 300Y = -1/2T
In the last 300 years, half of the trees in America have been cut down. Of all the many reasons, growing beef for human consumption has been the cause of 85 percent of all deforestation and the resultant loss of millions of tons of topsoil and most of the water pollution in the United States.

3. 1#W = 25 G or 1#B = 5200 G
One pound of wheat (1#W) requires 25 gallons of water to grow. One pound of beef (1#B) requires 5,200 gallons of water, including the water required to grow the grain to be fed to the cattle.

4. 1/4# = 55 sq ft
Each quarter-pounder (1/4#) burger sold in America's fast food restaurants requires the destruction of 55 square feet of tropical rain forest. This is due to the slash-and-burn policies of beef farmers in those countries, which results in the loss of topsoil in rain forest areas, creating a permanent desert. Because of this information being made public, the nation's largest fast food chains stopped importing beef from countries with tropical forests. However, since the U.S. now imports the same 10 percent of its beef for other culinary interests, the same dynamic is occurring. Our dinner diet is responsible for much world deforestation.

In my lecture, I also pointed out that the trend of land use in America is particularly destructive. Intensive agriculture in the form of Contained Animal Feedlot Operations, or CAFOs, commonly known as "factory farms" have taken over the smaller family farms, which can no longer compete with the larger establishments. In 1945 there were 2.5 million farms in the United States. Today, there are 400,000 and within five years there may only be 200,000.

What I wanted was for everyone to have a wallet-sized cheat sheet for making their environmental arguments have bite, and it worked. Many of the attendees reported back that they had subsequently been able to impress their friends and families with the knowledge they memorized in that meeting. Five years later, I was able to borrow that same index card from one of our members, who still had it in her purse, to write this section for you.

Continuing Success
Overall, the results from our vegetarian club were dramatic. Within our first few years we had accomplished several significant things. There were a dozen restaurants with at least one new item on their

menu, just for vegetarians. They weren't all vegan, but it was a start. Now we could at least go out to eat without having a battle. That situation has only improved: After fifteen years, we have scores of restaurants countywide offering vegetarian choices. Two restaurants have actually researched and created entire vegetarian menus for us apart from their regular meat-centered menus. The local restaurant association has begun teaching its members that when you turn away a vegetarian, you turn away not just one, but four or five customers. This is because any carload of passengers going to lunch will often cater to the person with the most restrictive diet.

Our group has evolved as well, both in width and depth. After running a few years under another nonprofit I had started, the Vegetarian Club of Canton obtained a separate nonprofit status with the Internal Revenue Service. As a 501(c)3 organization, we have begun to write and receive grants for student educational activities and general operations. We also have more members, and many of them have become very well informed. Some have gone on to teach others. One of the biggest problems with an organization like ours, however, is turnover. After one or two years, when members finally feel satisfied with their level of knowledge, they tend to stop coming and I am constantly reminding them that, although they no longer need to attend for their own benefit, they need to keep coming for the benefit of others. We need to continue to pay for the same learning curve year after year to give the ever-changing restaurant owners, managers, cooks and even new servers a chance to learn about vegetarianism, and to continue our speakers' forum for new vegetarians to grow through.

Every year the Vegetarian Club helps to promote the national Vegetarian SummerFest organized by the North American Vegetarian Society (NAVS), our national club affiliate. For several years, NAVS has held their annual conference only four hours from Canton in Johnstown, Pennsylvania on the beautiful campus of the University of Pittsburgh. One year we had over twenty Vegetarian Club of Canton members attend. Other VCC members have gone to Ontario, Canada to the Toronto Vegetarian Food Fair, which features speakers and draws over 10,000 people. Nothing does more to deepen both knowledge and commitment than attendance at one of these conferences. One of my goals has always been to create living exponents of the knowledge of vegetarianism. We now have many in our community. VCC has become a well-recognized part of our community, reaching into every neighborhood to touch people's lives.

Animal Activism

After a few years of attending our vegetarian meetings, local animal activist Deborah Akel came to me for help on her proposal to ban leghold traps in the City of Canton. There had been an unfortunate incident involving a cat who had lost a leg in a trap placed behind a garbage can to kill off nuisance animals. It had gotten huge publicity and several letters had been written to the editor. Evidently, placing the trap in our dense urban area was not illegal, and while not checking the trap for several days may have been a violation of cruelty laws, no charges had been pressed. Deborah felt the atmosphere was ripe for a new ordinance. Large metropolitan areas are clearly no place for indiscriminate weapons, since there are too many beings, including small children, who might become unintended victims.

There was already an ordinance banning hunting and the discharge of firearms in the city, so one would have assumed the ordinance would be easy to pass. The state trappers, however, immediately positioned themselves to fight the ordinance, fearing that this would be the thin end of a new anti-trapping wedge. Once trapping was banned in Canton, they feared, all cities and then rural areas would be targeted, and eventually their guns would be taken away.

The Vegetarian Club, therefore, created a new position for Deb— vice president of ethical and animal issues. With the group behind the new appointee, we felt she would have more clout. Then we pitched in to help her, and, although it was a tough and emotional debate, the ban passed Canton City council 11 votes to 2.

One would not expect that our vegetarian group would ever have had to deal in any way with violence. However, this has turned out, unfortunately, not to be the case. The closest we usually get to a physical confrontation is if we have a speaker talk about the violence in "factory farming" or describe the methods being used in slaughter-houses by multinational corporate meat-producers.

On one such occasion, one of our dinner meetings ended in a fight between one of our members and a beef-eating customer of the restaurant. I set up a meeting in a separate room in a well-known steak house that had previously been lousy at catering to vegetarians. Until then, all the steak house had had for vegetarians to eat had been a salad bar. Nevertheless, the owner/day-manager was fairly cooperative and encouraging, and told us he would work with us. However, when we showed up for the meeting months later, the evening manager was hostile from the beginning. It was clear that he hated us and felt we were a threat to his entire belief system and probably his livelihood.

"I can't let you use the extra room," he said to me. "I have it full of customers, and I'm not about to move them." Sure enough, he had not emptied the meeting room in time for our group and proposed to put us out in the middle of a big dining area that was partially walled off.

I was frank with him. "Sure, we can eat there," I said. "But you are going to have a major problem when we get to our speaker tonight. It could upset some of your customers." I went on to explain that we planned to watch a short movie about chicken farms that was graphic and disturbing. The manager acted like it was my problem. Just before we were to run the film, I asked the manager again to consider moving one table of three rough-looking men I had spied out who would be forced to both watch and hear the film clip. He refused.

After the movie, while our speaker was beginning to explain the problems around cruelty in factory farms, one of the three men got up and came into the archway at the end of our group. He was a tall, lanky guy with a scraggly beard.

"You people are a bunch of f—ing idiots!" he screamed. "You don't know what the f— you are talking about! You guys piss me off."

I was at the other end of the long table of forty. One of our new members, a city employee sitting next to my mother, rose up and took one step toward the guy. He put up both hands with palms up and fists unclenched.

"We'd appreciate it," he began, "if you didn't cuss in front of all these..." He got no further, as the irate customer stepped forward and decked him. Then the irate customer jumped on the city employee and they both landed on my mother's lap. Everyone turned to me with a look of panic and in a way that told me they expected me to do something. I turned to my date, who knew the whole story about the manager.

"Now, where's the manager?" I asked. "This is his fault. And you know what's really ironic? Now I suppose I'll have to go over there and break up this fight."

I did. Actually, I got the customer's two buddies to help. They were standing watching to see whether they would need to jump in and help their friend battle it out with our fanatical vegetarian pacifists. Instead, they helped pull their pal off our club member and restrained him while I helped our man off the floor and put him back into his seat. I then checked on my mother. I apologized to the customer for upsetting him and helped to steer him back over toward his table.

Our lanky friend was, however, beyond reason and continued to scream, and so I went to call the police. The hostess, a fragile old lady, wouldn't call the police without the manager's agreement and wouldn't let me use her phone. The manager was noticeably absent. Finally, after finding a quarter, I brushed past her in exasperation and went out in the hall to the pay phone. By the time the police came, the customer was having second thoughts and on his best behavior.

The police talked to me, our club member, the customer and the manager. Finally, the police came over to me.

"Well, the manager says that he will not file charges against you," they said, "if your guy agrees not to file charges against the customer who attacked him."

"What?" I replied, incredulously.

"The manager says you assaulted his hostess. But he agrees to drop his complaint against you if your member agrees to drop his complaint against the other customer as well." So that's how this works, I thought. What irresponsibility!

I told our man, "Obviously, they don't want this altercation in the newspaper. My advice is that you do whatever you need to do. If I were you, I'd drag that guy into court in a heartbeat. He's probably already on parole. But don't worry about me. My incident is unrelated to your being assaulted. I'll fend for myself." In the end, the meeting ended and the charges were all dropped. We never went back there, nor could we. The steak house went out of business later.

The only other time any members of our groups have put themselves near violence has been in some of the actions of the few members who are animal rights activists. I have been among them. These actions have primarily included fur store protests, leafleting at McDonald's, hunt protests and pigeon shoots, about which you can read in the next chapter. While I have never helped any "hunt disruptions," I have counseled some young people who have done so. Disrupting hunts is now illegal in Ohio, and I can't say I am not in some ways relieved. There was always a risk of injury when young people were deliberately going out and confronting hunters who were not only armed but locked and loaded and eager to shoot something.

Misunderstandings

In spite of all our educational work, the level of misunderstanding about vegetarianism still amazes me. I was once confronted by a man in a restaurant who was sitting at another table, but whom I had not even been addressing. He stood and argued with me very forcefully that chicken and seafood were not meat! He even began to yell and turn red about how stupid I was. Obviously, the whole idea threatened everything he had been brought up to believe.

The whole encounter led me to start telling a new educational joke at our meetings: "We are often asked to define vegetarianism. Everyone knows by now that there are three kinds of vegetarians. First, the purest kind is a vegan. Vegans eat fruits, vegetables, legumes and grains. If you add dairy products and dairy by-products to the diet, that is the second kind, a lacto-vegetarian. If you then add eggs to the diet, that is the third kind, a lacto-ovo vegetarian. Then there are those people who think they are vegetarians, but still eat chicken and fish. We call them 'Catholics.' " I mean it facetiously, but it is astonishing how often I've found it to be true!

We have definitely made progress in Stark County. In a county where over the years I've had several waitresses actually panic when I told them I was a vegetarian and run off to get their manager to talk to me, I recently ate at our downtown McKinley Hilton. When I started off with "I'll need your help tonight. I'm a vegetarian," the waiter smiled and said, "That's great. Are you vegan or lacto-ovo?"

Our vegetarian club has had a successful impact on its members and the community because of good organizing skills and volunteers who have carried out the necessary tasks year after year. Stunned that a small conservative Ohio town is doing more to promote healthy vegetarianism than many major metropolitan areas, our guest speakers and other visitors to the area have often asked Vegetarian Club members, "What's in Canton?" I've been told that they usually smile and say, "David Kidd." I would argue in response that, except for some innate organizational skills, there is nothing really unique about me. Anyone who is old enough to think of a good idea is also capable of starting a nonprofit grassroots community action organization.

Vegetarianism, my commitment to nonviolence, my TM training and the organizational know-how I learned in the army have taught me to ask myself an essential question: How do we know what to act on and when to act? I believe that awareness equals responsibility, and that if you have enough consciousness to see the need, it is therefore your responsibility to act on filling it. To put it another way, if you do not know about a problem, you are not karmically responsible for it. However, the moment you do know, then you are also responsible. Not to act then would be both bad karma and a sin. Nevertheless, since there are so many social needs apparent to those who are awake, it is only necessary to pick one issue and become an advocate for it. All that is needed after that are good organizational skills and a willingness to get others invested. After that, you simply watch it grow!

Figure 7:1 Dead and wounded birds collected by "trapper boys" at Hegins

Figure 7.2 Real Men Don't Shoot Pigeons!

7: Real Men Don't Shoot Pigeons

I HAVE NOT only been an animal activist in restaurants, but on several occasions in my life I have had the opportunity to put my beliefs into practical use in situations involving both humans and animals. There are times when events are so contentious that good people need to stand in the way of violence and demand that it stop. One of the most provocative and compelling issues in which I have been involved was the Hegins Pigeon Shoot (pronounced "ha-gins").

I first heard about Hegins at the annual Vegetarian SummerFest conference sponsored by North American Vegetarian Society. Hegins was one of the issues at the top of agenda for animal advocates around the nation from the late 1980s to late 1990s. I went to see what the big deal was, and ended up attending for several years to help protest the event.

Hegins, Schuylkill County, PA, Labor Day, 1994 to 1997

Pennsylvania still permits the shooting of live pigeons for sport. It is a very popular practice across the state in private gun clubs. Three other states also allow it: Texas, Louisiana and Tennessee. But there are no known shoots held in those states today. The rest of the nation has, state by state, outlawed this practice as the barbaric and cruel act that it is. Hunters in these more progressive states have moved on to shooting clay pigeons, or skeet, and now the newer and more fun variation, sporting clays.

In Pennsylvania, however, every weekend, during good weather, there are numerous live bird shoots. Today, they are held in private clubs. However, for sixty years, the county park in the town of Hegins in Schuylkill County sponsored an annual shoot each Labor Day on their public parkland. The shoot was the big fundraiser for the park, which was the site of the local swimming pool, and brought in substantial sums of money for the community. In some years, nearly two hundred shooters would come from all over the country and pay to participate. Large cash prizes were awarded and usually between 6,000 and 8,000 birds would be killed. Paid attendance would vary from 10,000 to 20,000.

For many years, animal activists documented the extraordinary cruelty involved in this pigeon shoot. Even though the event drew some of the best shots in the country, surprisingly, a large majority of the birds released were not killed outright. Instead, the wounded birds would fly to a nearby tree or land on the ground where they could suffer for hours or even days before they died. Some were missed outright. Local enthusiasts for the shoots would encourage young boys and girls to become "trapper boys." The children would load the traps and gather up the killed or wounded animals after each round of firing. The children were taught that the pigeons were just "rats with wings," and that any concern for the pigeons' welfare was misplaced. So, the children would stomp on the birds, who flopped about helplessly, or broke the birds' necks with a twist before flinging the bodies in a trash barrel.

In the late 1980s, after they had heard from eyewitnesses what was occurring, a coalition of Pennsylvania animal rights activists from local groups began to protest at the Hegins shoot. Hegins was a more conspicuous target than shoots in private clubs because it was held on more accessible public land. Soon, these groups were joined by major national animal rights groups, such as the Fund for

Animals and People for the Ethical Treatment of Animals (PETA). The Fund had been started by author Cleveland Amory in 1967, while PETA had been founded by Ingrid Newkirk and Alex Pacheco only a few years prior to the protests. The protesters included many out-of-staters, students and other members of social justice groups that traditionally are seen by those in power as "professional protesters." However, the groups also included mothers with children at home, businessmen and -women and lawyers. By 1994, the year that I first attended Hegins, the Labor Day weekend protest had reached a peak.

To get a sense of the scene, picture 20,000 valley residents driving into the park, then walking, some with shotguns over their shoulders, from the huge grass-covered parking lot with their families to enter the front gate after having to pass through a gauntlet of 1,500 vocal protesters. Inside the park, although it is still early morning, the beer is already flowing freely, ribs are cooking in open pits and the local Rotary Club, Lions and JayCees are selling food and soft drinks, engaged in their own fundraisers.

The shooting starts around 8 o'clock in the morning. One at a time, the hunters line up in front of seven small wooden boxes, each containing a pigeon that is either a captured "nuisance" bird or a bird raised in captivity for the event. The birds are stored in a hot hut until they are delivered to each of the seven killing fields. The birds usually arrive dehydrated, underfed and unused to the bright daylight.

The hunter takes his or her stance, shoulders the loaded gun, takes the safety catch off and yells, "pull."

A string is pulled by a trapper boy, allowing the spring-loaded lid to pop up on one of the boxes. At the same time, the bottom of the box snaps up a few inches, throwing up and out the scared and hungry bird. Most of the birds burst into flight, some of them flying free for the first time in their lives.

Blam!

Within seconds they are shot at. Unlike clay pigeons, you never know which way live ones are going to go—but that is the extent of the "sport" in the practice of shooting live pigeons. The hunter has two shots to kill each bird. Some of the weaker birds simply rest on the edge of the box or land on the ground nearby, where they are easily picked off. Others take off at strange angles and evade being shot. The crowd roars with each kill, the more gruesome the better.

When I was there, the shooting went on without a break until nearly dark. The seven killing fields faced away from each other on opposite sides of the park. The reverberating concussion of the 12,000 or so shotgun shells loaded with extra heavy amounts of gunpowder was in itself a mind-numbing experience. For anyone unfamiliar with the discharge of weapons, the constant noise of many guns firing together is enough to cause a deep shock to the system. However, watching thousands of birds die is worse. Among the activists, I discovered, nearly everyone cried for at least the first few minutes, while some screamed in disbelief and others broke down in hysterics after watching for several hours. A few were so shaken emotionally by day's end that they needed to be taken away in ambulances. I observed one woman running screaming across a field to get away from the noise; even hours later, she still could not be calmed down. Most of the activists were like me. We cried for a while, and then went to do our jobs.

Such disturbed feelings were, however, not confined to the protesters. It was not uncommon to see the youngest children of the local attendees crying when they heard and saw the gunfire and violence for the first time. The children were harshly teased or chastised for their sensitivity.

The Fund for Animals sponsored a two-day training workshop each year at a hotel in nearby Harrisburg for those interested in participating in the protest. They discussed the overall concept of the protest and their mission to have the laws of Pennsylvania changed to outlaw such practices. Then the Fund invited attendees to decide what level of protest activity they would participate in. The choices of roles were as follows: 1) protesters who would protest verbally outside the park and try not to get arrested; 2) protesters who would enter the park to deliberately attempt to delay or disrupt the shooting and be arrested; 3) documenters, who would sit in pairs at each of the shooting fields inside the park and watch every bird and record the number of dead, wounded or missed; 4) bird rescuers, who went into the park to try to recapture as many wounded birds as possible and run them outside the gate to the veterinary tent for emergency treatment; and 5) peacekeepers to help avoid or break up fights. Each job had its own risks and rewards. Each job had its own training workshop. Safety was a major element of the training. The safest job was to protest outside the gates without the intent of arrest. Even then, altercations sometimes arose between locals attending and protesters. In these cases, regardless who started it, both parties were immediately arrested and booked, with the judge later on ultimately deciding who was at fault.

One strategic goal of the Fund was to have a lot of people arrested, especially women. Men who were sent to the county jail were not treated kindly. However, there was no prison for women in Schuylkill County. Consequently, women arrested who did not post bail had to be kept in a nearby hotel at the county's expense. And most needed vegetarian food. If the women paid their fines, they were released. But if they refused to pay their fines, they could be given a couple months in "jail" at the hotel to "work" them off by serving time. It was felt that making such arrests into a great enough expense for the county would put pressure on the park to discontinue the shoot. In some years, over 125 people were arrested.

Most years, the fines were negotiated ahead of time between the state police and the Fund for Animals. In their workshops, Heidi Prescott, National Director for the Fund, would say, "If you want to be arrested and pay your fine, that's great. We need some of you to do that. If not, here's a sample schedule [not actual] of fines this year: For running on the shooting field to delay the shoot, you will be charged with 'trespass.' That will cost you $150. If you release birds from their boxes [freeing them and causing further delays] you will be charged with 'trespass' and 'theft of county property.' That will cost $300. If you run off when they try to capture you, that's 'resisting arrest.' Add another $200, bringing the total to $500. If you lie down and make them carry you off the field on a stretcher, that's also 'resisting arrest.' And finally, if you roll off the stretcher to further slow things down, that's considered 'escape.' Add another $200 fine. That's the maximum this year, $700. But what we really need are people who will agree to get arrested and not pay so they can remain in jail as long as possible."

Getting arrested was also a greater physical risk. Violators were chased and sometimes tackled. Abuses occurred and people were hurt. In the early years, before the state police got involved, protesters were dragged off the fields by their hair or by a limb, sometimes by local volunteers coming out of the audience. Even the documenters, sitting quietly on the sidelines, were subject to attack. They were verbally abused, spat on and kicked.

However, it was the bird rescuers who had the most physical contact with the locals. Wounded or missed birds would sometimes fly out of the park, but many would circle back and land in a branch of a tree in the heavily wooded park. Locals would then stand beneath the trees with birds in them, chanting and waiting for them to fall so they could quickly kill them before they were rescued. Rescuers had the job of darting in and grabbing the birds, and, while holding them close to their chests or under their shirts for protection, run to the front gate of the park and out to the veterinary tent. In this way, at least some of the birds could be saved.

It was often the case that ten to twenty locals and one or two rescuers were after the same bird, and it sometimes got very physical. Many protesters and locals were arrested when the slightest contact was made. One year, one of the locals was videotaped taking a rescued bird from the clutches of a female rescuer, biting the bird's head off, and then shoving the bloody carcass back onto the front of the female rescuer's shirt. That graphic clip made the TV news statewide.

I was invited by Heidi to be one of the two leaders of the peacekeepers. The man in charge was a very committed Buddhist named Norm Phelps. He and I were to offer training to would-be peacekeepers. Norm talked about staying calm while I talked about and demonstrated practical tactics. We made it clear that staying calm was the first rule of the day and that under no conditions was it accept-able to be violent. As we made clear, we were there to prevent or to break up fights, not to start or participate in them.

Norm explained to our workshop that there had been a serious lack of communication between the police and the protesters in the past, and that, should we need assistance, there had been no way we could let the police know. In previous years, when only the local police had been in the park, the officers had seemed to deliberately delay coming to anyone's aid, partly because they didn't want to have to arrest their friends and drinking buddies. After all, they had to live with them for the rest of the year. The park covered many acres, so sometimes the officers simply didn't know someone needed help. Now, however, the increased amount of activity at Hegins meant that the state police were in charge of security operations. Consequently, there was greater protection and it was more fairly provided than before. But there still needed to be a solid line of communication between the activists and the authorities. So Norm had a number of radio handsets, which he issued to peacekeepers and data collectors. He would spend his day on the roof of a nearby building alongside a major in charge of the state police detachment coordinating commu-nications. He was to be our lifeline.

The mornings usually started off quietly, if the steady thumping of shotguns can be considered quiet. By early afternoon, though, beer had gone to the locals' heads, and the event usually got rougher phys-ically. Each year people suffered from major and minor injuries. It was not unusual each year for a few lone protesters to get surround-ed by a packed crowd of men and boys and get kicked and punched. Bloody noses and broken ribs were common injuries.

I began with questions: "Is there anyone in here who loves a good fight? If so, you are in the wrong workshop, and need to leave now. We can't use your help. Tomorrow there will be people injured. It happens every year. Some not seriously, others seriously. Our job is to try to prevent that from happening. If the thought of being so close-ly involved in such dangerous situations scares you so much that you feel you will freeze up and not be able to do your job, then you too are in the wrong room. We'll find something else for you to do." A couple of people left.

My primary recommendation in the training was that we should help remove any protesters who were being verbally or physically abused or had become abusive themselves and take them out of the gate to the vet tent, where most of the media were situated. There were usually several huge TV trucks parked there with satellite links and there was almost always a video camera running. We considered that area to be our safe haven. Once in front of a camera, locals were less likely to commit an attack. We simply had to remove our endangered and upset protesters to this base until they calmed down and felt it was safe to go back inside.

I gave very specific tactical advice that I had thought about on on the drive over to Harrisburg. "When you step between two people who are fighting, if you turn toward the angry local and yell or push at him, you're certain to get punched," I instructed, demonstrating with two trainees. "So, instead, shock him. Turn your back to the local, face our protester, and yell at her or him instead: Say 'You're out of line, and I'm taking you out of here.' Then grab the protester's shirtfront and start walking or dragging them toward the front gate. Stay between them and the attacker. The others will follow your lead and go along with you, but by then you are in control."

All of our protesters would be informed that the peacekeeper's job was to remove them from bad situations and take them to a safe place. None of our protesters was encouraged to start any fights. So we would let them debate and argue all they wanted, but some of them did get angry when after hours of being picked on they forgot themselves. That is when we would intervene, because that is when the angry protesters were in the most danger. Remember this about a fight—this first one to completely lose his or her temper loses the fight. Many protesters became so focused on one person that they didn't even know when they were surrounded or in danger.

To their credit, the Pennsylvania state police were completely unbiased, professional and very intolerant of local shenanigans. In some years, there were 300 police working that holiday weekend, some on horseback. Our peacekeepers were to keep Norm appraised of trouble by radio as soon as it arose. Norm and I devised a quick code with three levels to handle problems discreetly on the radio. (You never know who else is listening.) Our Code One was a verbal incident, easily handled; Code Two was a situation with yelling, pushing and shoving, again manageable; and Code Three was the most dangerous—a fight in progress or weapons visible, where police were needed immediately. Depending on what I reported, sometimes Norm would call other peacekeepers to move in our direction. If we got in over our heads, we could call for police help over the radio. Norm stayed all day on top of a nearby building deemed the State Police Headquarters with their ranking officers and big telescopes. I roamed freely in the park. If I was needed, Norm would direct me to the trouble spots, although, as you might imagine, I often found them first. All I had to do was go in the direction of any new roar of the crowd. That was where the action was developing.

On one occasion, I heard a swell of noise from the gauntlet outside the gate. It seems that a leading figure from the Ku Klux Klan had decided to show up with his assistant, both of them in the flowing robes that showed the full majesty of their ranks. They were here to support the shoot, the locals' right to bear arms and the National Rifle Association, which had a table to raffle off a gun at the event each year. Again, to their credit, the state police marched both robed men back out of the gate and searched them and their cars for weapons before letting them attend. As you can expect, the KKK considered the protesters to be anti-hunting, anti-gun, anti-freedom and completely un-American.

All day, hundreds of locals faced off against hundreds of protesters across two rows of fences separating the bulk of the attendees inside from protesters outside, screaming epithets at each other. The fences had police standing about every 100 feet, insuring their inviolability. The younger local men had not really dared to venture out of the gate into the crowd of protesters, who numbered more than a thousand. They mostly roamed the park in packs to pray on our iso-lated protesters who went inside to do their duties.

Another memorable incident occurred while I was outside the gate taking a lunch break among the parked cars. The yelling sud-denly increased. Out of the gate came a virtual conga line of about thirty young men, led by a short, grinning kid with crew-cut red hair, an enviable patch of freckles and a T-shirt bulging with impressive muscles. The men were pushing through the entrance gate crowd made up of hundreds of women. They danced and strutted their stuff, yelling obscenities and challenging everyone. I could just hear their brains chanting, "Aren't we cool? Aren't we cool?"

The conga line was looking for trouble and headed straight toward me and another friend, Chris. We were the only male targets in sight. I had on work boots and a pair of Army camouflaged pants with a bright yellow T-shirt. The back of my shirt read, "Real Men Don't Shoot Pigeons!" in red letters, something I had made specially for the occasion. I looked up at the police headquarters on the roof about 100 yards away. There was movement and pointing. They were watching with binoculars and were already on the radio. All right, I thought. They see it too.

I noticed that in the rear of the line coming out of the front gate were three or four very large middle-aged men, weighing in at 220 to 260 pounds. One was looking directly at me and grinning while he pushed at the kid in front of him, inciting him.

Ah, I've got it, I thought. That was the father of the kid up front. They even looked alike. I looked at the leader, then back to the dad. He nodded to me, glaring, as if to say, "That's right, buddy. You touch my kid and we're gonna come over there and clean your clock."

My old Viet Nam training kicked in: situational awareness. I looked over at the state police horse squad located about 50 yards off to my right. They were beginning to mount up. Good, I thought. Here comes the cavalry. But there was no way they could get here before the conga line arrived unless they galloped through the crowd. We were on our own.

I turned and hollered "Video cameras to the front!" It was well known that the presence of cameras would have a somewhat calming influence on those locals not eager to be caught on film starting trouble.

Several women with cameras came forward. One leaned over to me and said, "I have a camera, but I'm out of film."

"Come in close and pretend to shoot anyway," I said. "They won't know the difference, and you just might save someone's life."

At that moment, that someone was me.

Just then, Chris touched my shoulder.

"I'm right beside you," he said, "no matter what happens." That felt reassuring. Chris was a nice guy, about six feet tall and athletic, and looked like he could hold his own if he ever got into a fight. To her credit, my girlfriend Kelly stayed right beside us as well.

Let's just hope they don't have knives, I thought.

I watched the conga line push its way through the screaming crowd. Both sides were hollering. I thought, How can I love this kid enough to stop him in his tracks? He and his followers clearly had a violent intent. When the kid in front got about three feet from me, he stopped and flexed his arm muscles, fists ready for a fight. I looked him over. He was breathing through the mouth, a bit heavily, and I could see how tense he was.

"How do I get a dialogue going with this guy?" I wondered. We needed to calm things down for a few more minutes.

My eyes were drawn to an incredibly ugly tattoo on the kid's left shoulder. It was a vivid image of a white skull with long fangs dripping red blood. I gave him a big toothy smile and gestured at his shoulder.

"That's the ugliest tattoo I have ever seen my life." It was true.

His grin got even bigger. "Ain't it great?" he replied.

Jesus, I thought, he had taken it as a compliment. I decided to follow that thought. At least we now had us a conversation.

"Where the hell did you get such a thing?" I continued.

"There's a guy in town that does this."

"God, it's hideous. I would never have the guts to wear a tattoo like that. Listen, I know you're looking for a fight, but there isn't anyone here who wants to fight with you, unless you want to fight all these women." He looked around him, disappointed. "And I don't know what everyone has been telling you, but nobody here wants to tell you what to do. We're not here to change you. We're just here to help change the laws in Pennsylvania so it can catch up with the rest of America."

He wanted to argue with me, but didn't quite know where to start. Realizing he wasn't going to get into a fight, he began to calm down. He closed his mouth and took a deep breath through his nose. Gotcha, I thought. We continued to talk, heads leaning close so we could hear. There was still a lot of pushing behind him and yelling from his supporters inside the park. His friends would be proud of him for facing the enemy head-to-head and would think he was giving me an intense earful.

Just then a scrawny, pimply-faced young male activist pushed through beside me and started screaming at the whole line of locals. It was his first close contact with the enemy, and he was practically berserk with anger and babbled at them incoherently, stumbling on his words. As one, they all raised up and turned, reaching out, and made ready to pounce on the new target. The air was instantly charged again. Just as I had counseled the peacekeepers to do, I stepped in front of the new kid with my back to the locals and grabbed the young protester by both shoulders and shoved him back through the crowd until I passed through about five rows of people. I went so far that people didn't know me, and thought I was one of the locals after one of their own. One woman said, "Hey you, take your hands off of him." I told her, "I'm on your side. Now take hold of this kid and don't let go of him. Sit on him if you have to. He's about to get us all killed with his big mouth."

"OK, I will," she said, taking hold of him. I pushed back to the front.

Just then the state police rode through the crowd on horseback, cutting in from the right in a column of twos. They rode directly behind me, essentially dividing the two groups. Then they actually walked both columns of horses apart sideways, something I didn't know a horse could do, separating the two groups. Unfortunately, they put me on the wrong side, pushing me into the guy with the tattoo. I turned to the nearest cop and said, "Hey, you need to let me go on the other side."

The police officer took a look at my camouflage pants and T-shirt. His eyes said, "Ya, right." He was about to say forget it when I showed him the back of my yellow T-shirt. I was allowed to pass through and the local boys were turned around and ushered back into the park. Relieved, I went over and sat up against the wheel of a pick-up truck and did my afternoon meditation. I never did get to use my best tactical idea, which I would have called for if a fight had broken out. We would have immediately yelled for every protester to sit down wherever they were. This would have left the line of angry locals standing exposed among a sea of women, no longer threatened and faced with no one to fight, unless they kicked the women who were sitting harmlessly on the ground.

Later in the park, I was called over to help some documenters, two young girls, who were being kicked and spat on by several men. I moved them over to their left about sixty feet in front of the nearby bleachers, where their backs were protected. The calmer and older locals watching the shoot agreed to keep an eye on them. The guys harassing them then taunted me and challenged me to a fight. They spat beer on me while I took their picture. Taking their picture was another safety move for me. One gave me the finger for the camera, giving me a nice shot for my local vegetarian newsletter.

My daughter Sara, then a student at Kent State University, wanted to attend the event with me in 1994. She chose to be a documenter. She was assigned to sit all day with Sara Steelman, a state representative from Pennsylvania who attended anonymously with the protesters to get an inside look at the event. She got an eyeful of hate, some even directed toward her. Late in the afternoon, as the shooting fields began to shut down, my daughter was freed up and came to ask to join the peacekeepers with me. She had already been trained.

Within her first hour, I saw her walking by with her left hand on the chest of a yelling local youth and her right hand grasping the shirt of a young male protester whom she was leading out of the park. Surrounded by six more hovering locals, Sara nevertheless managed to keep the antagonists safely apart.

"Sara, you need any help?" I called out to her.

"No, I don't think so," she replied. She clearly had everything under control. Sara probably kept that young protester from getting beat up in the back of the park. It was an act of peacemaking that is amazingly empowering experience for a twenty-two year old girl. As for her dad, it made me so proud that tears came to my eyes. It did occur to me that I was glad her mother was not there to see what Sara had done.

Later, Sara happened to be near a wounded bird that had fluttered down from a tree in the back of the park, and had been chased under a car by locals. Although Sara had not wanted to be part of the rescue operation, she dove for the bird, knowing that if she didn't it would be dead within the minute. She was able to grab it and bring it to her chest while almost halfway under the front of a pick-up. Seven or eight local boys both on top of and around her were reaching in, trying to tear the bird from her grasp. This is when I appeared.

All I could see were asses and elbows, but I knew who was in there. I got down on my haunches.

"Sara, are you OK?" I asked.

"Yeah," she replied, gasping. "But I've got to get out of here soon." It was a stalemate. If she tried to back out, the locals would grab the bird from her chest.

I began to drag the locals out one at a time by the back of their pants. I stood each one up respectfully and said, "You're out of this one right now. Just give it up. Maybe you can win the next one. But that's my daughter down there, and I don't want anything to happen to her." They respected that and stood back.

As it turned out, the last guy up was the jerk with the beer can and the finger who had been stalking me and giving me a hard time all day and whose photo I had taken for my vegetarian newsletter. As Sara ran off to the rescue tent with the bird, the local boys turned to abuse me. One of them went to his truck and brought out his crossbow, while the others were daring him to use it on me. He loaded a bolt, but wisely kept it pointed up and never brought it down to bear on me. I walked away, feeling an itch in the middle of my back.

When Sara arrived breathlessly at the vet's tent across the park and outside of the front gate, she handed the wounded bird over to the triage assistant, but it was already dead. She looked at the blood on her shirt and just sat down and cried. I came by shortly thereafter to check on her and could only offer a hug. Now even more determined, by the end of the night she was able to rescue two more birds that lived.

We assisted our people both inside and outside the park. A few times, after helping people out of a tight spot, when someone inside was really gunning for them personally, we decided that they should stay out of the park for the rest of the day. In several instances, when individuals had been singled out and seriously threatened, they just went home. Safety first. There was no more they could do that day, anyway.

Late in the day, as I stood with Sara near the last field of fire open for the final shoot-offs, one older, sour-looking man approached us with a small group of friends. He was wearing a black baseball cap with KKKK on the front of it (obviously for Knights of the Klu Klux Klan).

"We don't need you goddamn queers from New York and New Jersey coming down here telling us what we can and can't do," he yelled in my face.

I smiled and nodded to him, seemingly in agreement. I knew there were some gays and lesbians among the protesters, but I wasn't one of them. There were also a surprising number of married folks with us. And here I was standing there with my arm around my daughter's shoulder.

"Actually, I'm from Ohio," I said.

He continued, not amused, "And where were you, goddamn it, when I was getting my ass shot off in Viet Nam in the sixties?"

Sara looked at him. "Well, personally, I wasn't even born yet," she said quietly. Then she looked at me, expectantly.

"Well," I said. "I was in Cam Ranh Bay and Phu Bai for two tours in the Army. So don't give me any of that unpatriotic protester bullshit. Besides, we're not here to tell you what to do. We're all here just to help change the laws of the state to stop this shoot."

He yammered awhile longer.

Feeling a bit emboldened, Sara asked, "What does that KKKK on your hat stand for?" I thought she was being cute, but she really didn't know.

He looked down at her and said with a straight face, "Well, honey, that means I shop at the Kuh, Kuh, Kuh K-Mart."

Later Years

One year, I remember standing outside the gate with both Heidi Prescott of the Fund for Animals and Ingrid Newkirk of PETA. We were watching all the protesters leave the park. That time of the evening when protester numbers dwindled and the vet tent was being packed up was one of the most dangerous for those few remaining. I asked them both a question, "Are you willing to have someone killed or seriously injured if that's what it takes to stop this shoot?" They both answered without hesitation, and almost simultaneously, "Absolutely not."

I observed that in view of the day of rage that had just occurred, and the minor injuries that had happened, it was hard to imagine the next year being anything but worse. It seemed highly likely that someone would be seriously injured or worse. I also suggested that the protesters seemed to be having too much fun. There clearly were some who came now just for the fun of yelling and screaming at the locals. I was particularly disturbed that day by a woman who singled out and yelled at little kids that their fathers were murderers as the hunters entered the park with their families, carrying their shotguns over their shoulders.

"Wouldn't it be possible to invite protesters to come and protest in silence?" I asked. Through the next year, Heidi and her staff planned the next year's protest to refocus the event on the rescue of injured animals. The Fund took over the protest, focusing on legislative changes, which was one of their strong points, and asked protesters to stay away that year. Many obliged, although three hundred showed up anyway. It was difficult to enlist them, but one by one they lined up outside the park fence and turned their backs on the shoot, standing completely in silence all day. When they talked to each other, it was in reverent tones. It was eerie.

One petite woman in particular, whom I had observed as one of the mouthiest protesters the year previously, at first didn't like the idea at all. But by the end of the day she came up to me and expressed her amazement and satisfaction. Not talking was obviously something new to her, but it had made a powerful impression. We literally had groups of locals approach the line to taunt everyone. In several instances, after several attempts to evoke a response, one of them would say, "Aw, gee, you guys are no fun. We just came today to yell at you all. But this isn't any fun at all. We're goin' home." Victory! We loved it. I could tell that the locals were absolutely in awe of the rigid silence that the several hundred protesters were able to maintain all day with such discipline. Paid attendance at the event dropped back to normal levels and, in turn, the Fund was able to increase its efforts on the legal and legislative front.

The Hegins/Schuylkill County park pigeon shoot was ended by a judge's order in 2000. In his decision, the judge railed at the inhumanity and cruelty of the shoots. This court judgment actually only upheld the right of the ASPCA cruelty officers to have jurisdiction in the rural county. They had been arresting locals who killed wounded birds, which they felt fell under the state cruelty statutes. However, the court was seen as turning strongly against the shoots. The county park saw that the courts had turned against them and subsequently caved in on holding their annual shoot.

Pigeon shoots are, however, still legal in Pennsylvania in private gun clubs and are still regular events. Meanwhile, the legal fight goes on. The Fund has two separate cases pending, either of which could help end the legality of pigeon shoots in Pennsylvania, and they continue to lobby the Pennsylvania House and Senate to change the law through legislation as well.

One irony in all of this is that many hunters I have talked to around the country are almost uniformly disgusted by the whole event. All over the U.S., there is a consensus that holding pigeon shoots opens up hunting in general to attack by animal rights activists and that, by continuing the shoots, the locals may win the battle but lose the war to protect hunting overall. I have also seen hunters who came to Hegins to see what was going on. One Pennsylvania hunter visiting Hegins deliberately walked up to me and told me, "I am an avid hunter. And I'm here to tell you that this is not a sport. It's disgusting, and I'm embarrassed that this is happening in Pennsylvania. Live bird shoots are giving all Pennsylvania hunters a black eye."

There were many lessons learned from the Hegins protests. If there was a good side to it all, it was that for several years Hegins became a national rallying cry and a protester development school. This event brought hundreds of new people, some surprisingly conservative, into the animal rights movement to stand against an obviously cruel event and gave them their first experience in facing the kind of insensitive people who perpetrated it. There was also a lesson in teamwork. The Fund was well organized and networked scores of groups together. At Hegins, there was safety in numbers, because single individuals were the ones most often targeted for harassment and physical abuse. The various groups participating were painfully aware of this and usually put people into pairs to do their work.

The protest also serves as a model for any animal rights event. The first rule is to take a stand, however impossible. In this case, it was to "stop the shoot." The second is to be brave—in this case, to risk verbal abuse, arrest and sometimes injury. The third rule is to be prepared for setbacks. There were early disappointments, and it took many years before the state police, legislature and courts began to move in the desired direction. Eventually, as we discovered, the mood changed. Today, the Fund reports that even legislators who were violently opposed to stopping the shoot say things like "Didn't we do a good job in ending that?"

Finally, there was a lesson in nonviolent action. It worked. The protest leaders never encouraged any acts of violence to be committed by the protesters. Although a few violent acts occurred, most fights were in self-defense. Many acts of civil disobedience were, on the other hand, carefully calculated, timed and carried out. It became clear to me that even yelling at the opponents (and often at their children) was itself an act of violence on the part of the protesters and inflamed and enraged both sides. There are times when this tactic is necessary in an argument to get someone's attention; but once you have that attention—and we did at Hegins—you cannot change people's behavior by yelling at them. Switching to talking calmly and softly worked best. It is unnatural for people to continue to yell at you when you lower your voice in response, because they are no longer being threatened. Pretty soon they realize they are the only ones yelling and automatically lower their voice to match your tone. Eventually, they calm down, anger dissipates and reason begins to show up. Reason prevails. With reason, we can get through and change people's understandings and beliefs.

True, it was hard to stand there and get yelled at and chanted at all day without responding. But a thousand little instances over several years have shown me that being calm against anger, being kind against meanness and turning the other cheek as often as one could often won the day. Hegins was a great lesson for all of us: that nonviolence can win against horrendous and unthinking violence.

Personally, I couldn't help but feel intensely the incredible parallels that existed between my walking alone from shooting range to shooting range inside the county park at Hegins while looking for trouble spots, at first feeling vulnerable and surrounded by the enemy, and my walking from bunker to bunker at night in Viet Nam twenty years earlier as a sergeant of the guard. Why do people go to war? To test their mettle. I did that in the 1970s. Now Hegins became my personal refresher course in the 1990s of my ability to feel safe, to feel protected and to be able to love everyone, everything. It became my place to practice minute by minute my Unity with every other person, animal and thing, at least on the deeper levels, because it was clearly not so apparent on the gross surface of life.

8: Ten Tips for Proactivists

MORE PROACTIVISTS ARE needed in every field. Know that you can make a difference, right now, whether you are a student or a senior citizen. Everyone has something to give. For many, the problem is getting started.

1. Follow your goose bumps.
I've been asked many times by people of all ages how I know what project to get involved in within my community. For me, the answer is quite simple. The best project is the one that excites you the most and gives you the most pleasure. There has to be a good spiritual reason that some particular project excites you. When the hair goes up on the back of your neck or on your arms, or when you feel the goose bumps rising, your body is resonating at that moment with what you are thinking or hearing. Your spirit is speaking to you, telling you to pay attention.

Having said that, if something doesn't inspire you, you can simply pick a need in your community and assign yourself to serve that need. Unless you have a real career interest, you may want to start as a volunteer. In that way, you will systematically eliminate the things that are not fun for you. Keep moving from unpleasant jobs to other tasks or fields that please you more. By finding what you don't like, you will eventually find something that you enjoy a lot. My advice is to be sure to not settle in and get stuck with something you don't enjoy. Never be afraid to follow your feelings and go on to something more interesting, more satisfying. When on a Monday morning you find that you can't wait to get up and go to work or to your new volunteer job, then you have arrived at the right project. This may sound like selfishness, but it is really best for all concerned, including you, the people you work for and the ones your actions serve. Whatever excites you most is serving your highest good and is therefore most evolutionary for you. If it serves your highest good, then it will also serve best the needs of those you are working to help.

Sometimes, instead of going to work for an existing agency serving a need in your community, you will, as I did, find your own niche—an area that is not being addressed adequately. When that happens, you might need to start your own project. If so, here are some additional tips that might help you in your activism.

2. Put a positive spin on it.

When you decide upon a community project or action, it is best to put a positive spin on it. Be *for* something. Even if your action is aimed directly against someone's else's efforts, you can hold yourself out to be *for* something instead of *against* something. This is a really hard concept for some people to grasp, but it is critical if you need to gather other people and resources around you.

If, for instance, you want to stop a corporate giant from building a landfill in your neighborhood, it is better to call your group Citizens for a Safe Community rather than Citizens against the New Landfill. Polluting businesses and legislative committees use this tactic all the time. Why? Because it works. The reasons for using a positive name are both psychological and metaphysical. Most people would rather rally around something positive than something negative because it is easier emotionally to be for something than against something. Why not fight the hunting of mourning doves because you love birds rather than because you hate hunters? How about planting trees because you love this planet rather than because you hate loggers? Let's feed the hungry because you love them rather than because you hate the system that created their poverty.

It is important to note that taking this attitude will not adversely affect your actions. You may end up doing exactly the same things in exactly the same ways. What it will do, however, is make the work personally evolutionary instead of harmful. That is the metaphysical reason for putting a positive spin on your project. A further benefit is that the vast majority of donors, corporations or groups do not want to have anything to do with a group that is seen as reactionary or negative. However, they will help you to do the same work if you hold yourselves out as a proactive organization instead of a reactive one. Trust me, I know.

Given all of the above, I recognize that sometimes the actions being protested are so harmful, so cruel or so violent that the only way to get involved is to jump right in and confront the perpetrators. Sometimes we need to take an immediate and strong stand against something. Here, too, by doing this we are taking action that will benefit not only those we want to protect, but also ourselves and even the person or persons whose misbehaviors we are stopping. This is exactly what the police do.

The major problem with this negative mode of action is that some of the people I've met who are heavily involved in protest actions do not know any other manner of functioning except to be negative. When I see such individuals screaming and hurling abuse, I always wonder how they treat their spouse and kids. For some, such activism has become an entire lifestyle. Many activists are using a club to invoke change when soft words could accomplish the same thing.

What I therefore advise activists to do when presented with a situation that offers more than one tactical route is to avoid unnecessary negativity and choose the gentler approach. We always need to think about what is effective in the long term, and we don't need to cultivate a righteous anger to be an effective activist or protester. We need to cultivate the ability to act from love and not anger. Anger needs to become simply one of the tools we mentally turn on or off to get things done. The danger is that it is addictive, and one can get stuck in that mode. If our anger consumes us, then we and not the objects of our anger are the ones with the problem. If we don't come from love, then in the long run our actions will not be as successful or sustainable.

3. Get organized: Setting goals and objectives.

Once you have developed the seed of an idea you need to write it all down. Try to get that idea on paper in a logical fashion. If you need to, draw pictures and graphs to better illustrate the concept. Work on both sides of your brain. The left side is the scientific/logical side; the right side is the artistic/creative side. Use them both if you can.

A few projects can be implemented directly from a mental idea into physical action without writing them out. Most, however, will need to be written down and outlined. I find it is best to do this at the outset—not only to make the idea clear to ourselves and to discover what we have missed, but also to make it presentable to others. These others may include those we want to help and potential donors or volunteers.

You need strategic goals and objectives. Your strategic goal is the same thing as your long-term goal or purpose. This is the big fight you want to win—whether that means stopping a pigeon shoot, planting trees or educating the community about organic foods. Your goal needs to be clear and have a timeline, such as: Our purpose is to distribute and plant three million free trees in the next eleven years in this county. Your short-term goals are actually called objectives and they involve tactics. Objectives are specific steps needed to accomplish your overall strategy, such as: In year one we need to raise $25,000, buy 100,000 trees and distribute them free to schools, churches, groups and individuals. Tactics help you develop a plan of how to get to each objective. Next, you should step back and take a fresh look at your project. Are you doing all you can do or just doing what is comfortable? Can you grow it into something bigger?

4. Dare to make it bigger.

I've received hundreds of calls from teachers who want to buy twenty trees for their classroom to have a "free tree" project. The teachers feel they are taking a bold step by calling me and launching a new project. After discussing their plans and explaining how little work is involved, I always ask them to consider making their project bigger. How much bigger they want to go is always dependent on their comfort level. My job is to push everyone to their limit.

There are two ways to enlarge the concept of a project. The first is to make it bigger in size by quantity. If one is going to raise money and call a nursery and buy trees, it is just as much work to order 100 trees as it is to order 1,000 or 5,000 trees. For instance, I always ask such teachers, "Can you take a moment to get out of the mental box you are in? It's great that you are thinking about helping the students in your classroom. But why not invite all the other science teachers to participate with you and buy trees for all the students in your building?" For some, this is too big a notion, but many get it right away. A lot of projects involving 100 trees have instantly grown into projects with 1,000 trees. Some teachers have even realized that they could e-mail their whole school district and buy trees for every student in every grade in every school building. Suddenly there are 5,000 or 10,000 trees involved.

Size does matter, and size can be increased by time. I will ask, "How many years will it be before you retire?" I then suggest that the teacher make a formal commitment to continue his or her new project idea for the next five or ten years. If he or she decides to do so, the project can grow by a factor of ten. My pitch ends with, "What else more important have you got to do every year until you retire than doing this tree project? If you do this in a big way, you will have something to be really proud of when you retire. This could be your legacy to the community."

(A further benefit to thinking large is that the media will get a lot more excited writing about the launch of a 100,000-tree project than a 1,000-tree project. The visionary size of a massive ten-year project often inspires more volunteers and donors as well.)

Now that you see how simple it is to think bigger, you can visualize your success right up front both in terms of quantity and time. Then don't be afraid to claim it. My belief is that if you can think big enough to identify a larger problem, then you are qualified to help solve it; as we grow in awareness, we grow in responsibility. Our goal as activists needs to be to always strive to first grow our awareness to the highest level, then go out and perform action until we reach our level of discomfort. We need to continue to reach higher to challenge ourselves. Why? Because anything short of that means we are not learning anything new and not evolving.

5. Add an altruistic twist.

Now that you have selected and defined a project, you need to find out how to make it better. One way is to make the project as unselfish as possible. For example, in my tree projects, we could have bought trees and sold them cheaply, say for ten cents each. Or a nickel. But tree seedlings were already for sale everywhere and not many people were buying them. The first response from some of the Rotary clubs I approached was to say, "Great, we'll buy them for ten cents and sell them for a quarter and make money." If we had done this, the project would have been seen as just another fundraiser and, as I indicated earlier, the media would have largely ignored it. Furthermore, selling trees and collecting the money would have been a logistics nightmare and the poorest students would have been left out. What gave my project pizzazz was the decision to buy the trees and give them away for free with no strings attached. Naturally, the people who received trees had to commit to plant them in their yard, but otherwise the gesture was completely altruistic.

As I noted in my chapter on the "free tree" project, the media loved the idea. Why? Because there were no hidden benefits to organizers or sponsors and no remuneration for me. Even after I landed a contract from the State of Ohio to start projects throughout the rest of Ohio, I continued to run our local project without pay. I tried hard to keep the Rotary clubs in the front of the media stories as the ones who "owned" the project, while I stayed in the background. But, as I have said, you cannot be responsible for how people will see you. After about 400 stories in thirteen local papers over ten years, I was accused of being a "media slut" by one of our prominent community members. "Thank you," I replied, accepting the statement as the compliment it was not meant to be. He thought I must really be "full of myself." My experience is that people are quick to transfer to you the feelings they would have if they were in your situation.

Here is another example of altruism. What if you were to raise money and give a scholarship each year to a needy blind child to attend a special School for the Blind? Your corporate sponsors would usually want their name all over such a project, maybe even having you name the scholarship after them. That would probably work. But how about choosing instead to keep the donors secret and appeal to that spiritual ethic in your donors and yourself that teaches us to "pray in a closet" instead of in front of everyone? This would make the whole scholarship truly altruistic. Then no one could be accused of supporting it for his or her own benefit. If you come in a genuine spirit of altruism, you will be amazed at how many people will rise up to assist you, proud of being associated with such an honorable cause.

6. Always give political leaders a "heads up."

Your county supervisor or county commissioner, mayor and city councilperson may not have helped you to start your project. They may not even lift a finger to help you fund it or run it. But after you announce the plan publicly, they are the ones who will be questioned about what they think of it. They need to be in the know at the very beginning. You owe it to yourself to keep them informed up front, before you make your first announcement.

Whether they are speaking to the media or a community group, or out golfing at the country club, your political leaders need to know what you are doing in "their" district. This is important because, if they are uninformed, they might criticize your project out of ignorance. And their voices count. Donors will be reassured if your mayor says that the project is a great idea. If the mayor says that he doesn't know anything about the project, then it will be harder for you to raise money. Donors may believe that your project must not be that important if the elected officials don't even know about it. To raise money after a mayor has made negative comments is even harder, since the fundraising could become a partisan issue.

When you, the project's director, fail to inform elected officials of what you are doing they become, in a word, embarrassed. It's their job, after all, to know everything important going on in their district, and, for them, knowledge is power. You are doing them a favor by tipping them off ahead of time. That said, you don't need to approach the elected officials to seek their approval; it's enough simply to let them know what is about to happen.

So whatever you have planned, unless it has an element of surprise in it, it is usually best to give political leaders a "heads up." Even if you plan a protest or have people who want to get arrested, you can tip off the leaders ahead of time. They may want the police chief in on the meeting. This could prevent an overreaction by police. People —even police—are most afraid when they do not know what is going on. Think safety first.

7. Include your worst critics.

Invite your worst potential critics to participate in your project. This rule is as important as the ancient idea of keeping your enemies close to you so you can keep an eye on them. Sit down and try to calculate who might have a reason to be critical of your project in the future. It might be someone who would oppose you conceptually or a potential supporter who needs to be included up front or he will feel left out. Once you've identified them, you should offer these people positions of respect in your project. Even if they refuse, at least they will know they were asked, and may therefore be less likely to disrupt or oppose your project.

As you will recall, in my tree projects I invited every local tree expert I could identify to be on an advisory board and gave them a real function to accomplish (under my guidance). They selected the mix of trees I would distribute in every county. I never asked their permission to run my project; if I had, some of them would have said no. I told them the deal was set up and funded, but that I needed their technical expertise. Every one of the local tree experts then became an informed proponent of my project. They were walking advertisers for the project; they had inside information.

Unfortunately, in a few instances across Ohio, some of the people I failed to include became our critics in the media. This was not because planting trees was bad for their community, but because they had had their feelings hurt by being left out. Since they didn't get any "power" from us by being part of the project, they tried to take "power" from us by being critical of it. My job, as I saw it, was to see the good in everyone, and to hold that space open for them to grow into.

8. Secure funding before you release the project to the media.
How many times have you read in the newspaper that someone has come up with a great new idea? They announce it in the newspaper, claiming credit for it, and then the story usually ends with a call for financial support from the masses or local businesses to help to pay for the project.

In my opinion, this is the worst way to fund a program. This kind of public appeal seldom produces offers for funding and rarely garners widespread support. It is seen for what it usually is—another inept attempt at changing society. These articles almost always end up being perceived as self-serving, because they feature the person who came up with the idea. Even if that is not true or the real intent of pitching the idea, that is how such stories are read. If you took such a newspaper clipping about how you have this great idea and laid it on the desk of a potential donor, they would more than likely retort: "Yeah, I saw that article. But what do you want from me? I read in the paper that you are going to do that project."

What the donors are saying is that they know that we usually only get one real big chance to tell our story to the public in the media. After that, the story goes to page two (or twenty). You already wasted that one chance with your initial appeal for help. The problem was that your appeal was about you and it should have been about your donors.

My experience has been that it is always better to find your money quietly first, then release the project idea with the announcement that it is a "done deal." Then you can tell who the donors are in that same article. The donors are thrilled because they get the maximum possible coverage. Remember, for many donors, you are really selling advertising. Their foundation or corporate name almost always needs to be put out front, unless they instruct otherwise. Now you yourself may get relegated to the background, but that simply makes the whole idea less self-serving. With this way of beginning a project, you will not only be seen as innovative but entrepreneurial because you cleverly put the whole idea together. A funded project is one that is actually going to happen. Everyone likes to read about happy endings.

In my tree projects, I actually used the term "embargoed" during the organizational and fundraising stages to help key volunteers and the media know that we did not want to have any press leaks on our projects until they were ready to be announced—and by "ready" we meant that we had our funding arranged. We saved the big story until the donors could be named. In my case we told the media exactly when that release date would be; an early story or leak was a mess. It was disastrous to have hundreds of calls from people looking for free trees when we didn't have any to give. So, when we announced our projects, we not only announced the idea and the funders, we went right on to announce how to order free trees. It was very practical. If we didn't do it this way, our second story about how to get trees would also be relegated to a tiny corner back on page twenty.

9. Deal with problems when they arise.
When I was in the military, we were trained to run toward the sounds of gunfire. As unnatural, idiotic and brainwashed as it sounds, that was what I was trained to do. During incoming fire, while everyone else was running for shelter and a good hidey-hole, I was concerned with getting my team armed and moving toward the trouble. It was clearly understood that, in the long run, fewer people would be hurt

or killed by having a few men react by facing the danger head-on than by passively waiting for trouble to come looking for us. In the marginally less violent structure of nonprofit organizational management, this rule still applies. It is called "crisis management."

If you intend to be an effective activist and leader, you will need to learn to face all problems head-on as soon as they arise. Never put off a problem if you can avoid doing so. Our psychological need for peace and harmony often causes us to go out of our way to avoid facing someone who might be upset with us or what we are doing. Indeed, keeping the peace is often so important that we take great steps to avoid facing a problem (or even a person with a problem), fearing that by dealing with them we will actually be disturbing the peace. This is a common idea and, unfortunately, it is always a misunderstanding.

When I was starting my tree projects in other counties in Ohio, I often faced stiff opposition from, of all things, other established tree-planting groups and, in a few cases, state foresters. Complaints would be directed to the State Division of Forestry, who would ask me to deal with them. I immediately called up the offended group or agency, much to their surprise, and asked for a chance to come and speak to their whole body as soon as possible. Once I made my presentation and answered questions, I found most of the problems had evaporated. I discovered that most problems are based on the fear of the unknown. If, after the presentation and discussion, there were still issues to be resolved, we worked to iron them out and made commitments on the spot. This technique worked in about thirty cases, but failed in one or two instances where ego-driven control problems and turf wars prevented me from moving ahead. Even in these last instances, I could sense that some of the members of the other group wanted to cooperate but were unable to move ahead with us because the political price in their group would have been too high. After all, they had to continue to live and work with the ego-driven control freaks who were afraid of us.

In closing one of the worst meetings, I remember asking one of the tree-planting groups the following rhetorical question: "Imagine that we actually succeeded in planting 20 million trees across Ohio over the next 20 years, and every one of our 88 counties received between 250,000 and a million new trees—except your county. Wouldn't it be ironic if, when asked about that years from now, we would have to say that the only reason we didn't get to plant trees in your county was that the organization most responsible for planting trees here was afraid to let us do it?" That helped bring on a few more counties who might have otherwise said no. In the end, we started projects in 87 of Ohio's 88 counties. The 88th county could be a chapter in itself.

Problems fester and grow like mushrooms when kept in the dark. The bogeyman of your imagination is always bigger than the one that exists in reality. Therefore, it is almost always best to bring problems out into the open light of day and lay them out to see and discuss. You will find that you can resolve your differences and move on by doing so. You will also find that all parties will respect you for having the maturity and nerve to deal with the issue head-on.

10. Never use the "command" form of speech.
While this is a good idea to use with anyone in everyday speech, it is especially true with volunteers.

If I could change one thing in the English language, it would be to eliminate the command form of speech (the imperative form) from common usage. I've found that most people use it unconsciously, a carry over from their parents. It does more damage than good.

Like our adrenal glands sitting quietly on top of our kidneys, the imperative form of speech should be held in reserve for emergencies only. It is meant to be our back-up language when something is really urgent. But just as running every day on hormones from our adrenals is not sustainable, using the imperative all the time can offend everyone around us and, in effect, wear out the command form so it doesn't work when we really need it. Have you ever seen someone yell at their kids and not be listened to? It's like crying wolf.

If suddenly someone began shooting at us, and I was the one to figure out first what was happening, I would need to yell "Duck!"

That's an imperative. It does not present an option. It says, "Get down now!" It doesn't say "Hey, let's discuss that incoming fire and consider our options." This is an example of a time when it is suitable to give an order to someone else in a command style and even with a command voice: in an emergency. In my opinion, it is one of the few times when such a style and voice may be valuable.

I cannot count how many times I have heard supposedly experienced leaders running around in the midst of a project obnoxiously giving orders. While often tolerated, such behavior is a sure way to offend everyone and lose good volunteers. Volunteers simply need to be *asked* to do things, not told. After all, they are already there to help and wouldn't be there if they didn't intend to assist you. It is completely unnecessary to give them commands. In any case, within a polite request from a leader who is clearly in charge is the implied command; giving it is overkill. Those commands almost always come from ego. I once had to fire a volunteer who was so bossy and obnoxious that everyone else threatened to quit that project if he was to help the next year.

When I was a lowly enlisted man in the Army, I found myself receiving orders from men who were often not as qualified as I was to do what needed to be done. They just happened to be in charge that day. It was really annoying for me to have to take orders from incompetent senior Non-Commissioned Officers (NCOs) and officers. But I listened and did my job, even though I didn't like their management style. I didn't mind orders from good commanders. What I liked even less was when an insecure officer would throw his weight around by making everyone stand at attention while he belabored some minor point—just to show who was really in command. Those inane commands were always the most insulting.

On the company flight line in Cam Ranh Bay, Viet Nam, I once caught a pilot screaming at one of my mechanics while holding him at attention, all because the mechanic looked sloppy and needed a haircut. I knew that that sloppy "kid" had stayed up throughout the night and had changed an engine, and wanted to watch it start up. I took the pilot aside and proceeded to tell him never to approach my men with any complaint again. "Why would you yell at someone who holds your life in their hands?" I asked him. "We have enough morale problems already. Come to me with your problems instead. I'll handle them." He was, as you might imagine, less than pleased to hear that from an E-5.

Later that night in the officer club, when the pilot complained about my mechanic and me to the captain in charge of our flight line, the captain bawled him out. What had happened was that I had tipped off my flight line captain beforehand. That night he asked all the pilots to direct all of their complaints either to him or to me, and not to my men (the chain of command works both ways!). We never got any further complaints after that.

I have since come to understand that people who pick on others have low self-esteem. They are trying to build themselves up by putting other people down. They are trying to take power away from others to fill their own lack. When I experienced it in the Army, I swore then to never use the command form of speech, and I have tried hard to uphold that oath ever since—not to speak down to those who are there to help me. If you plan to recruit and train volunteers, you will need to learn how to work with them as equals. They are not beneath you, regardless of what the organizational chart says. This is the ultimate case of self-preservation for you. Why? Because, being volunteers, they can just as easily get up and walk out as they can enthusiastically stay in your organization. Never give them that excuse.

9: The Future of Environmentalism

THERE IS NO shortage of environmental work for any activist to pursue. There are currently many opportunities to go out and do great work for the environment. New opportunities will continue to arise. In fact, I believe that if I had a few more lifetimes, there are several more major projects I could do that would each need several years of concentrated effort to launch, then a couple of decades to implement and get firmly established.

In this chapter I will highlight several issues and opportunities that activists may wish to consider. I will also introduce several new ideas. The reason why I am writing about several of my key environmental project ideas is, first, to let readers see how easy it is to take a fresh look at their state's environment and come up with ideas themselves; and, second, to inspire a few people to commit themselves to tackling one of these ideas. I could use some help. Then I won't have to wait until another lifetime to get them done!

I have sorted these ideas for action into local, regional, statewide, national and international issues.

A word to students: Don't panic! None of these issues will be finished before you graduate; so you have plenty of time to research the problems and plan your actions. Or, better yet, you can pick one and try to solve it now. Don't wait. Age is no barrier to environmental action, nor is the fact that you are not yet out of school. You might consider getting involved in one of the local actions first. How about in your own home or backyard?

Local Action 1: Get your own house in order.
The first place to look is in your own home. First, look at your household operations: How can you live more simply and sustainably? Can you recycle, reuse or reduce more paper, plastic, gasoline, water, electricity etc.? Can you reduce your mowing, or drive less, or grow your own food?

Could you take your newfound knowledge and teach it to others? Could you become a role model for your friends and family, or neighborhood? Could you help others? It's important to start with yourself first, because only after you have your own life in order, by living more sustainably, have you truly earned the right to consider becoming a community activist. Before that, all of us would be justly labeled hypocrites. But don't let that keep you from taking any worthy action.

Look at how you live your life at home. First of all, let's talk about television. For about ten years after my divorce, I didn't own a television, but I finally got one, primarily to play rented movies for my kids. I didn't hook up to cable TV until I had to a couple years ago to get access to a high-speed Internet cable. Even so, it didn't take long for me to become aware of how addictive television is. TV can provide an exhaustive body of both useful and useless programming. In moments of weakness, I too can sit down and surf the TV cable network, looking for something brainless to distract me while I take a break from the concentration of my work. Typically, just like the worst of TV addicts, I find that a well-intentioned few minutes of break can easily turn into a couple of hours wasted. Fortunately my house was struck by lightning the week I started to write this book and my TV went up in smoke. No more distraction there! I don't own another one yet.

I have often wondered what I would have accomplished if I had been hooked up to cable TV during my post-divorce/depressed years. Since I didn't have television, I went outside and did things myself. Rather than watching other people discover nature on the Discovery channel, I was out canoeing, backpacking, rock climbing, and observing and learning about nature. Instead of watching sports, I was playing racquetball, and competing in area mini-triathlons. My suggestion is that you don't waste your life watching it go by on TV.

Ever notice how some people take their TV so seriously? One would think that they believe they might earn a higher place in the next life for watching every *Cheers* rerun or for not missing any football game for five years. Every minute sitting in front of a TV is another minute of your precious life wasted.

A Call to Action: I am often asked, "What should I study to be an activist?" The real answer is: "It doesn't matter." Study what excites you. Study whatever is a passion in your life. The important thing is to turn off your TV and study. Read. Think. Then go do something great. Why not try to see how long you can go without watching TV? Start today. If you can't easily do that, then recognize now that you have a problem. Why not have the cable disconnected for a few months? You'll probably climb the walls for a few days. Gosh, you might have to take a walk, or read a book, or do something else to stay busy. How about making a New Year's resolution to get out of the TV habit and exercise for six months? Or give it up for Lent. Make it a spiritual quest! Or why not offer to give it up voluntarily the next time you need to be punished for something at home?

Local Action 2: Start in your own backyard.

In 1988, I moved into a tiny 100-year-old cottage house near Myers Lake. In the first week, I mowed the two-lot half-acre lawn. It took over forty-five minutes. I sat on a rock afterward sweating and said to myself that I had just mowed the grass for the last time. What a waste of time and gasoline! I decided I had better things to do for the rest of my life.

I immediately apologized to all the wildlife around me for what I had done and vowed to do something better with the land. It only took a few minutes to decide on a plan of action. I staked out a wavy line twenty to thirty feet inside the perimeter of the rectangular property. I agreed to mow the center of the yard but to allow the outer area between the wavy line and the perimeter to become reforested as my own private "greenspace." I gave it back to God. This was my first "greenspace" project, my own backyard habitat for wildlife.

Within a month, my yard had a very well-defined mowed area that contrasted with a distinctive outer area with much higher grass. In that area I made a few piles of rocks for nesting, threw in dropped limbs from trees, and put in a large compost pile to accommodate the leaves from my three 200-year-old oaks. Next I planted over 100 seedlings of different hardwood trees and a variety of bushes, including raspberry bushes, honeysuckle, white and purple lilacs, Rose of Sharon, wild cherry, dogwoods, butterfly bushes, a few pines, ground cover and perennial flowers along the borders. Ivy lined the northwestern border. In went some birdbaths. Now I had all the ingredients for eventually supporting wildlife: food, water and shelter. Within ten years those trees would completely block visibility to and from all of my side-yard and backyard neighbors. My mowing time dropped to about twenty-five minutes.

There were the inevitable problems with my neighbors. In any community where there are zoning regulations, one has to be considerate of one's neighbors. A house that looks unkempt can be an eyesore that can decrease the real value of the neighboring homes and sometimes the whole neighborhood. Our zoning laws required all grass to be kept mowed to less than nine inches. I figured that since my house had been an eyesore before I had bought and painted it, I was safe from criticism. I was wrong.

When the grass got to be about fifteen inches tall in the greenspace, I received a visit from the Township zoning inspector. Although no one had had the kindness or nerve to walk over and ask me what I was doing, a neighbor had reported me. This annoyed me, since I could have easily explained my plan to them. I wouldn't even have yelled at them! But I hadn't followed my own principle of letting everyone know what I was up to.

The inspector wanted me to show him my backyard. I took him out back. "We have received a complaint," he said. "You have to mow your yard. If you do not mow, we will have to come and do it for you, and we will give you a very expensive bill for the work. Why aren't you mowing your yard?"

I walked him over the mowed area. "I do mow my yard. You can see that I have kept this area mowed very carefully," I responded.

"But what about this area?" he asked, pointing to the edges of the property where the grass was about to go to seed.

"Oh. You don't understand," I said, thinking fast. "That's not a yard area that needs to be mowed. That's a landscape area that needs to be weeded."

"Well," he stammered. "When do you plan to weed it?"

I showed him my overall plan, and, in particular, the hundreds of tree seedlings buried in the thick tall grass. Clearly, if I used a weed eater to cut the grass low, I wouldn't be able to avoid cutting down the hidden seedlings. I offered to cut the tops off the grass twice that year, just high enough to create a look of uniformity and prevent the grass from going to seed. I knew that for some people, in addition to the unsightliness of high grass, the seeds created pollen, which is an allergen. The inspector agreed to my plan and reported my plan of action to the neighbors.

Within a couple years, the trees were above the grass and leafing out nicely. It was easy to see by then that I did indeed have a miniature forest sprouting up. In the end, many of the trees that grew were those planted by squirrels burying nuts and birds dropping cherry pits. These came up automatically when I stopped mowing.

Suddenly, again without announcement, into my yard walked the same zoning inspector.

"David," he said, "I have had another complaint. This time we've been told that you have rats running around in your backyard every evening."

I smiled, and beckoned him to follow me quietly. I took him out into the center of the backyard and, pulling apart a thick clump of day lilies in a flower bed, showed him a cozy nest full of beautiful, tiny quivering bunny rabbits. "Here are your rats," I said. He laughed, shaking his head. He never came back.

Today the yard in my Plain Township house has a perimeter of trees that are twenty to thirty feet tall, and it's a regular jungle out there. Each fall, I rake up all the leaves that fall in my mowed area. Most of them are composted. The leaves that fall into the landscaped area stay where they land and have created, along with some ground ivy, a thatched understory that has become a great habitat for a score of rabbits, chipmunks and other critters. Each fall I watch as squirrels come hopping over from several manicured lawns into my yard to fetch mouthfuls of leaves and other material to take back to their trees to build their nests. I guess the word has gotten out in the 'hood about my craft supply store out back.

You can easily create your own wildlife habitat area in your own back- or side-yard. You don't have to be as dramatic or confrontational as I was. You could simply take a back corner of your yard and mark off a triangle about twenty feet on each side. Pile in some rocks, plant some bushes, and stop mowing it. Every yard needs a designated wild space and wildlife needs its privacy, free from human invasion. Every yard needs a portion that belongs to and is managed entirely by God, not humans. As my Transcendental Meditation teacher, Maharishi Mahesh Yogi, once said, "Nature knows better than man how to organize." I call it tithing to Mother Earth. Have you given ten percent of your land back to God?

The first major backyard habitat program offered to the public was through the National Wildlife Federation (NWF) in Washington, D.C. For over twenty years, in a brilliant demonstration of nature education with a practical purpose, the NWF has been providing all the information necessary for the creation of food, water and nesting areas that are critical to the attraction and sustenance of wildlife in urban backyard settings. You can visit their Web site at www.nwf.org. NWF has sold their packets of information to tens of thousands of homeowners, and has registered many thousands of backyards now as "certified backyard habitats."

The NWF program has since been copied across America by many of the state departments of natural resources (DNR). In Ohio, for example, you can contact ODNR's Division of Wildlife to receive a packet of information with specific recommendations of which trees and bushes to plant to attract your desired animal or insect. When you look at their materials, it turns out that what we suspected is really true: A weed is a wildflower that we simply don't yet know the name of. Some flowers specifically attract bees, others butterflies, still others hummingbirds. You may decide you are interested in helping songbirds, who are having real difficulty surviving at this time, or you may want to help out rabbits, raccoons, skunks or other so-called nuisance animals.

A Call to Action: Go wild in your own backyard. Be sure to tithe there, too.

Regional Action: Wildlife Habitat Conservancy
After fourteen years of starting and administering "free tree" programs for my nonprofit American Free Tree Program, I resigned from that organization in 2001 and left the board in 2002. AFTP has since scaled back its Ohio operation from starting and running "free tree" giveaways to simply encouraging ongoing projects. Recently, the organization has decided to move more solidly into the direction of urban forestry (large trees) and forestry education. There is a real void in those areas in Canton.

I will continue to promote new free tree projects via the Internet on my Web site, www.davidakidd.org, and I will still travel to lecture on the subject. Anyone interested in a new project can now go to my site to learn how to start and run a project in more detail than is covered in this book.

Before I left AFTP, I had begun to take it into a new focus of operating as a land trust. Three years ago, after we had completed planting over eleven million trees, I looked at our overall financial statement. After raising over $1.7 million dollars in 13 years, AFTP had a net worth of $5,000. We had done some great, award-winning work involving the distribution and planting of millions of trees by over a million volunteers, and we had absolutely nothing to show for it. On one level that was a sign of our success, because we planned to have nothing left in the end.

Our decision at that juncture was either to close up shop and celebrate our success or to move in a new direction. My recommendation to our board of directors was to change our articles of incorporation to permit us to operate as a land trust. I wanted to preserve greenspace for the benefit of both humans and wildlife. The board agreed.

My goal was to acquire over one million dollars' worth of land within five years. I felt that by doing so, our organization would become one of the more successful land trusts in Ohio. Only then, with a heftier balance sheet and some success under our belts, might we be able to attract enough financial support to properly launch a really comprehensive land trust operation. In the past three years, we have obtained three parcels of land in two counties in Ohio. They total 100 acres and are valued at approximately $465,000.

My goal has been to only ask for scrappy lands. I want everyone's junk land—junk to them, but a gold mine for me and our wildlife. This "worthless" land contains ditches, streams, ponds, swamps, wetlands, lakes and rivers. It also includes reclaimed and unreclaimed strip-mined land, exhausted farmland and ridges and hillsides too steep to use for anything else. I am also after dead spaces in the middle of commercial and residential developments, narrow strips along roadways and areas cut off by highway development that are too small to build anything on.

I have found that many developers are sitting (and have been paying taxes) on what is, for them, useless (as in unbuildable) lands and wetlands from earlier development projects. They appear to be thrilled at the prospect of donating those parcels to a land trust and sorry that they did not think of it sooner. They will get a tax write-off in the first year, and will not pay taxes on the land for the rest of their lives as they often have already been doing for twenty or thirty years. Furthermore, the land is still there. Only now, it is providing a protected greenspace for their development's residents to enjoy.

The first property we obtained was an 82-acre forest with a 30-acre shallow lake in historic Zoar Village in Tuscarawas County, Ohio. The land and lake sit behind a levee that protects the village from flooding from the Tuscarawas River, which runs along the back of our property. I fell in love with that property the first time I walked it. We bought it on a contract with the seller with $10,000 down and a note for $100,000. The owners worked a favorable deal with us to benefit the community, knowing that the land would be going back to public usage through our land trust. The mortgage at Zoar Lake is paid by rents from an old duplex on the property.

AFTP's goal is to pay off the mortgage and eventually remove the duplex. Ultimately, we want the land to revert back to the community park it once was when the village of Zoar operated as a communal society in the 1800s. We took it out of private ownership after 100 years, and have given it back to the public to use. The Zoar Lake Wildlife Sanctuary is now open for picnics and hiking. It's a great birding spot, with local birders identifying an average of 35 to 40 species each month. About twenty great blue herons fish there.

AFTP also received donations of two other parcels of land in two townships in Stark County. The larger is Shoemaker Acres, a 17-acre property that was given to keep some farmland from being developed with over 40 houses. We were not attempting to acquire farmland or to stop any development, but the family involved already had a clear commitment only to let their land be developed if it could be done by a sustainable or intentional community with an environmental purpose. They had turned down several builders' offers to sell. We will be developing plans for the future use of the land soon. Trees have already been planted on its perimeter.

All these acquisitions were done using modest word-of-mouth efforts on my part and mentions by our director in our company newsletter. The market for obtainable small parcels of greenspace appears to be huge. I believe that if we really went after such land with adequate funding, this idea could generate over 100 parcels of greenspace in every county in Ohio within a few years. That would be of tremendous benefit to wildlife, especially in the coming decades when there will be even greater pressure to develop every piece of earth for humans.

Since leaving AFTP I have worked on starting a new nonprofit corporation called Wildlife Habitat Conservancy. It will operate as an Ohio land trust. I will be using this vehicle to support land acquisitions and management to protect wild spaces in both urban and rural areas in perpetuity. It has already generated some interest from supporters and land donors, and I expect great things from it in the coming years. You can also read about WHC on my Web site.

A Call to Action: Be a greenspace ambassador. When you drive around your town or county and you see a tiny parcel of land that seems to serve no purpose and would be great to preserve as wildlife habitat (however small), stop and find out who owns it. Or look it up at your county map office, many of which are now available on line. See if the owners would consider giving it to a land trust. Then find a land trust to work with in your area. If there isn't one, start one, or contact us at the Wildlife Habitat Conservancy to see if we can work with you or your group. Frankly, the land could also be held in protection by a local church, an environmental group, an animal protection group, a vegetarian club or even a local civic organization, many of which have been named in previous chapters. Try to work with local organizations before trying to work with us. But let me know of your successes.

Statewide Action: Ohio Wildlife Corridor (WildeCor)

Something unique has happened in Ohio that has created a small window of opportunity for a possible environmental action of massive proportion. After over 150 years of systematic deforestation, demolition and often ruination of Ohio's rural lands, in the 1990s nearly all of the coal mines in Ohio closed and scores of operators suddenly took their machinery completely out of state. The only remaining large operation still active is run by Ohio Power in southeastern Ohio on its own land.

As a result, there are currently over 500,000 acres of strip-mined land in the eastern third of Ohio suddenly available to buy. I drove along a hundred miles of this land one winter day and it felt like I was in Siberia. It was a treeless void utterly bare of the majestic hardwood forests or rich farmland that once graced this Ohio valley.

Much of this land is owned by private citizens. Nevertheless, there are about 150,000 acres owned by coal companies, most of which are eager to sell. I see these lands as a huge opportunity for a massive reforestation project. The beauty of the idea is that much of the land is available in large chunks for as little as $1,000 to $1,500 per acre. Unfortunately, the land has been greatly disturbed. It has no subsoil full of useful microbes and bacteria and only a very thin layer of topsoil. It is not good enough to farm on; most of it is not good enough even for raising horses or dairy cows. It has, however, been found to be adequate for grazing longhorn cattle, which, much to my dismay, some ambitious farmers have brought to Ohio for that purpose.

In addition to this reclaimed land, there are over 300,000 acres of strip-mined land that were abandoned by unscrupulous mining owners and never reclaimed. The state works hard every year to try to improve pollution problems from the worst of these sites, but topsoil or mining trailings are still running off into local streams, causing pollution and the death of fish and other animals.

I have calculated that at the rate the state can reclaim the remaining abandoned acreage, it would take over 200 years to complete the task. Sadly, it was often the same operators who, over and over again, defaulted on their modest cash bonds instead of spending the larger amount needed to finish their work. They simply declared bankruptcy and opened up a new company with a new name and often other family members as stockholders. In a hundred years, the state officials somehow never learned how to stay ahead of these operators.

My idea is to undertake a two- or three-year study to determine the feasibility of creating a 100-mile long, five-mile wide corridor of reforested land running north to south on the east side of Ohio. This corridor could consist of approximately 300,000 acres, and could be

Figure 9:1 A 43-acre strip-mined land on which 50,000 trees were planted ten years previously

reforested with over 300 million trees. My vision is of large parcels of land (5,000 to 10,000 acres) linked by a narrower band of connecting trails, like an emerald necklace. After completion of the study, we would know exactly what land to acquire and what the cost would be. The project needs to be implemented with a combination of federal, state and private funds, and I estimate it would take twenty to thirty years to buy the land, reforest it and create hiking, biking and horse trails. It could cost $500 million, and would be a significant public works project. There would need to be parking areas, campsites and guidelines for use of the nearly 600 lakes and ponds that would be on the land. The corridor could become linked with, or even part of the Wayne National Forest, which is located in south central Ohio. Any property tax revenues lost by local counties could be offset by increased land values on properties adjacent to the new greenspace areas.

Such a corridor would be of tremendous benefit to wildlife. It would create habitat for millions of animals and tens of millions of insects, also vital to the survival of amphibians, birds and mammals. The benefits to humans would also be substantial. For Ohioans, this new corridor would represent the only hiking trail in the state where a backpacker could hike a loop for a week or two and camp overnight. To do that today, we have to go to Pennsylvania or West Virginia. Likewise, the economic benefits to Ohio would also be large, with perhaps thousands of tourists traveling to some of Ohio's least populated counties to enjoy this recreation area. These tourists in turn would need to eat and buy gas and gear, and would visit specialty stores along the way. Eventually, the tax losses from the non-profit ownership of the land would be more than offset by increased sales tax revenues. Pressure for just such a recreation area will increase as northern counties continue their urban sprawl and every nature area disappears. By then it might be too late to put this deal together.

The United States needs to design and complete a large-scale and high-visibility reforestation project to help it to meet the carbon dioxide offset requirements agreed to in the 1992 Rio de Janeiro accords, even if our government didn't agree to the Kyoto Protocol. Planting trees is one of the best ways to remove carbon from the atmosphere in a visible way. Unlike promises of lower emissions from factories or automobiles or productivity cutbacks, which are hard to verify and difficult to coerce, you can go and see the trees growing.

If this land is not acquired in the next few years, it will no longer be available. Every month small parcels are sold off and put to other uses, which are mostly commercial or residential. My greatest fear is that our window of opportunity is closing, and could someday be completely gone before those most responsible in our government even knew it was open.

A Call to Action: This project is real, and is an exciting prospect for any aspiring environmentalist. Someone needs to help research this idea, which could be a real environmental coup. It would make a great graduate or Ph.D. thesis project. I would share my maps and preliminary files to help jump-start a study or research paper. If our Wildlife Habitat Conservancy were involved, we would need $220,000 for two to three years for the feasibility study, assuming maximum cooperation from every potential state department and the governor's office. Who can we find to support this concept?

Perhaps instead you know of such areas of land in your state. Why not work to put together your own wildlife corridors where there were none before? Here's a big hint: There are many coal companies sitting on remote lands of hundreds and even thousands of acres that have already been mined. They made their money on that land a long time ago, and are paying taxes on it every year. Coal companies are aware of their poor environmental image, so you can be sure that some of them would love to donate some of their lands to a good cause. Why not write companies in your area and simply ask them to meet and explore the idea? I'll join your meeting in a conference call to help get the process going.

National Action: The National Tree Trust (NTT)

One of the most enduring results that came out of President George Bush Sr.'s America the Beautiful initiative was the creation of the National Tree Trust (NTT). By an act of Congress, money was set aside to start an endowment to form a new nonprofit foundation whose purpose would be to help to provide trees for planting on public lands. NTT was very successful at getting the major paper companies to donate leftover tree nursery stock to them each year, which they shipped to participating groups across America.

The NTT program grew during the same years that AFTP was getting in gear. Most of our "free tree" projects gave away trees to be planted on private property and did not qualify to receive tree grants from NTT. However, we quickly included teaching about NTT grants in all of our meetings and workshops, and soon became one of their biggest customers. In some years, trees from NTT represented 10 percent of our business, and our projects represented 20 percent of theirs. Led for many years by a straight-shooting retired Marine Corps General, George Cates, NTT has made a name for itself as one of the most successful ongoing tree projects in America.

NTT offers other grants. One year AFTP received a grant that allowed two of our staff to travel the Midwest starting new tree projects in eight states. We particularly focused on reservations and parks. Some of the projects we began are still planting trees each year.

NTT also was the anchor donor in a project to plant 113 large trees on a major trailhead of the new Ohio and Erie Canal towpath trail, part of a national heritage corridor in Ohio. The beautiful trail-head/mini-park was constructed on top of an old dump along the Tuscarawas River. Since it was created to honor retired Senator John Glenn, Jr., I thought up the idea of placing a statue of Glenn as a young astronaut in the trailhead. It depicts Glenn in his uniform worn in *Friendship Seven*, when he was the first American to orbit the planet. Titled "Reach for the Stars," the statue depicts Glenn holding his helmet under one arm while reaching up to grasp several stars with the other hand.

A Call to Action: Why not contact NTT and pass their information on to a local tree-planting group in your community? Their contact information is in the appendix of this book. With a short drive-about, you could easily help identify a site that needs trees—a park, a ball field, cemetery, school property or golf course—any place that would qualify as public land under the NTT guidelines. Make an offer to the facility that you will put together the volunteers to plant the trees. Make it easy for them to say yes, and hard to say no. Free trees and ample volunteers are hard to refuse.

National Action: Earth Share
—A Breakthrough for the Environment

Imagine any federal employee in a federal office in any state. Once each year, this employee is given a booklet, a card and a pep talk. It is time to decide to which charities he or she would like to contribute each week from his or her paycheck as an automatic payroll deduction. In addition to the usual selection of a federation of social service agencies, one choice is now a federation of some of the best environmental organizations in the nation. The employee decides to give a little to both. Now multiply that by four million federal employees.

In the last twenty years, a new concept in fundraising has arisen that stands poised to be a major breakthrough for the American environmental movement. This new fundraising opportunity will significantly improve how national, statewide and even local environmental organizations are funded. For many grassroots organizations, it may become a lifeline.

The new idea is Earth Share. Earth Share, based in Washington, D.C., is a federation of environmental organizations that conducts campaigns for both public and private employers to allow employees to donate a few dollars from their paychecks to help the environment. If you are confused, just think of Earth Share as a United Way for the Environment; except when Earth Share enters a workplace to raise money alongside a United Way, the campaign becomes a "Combined Giving Campaign" instead of just a "United Way Campaign."

Charitable giving at the workplace began to take off during World War II. In the 1940s, federal employees and employees of large corporations (especially those with government contracts) were solicited each spring and fall for support for the Red Cross and United Service Organizations, and for sales of war bonds. Remember the Community Chest? The USO money went to several national community service groups. Later, these campaigns were combined into a United Fund, still later called United Way. They eventually came to primarily serve seventeen community social service organizations.

In the 1980s, other federations fought for the right to be included in this huge fundraising breadbasket. They argued, and rightfully so, that the small number of United Way organizations did not represent a complete picture of all of the hundreds of nonprofit organizations vital to each community, and that the United Way's resistance to the admission of other federations was discriminatory and monopolistic. Some of the other federations that were successful in gaining access to the federal employees were United Health Charities, Black United Fund and Community Shares, a social justice federation. These new campaigns, called the Combined Federal

Campaigns (or CFCs), are powerful. In 2001, 1.46 million federal employees out of 3.88 million gave an average of $165 from their paychecks over a one-year period. The CFC raised $186 million in 1989, increasing to $241 million in 2001, just from federal employees. Similar combined campaigns exist for state employees in most states.

The new kid on the block of federations for workplace giving is Earth Share. Earth Share is the first federation entirely dedicated to raising money for environmental groups. Since its formation in 1989, Earth Share has easily gained access to the Combined Federal Campaign. That means that every fall nearly four million federal employees have the option of designating their payroll deductions to go to an environmental federation. Earth Share is still working to gain access to every state employee-giving campaign. Because United Way members often sit on the controlling boards and help to make the rules for access, it is not a certainty that Earth Share will get into all the state campaigns in the near future. However, in spite of access difficulties, Earth Share has already become a major force in workplace giving for the environment. In 2002, Earth Share celebrated the raising of its one hundred millionth dollar for the environment—a great achievement after only 13 years.

In 2002, Earth Share formed a new affiliation with 15 statewide organizations that have already raised another $50 million over the last 20 years. Together, this new and stronger Earth Share partnership offers a breakthrough for the environment. Forty-one national nonprofit environmental groups and now over 500 smaller statewide and local grassroots organizations stand to reap the benefit of regular annual funding through employee pledges. For some of these groups, this is their first taste of stable funding. Earth Share has evolved out of the knowledge and experience of many early activist leaders in the American environmental movement. To me, all of them are heroes.

Members of AFTP helped to found Earth Share of Ohio several years ago. Today, twenty-five local and statewide organizations make up the board of Earth Share. After passing on taking a leadership role in Earth Share for seven years, I was Ohio's President for the last 18 months. I am extremely proud of the professionalism of our board members and staff. We are all excited to watch the state federation as it is poised for growth into new workplace campaigns in city and county governments, schools and corporations.

Working as a volunteer on campaigns has been fun, too. The United Way representatives in state or federal workplaces have always been very professional and easy to get along with. Most of the resistance to a new environmental federation exists now on the local level, where some people have their personal ego or often their job performance on the line. As a result, gaining access to a new organization is not always easy. In my first three pitches, I was 1) denied access by a county commissioner who said, "I won't do anything that might take a dollar away from United Way"; 2) told by a superintendent of schools that "I sit on the board of United Way, and I'm proud of the fact that our school raises more money than any other district in the county. I won't let Earth Share into my campaign, and if I did, it would never get equal billing with United Way"; and 3) told that a local city approved a campaign, only to suddenly cancel it after I delivered pre-printed pledge cards to give out with the United Way cards. They got flak from their United Way coordinator. In all three of these instances with public employees, the administrations committed blatant acts of discrimination, leaving themselves open to possible legal action. A private employer has the right to throw Earth Share representatives out of their office, but public employers are not allowed to discriminate. My job is to return each year and ask again.

A Call to Action: You can help Earth Share directly in your area simply by asking the right questions. Does your employer allow any federation to come into the workplace to solicit charitable contributions from the employees? If not, why not start? If so, would they consider permitting either an Earth Share state federation or the national federation to participate alongside the other federations (often United Way) in a combined giving campaign? Do you know any state or federal employees? Why not send them a personal note to remind them to watch for Earth Share when they make out their annual pledge card (usually in late summer or early fall)?

Contact Earth Share's national office to set up a new campaign. Donors are allowed to give either to the federation (undesignated funds), which will split it among the member groups, or directly to one of the members (designated funds). If you are not yet working, you can ask your parents to do the same at their workplace, or ask your teacher to introduce the idea in their school system. I cannot emphasize enough the incredible opportunity this technique of fundraising has for all environmental groups. If your company does not host a workplace giving campaign or offer an environmental option in its current campaign, Earth Share can help you to create one. See Appendix One for more details about Earth Share.

International Action 1: Restoring Paradise

We saw the smoke early in the day. Although the fire was still about twelve miles to the south, the wind was blowing it across our horizon in a long gray-white plume. With an eye to the smoke, we continued our driving tour of plots of former ranch land that have been replanted with trees in the Guanacaste Conservation Area of Costa Rica.

The purpose of my visit there in 1996 was to see firsthand some of the ranches on former tropical forestland that had been successfully replanted into tropical forest, and to learn about the techniques being used to accomplish the reforestation. I had already planted millions of trees in North America and was now visiting Central America to find the best country for the launch of a massive reforestation project in a tropical forest area. I had already determined through my research that Costa Rica was the best of all possible nations to work with on such a project. The critical question that remained was whether or not ranchland was too depleted to ever become a successful tropical forest again.

David Morales, then Director of the Program for Restoration and Silvaculture of the Tropical Forest for the Guanacaste National Park, talked about the impact of forest fires while we drove between sites.

He told me that the local ranchers fire their land every fall, primarily to burn off the grass and to kill all the tree seedlings that naturally regenerate each year in their pastures. This practice had gone on for centuries. From the conservation perspective, the main problem with seasonal burning was that some of the ranchland was inside or adjacent to the government-declared conservation areas. The result was that a fire on a ranch could quickly spread to protected land.

In Guanacaste Park, Morales showed me two nurseries in the Experimental Station in Santa Rosa used for growing various tree species to sapling size for replanting on newly acquired ranchlands. The nurseries contained seedlings grown from native seeds and nuts collected in the region by his forestry staff. In the Guanacaste area, the foresters had proved that they could restore former farmland and ranchland back to tropical forest, and, with the recent acquisition of thousands of hectares of land, they were now able to do it on a larger scale. Once forested, the main problem was keeping the tree saplings from being burned off until they were big enough to survive such fires. They need to be protected for their first seven years.

Morales explained the effect of the fires on the country. He started with the history of the use of land. Costa Rica was once 100 percent tropical forest. Today only about 27 percent of the country is covered with forest. About 12 percent of this remaining forestland is under the protection of the government, while the remaining 15 percent is controlled by non-governmental agencies (NGOs) operating as nonprofit and for-profit reserves, research or nature centers, and by many private citizens.

These citizens are often ranchers with a part of their land in old-growth forest. Most cooperate with the park and coordinate their seasonal burning activities to keep the fires from spreading. Ironically, the largest ranch in the area that is fanatically opposed to the national effort to establish the new government conservation areas to facilitate consolidation and reforestation efforts is owned by an American citizen, a clothing manufacturer from North Carolina with friends in high places. He and one other famous U.S. politician with land in Costa Rica have become the proverbial "ugly

Figure 9:5 David Morales, Director of the Program for Restoration and Silvaculture of the Tropical Forest for the Guanacaste National Park, Costa Rica

Figure 9:6 Logo for the Program at Guanacaste National Park, Costa Rica

Americans" of Latin America, according to several sources I talked with.

The researchers established a demonstration plot inside the park to show the effect of annual burning on reforestation. Two one-hectare plots have been set aside and marked along a main road. One is carefully burned off each year. It is rich in thick grass and the small sprouts of this season's tree seedlings, which get burned off each spring. The second, completely protected from burning, is now covered with trees of various ages that have come up naturally. Once they are big enough, the trees will prevent future fires, first by shading out the grass and virtually eliminating it, and second by having trunks thick enough not to be burned off or mortally damaged by fire if it comes.

While driving us deeper into the forest on off-road trails and paths that I never could have found even with a map and written instructions, Morales explained that Costa Rica's tropical forest is both wet forest and dry forest. The wet forest areas include the many types of rain forests so well known now around the world. They make up about 40 percent of Costa Rica's forested lands. The dry forests (the name is misleading) are less well known. The wet forests receive 2,500 to 4,000 millimeters or 98 to 157 inches of rainfall each year. The rain falls all year round, with moderate seasonal changes in temperature and humidity. Where there are forests, there is little risk of fire in any season; where the land has been cleared, however, fire is the greatest annual problem. The dry forest in Guanacaste, on the other hand, receives an average of 1,473 millimeters or 58 inches of rain. Most of this occurs in the six months of spring and summer. As you can see, compared with annual rainfalls of 60 inches in Ohio or 75 inches in Indiana, "dry" here is a relative term. During the other six months, this forestland is arid. The trees lose their leaves, the vegetation becomes dangerously dry and fires can spread uncontrollably.

Even before David and I saw the smoke, park fire brigade member Daniel Garcia had spotted the fire from the new fire tower on the *pedregal*, or rim, of the Cacao Mountain to the southeast. The fire tower was built to watch for unidentified fires in lowland forests. Garcia, whose nickname is "El Zorro," had called in the sighting to the fire brigade headquarters in the Santa Rosa area of the park. He had determined that the fire was of medium size and definitely heading toward the national park. It had been started on private property, probably by hunters (technically poachers) or neighbors unfriendly to the new concept of the conservation area. Although Morales and I continued our tour all day that Saturday, the fire we warily watched from a distance was destined to catch up with us later.

The Area de Conservacion Guanacaste (ACG) began over 36 years ago, when the first protected land was created as a result of the establishment of the National Monument of Santa Rosa in 1966. At that time, the National Government of Costa Rica acquired by decree a historic site in Santa Rosa called La Casona, along with 1,000 hectares around it. This was to honor those involved in the three different military engagements that had occurred to defend the freedom and independence of Costa Rica in and around La Casona since 1856. One of those battles resulted in the death of 120 soldiers under the command of an American, William Walker. Walker had decided to invade Central America with about 800 armed veterans of the Civil War, mostly from slave states, with the aim of establishing a personal empire that would allow the existence of slavery. Not surprisingly, this episode had not been featured in any history books I had read in school. In 1988, his disturbing story was made into a film called *Walker*, starring Ed Harris.

In 1971, with the formation of the National Park System in Costa Rica, The Parque Nacional Santa Rosa was created, including the monument. As a result of legislation in 1989, Costa Rica consolidated its parks into eight major conservation areas, and Guanacaste National Park and Santa Rosa National Park were combined to create the Guanacaste Conservation Area (GCA or ACG). Located in the northwest corner of Costa Rica, on the Pacific side, Guanacaste National Park has two volcanoes in it, Cacao and Orosi. The Rincon de la Vieja National Park (containing the volcano of the old woman, *la vieja*) was later added to the GCA. Another addition, the Horizontes Experimental Station, was the result of a donation of 7,317 hectares by an American citizen, arranged through the Nature Conservancy.

At the time of my visit, efforts had been made for two years to direct limited funding to create a forested connection between the GCA and Rincon known as the Rincon-Cacao corridor. This corridor has been referred to as a "global warming life jacket" by Dr. Dan Janzen, the world renowned biodiversity expert from the University of Pennsylvania, who has concentrated his study on this area for much of his life. His research shows that the proposed corridor would be of tremendous benefit to wildlife, including migrating birds and mammals, who need the shelter of trees to travel safely from one area to the next.

Today the GCA covers over 35,000 hectares, or about 84,000 acres. However, not all of the land designated for protection has been acquired yet, and legal and financial problems may continue to hold up specific parcels for some years to come. In spite of this, the GCA is years ahead of other conservation areas in Costa Rica, and Costa Rica is a decade ahead of other Central American countries in their reforestation efforts. The Guanacaste Conservation Area is just the first of eight designated areas in the country slated for expansion.

While Morales and I were driving around the Horizontes Experimental Station sites, Miguel, subdirector of the fire brigade, took a call from "El Zorro" about the fire. Because it was a Saturday and a holiday, most of the staff was gone. Many of the employees live at the brigade headquarters during the week and return to their homes on the weekends, and only a skeleton crew remained.

I had visited the fire brigade a few days earlier. The crew members were fascinated as to why I was there, and I was fascinated by their heroic efforts. Since their formation eight years earlier, wildfires had been reduced by over 90 percent in the park area, from 17,000 hectares burned to just 2,000. Their equipment was old and outdated, and they spent most of their time involved in community education and old-fashioned, labor-intensive, hand-tool firefighting.

This situation, however, encouraged innovation—including individuals carrying 80-pound backpacks filled with water right to the source of fires on the steep mountainsides. I was especially impressed with the way the group met and very thoughtfully discussed issues, trying to make decisions that included every person and not relying on the sort of top-down management style that one sees all too often in the U.S. The firefighters and administrators were very respectful of each other during a pension discussion meeting I sat in on.

As usual, this fire started in a field of jaragua, a grass originally from Africa that can grow to a height of four meters. Ranchers started planting jaragua after its introduction to the country by agriculture specialists in the 1940s. Jaragua is a good pasture grass that makes a field look like an African savannah. When an area is full of cattle, the grass is kept at a lower height by their browsing. It thrives in the Costa Rican countryside during the wet season, but turns to tons of kindling when the weather turns dry. Jaragua fires burn hot and fast. The fire brigade trains every year to control jaragua fires, and on a windless day it is possible to stop or at least control them. However, on this day, there was a wind blowing from the northwest with gusts of 15 to 20 knots. In these conditions, the grasses burned like a blowtorch, and this particular blowtorch was one kilometer wide and several meters high. Every living thing in the blowtorch's path would be vaporized.

When the fire hit the Inter-American Highway, it ran into a firebreak that had been burned off by the fire brigade. The fire brigade habitually burns about fifty meters on both sides of the road for about 50 kilometers within the park area to prevent forest fires from spreading. When the winds were light, this break provided a line of defense for the firefighting crews to attack the blaze and stop it. This day, of course, was different. The wind carried the large flaming sparks and debris into the air, across the road and firebreak, and into the park.

The fire roared on until eventually the wind turned it away from the park at the foothills of one of the mountains. Three hours after reaching the foothills, as the day was drawing to an end, the wind died down and the fire was controlled and extinguished. However, as a kind of parting gesture, the flames that had crossed the road burned several wooden utility poles belonging to the area's electric company. The bottom fourth of the poles was vaporized—seared off from ground level to about eight feet up, and completely missing. The tops had fallen over into some large trees, causing all electricity to be lost to Guanacaste Park and the community. Fortunately, the GCA telephone lines had been laid underground in that stretch, and were still intact.

When David Morales and I arrived back at the GCA for dinner and an evening meeting with Dr. Janzen, we found him in a crisis situation. Janzen was on the phone trying to find someone who could get emergency crews to the park on this holiday. He had been trying for hours, and was exasperated. The cafeteria for the park was dark and closed. The power was off, and so dinner was postponed. My meeting with Dr. Janzen was canceled, and every available trained hand had been sent out to help the skeleton fire brigade fight the fire. I found the subdirector of staff, Roger Blanco, also attempting to get assistance via the telephone at headquarters. Blanco agreed to let me ride out to the power-line break with him. We arrived at dusk.

For Janzen, the loss of power to the GCA was a biological emergency. He had hundreds of rare biological specimens in refrigeration units in his laboratory being prepared for the monthly shipment to San Jose for study by the National Institute of Biology (InBio). The park is the field headquarters for Dr. Janzen and his crew of parataxonomists who are working year round to collect, sort and identify biological specimens in the GCA. Some scientists speculate that while 67,000 insects have already been identified, there may be 250,000 in existence, most still undiscovered. Because the GCA contains 65 percent of the 500,000 species of fauna and flora in Costa Rica alone, it is a taxonomist's paradise.

What we saw when we reached the burn site left me stunned. On both sides of the road where the fire had crossed, the land was clear and blackened as far as we could see. Red sparks were still blowing

Figure 9:6 A new tree in a field of jaragua grass

across the road like a powdery snow does on a windy winter day in Ohio. Everywhere, the fiery glow of hundreds of small tree stumps— all that remained of several years of reforestation efforts—shone in the dim light. Only the larger trees—those with trunk sizes of two or three feet and larger—remained, and even they were charred and covered with soot.

We stopped near one utility truck that had miraculously appeared to fix the downed lines. Members of the fire brigade were wandering among the burnt tree stumps, putting out the worst of the hot spots near the utility lines with their backpack water tanks.

To help get the broken and melted wires along the road reconnected, the utility crew and a couple of firemen were attempting to stand up the remains of the poles that had been seared off. Getting the poles back up and the wires off the hot ground would offer a temporary fix until they could come back and install new poles the next week. They had two poles already tied upright with ropes, while several more remained on the ground. Roger Blanco joined two men working at the base of the next pole while three more men held onto ropes looped over the top. They manhandled the heavy pole about three fourths of the way upright, but were stopped by a wire that snagged in a limb of one of the few remaining large trees. They were stuck.

I stood helplessly watching while they figured out what to do. No one could really let go without dropping the pole back to the ground. I stepped forward and asked: "Do you have a machete? I can quickly climb up and cut off that small limb." Roger helped to translate my bad Spanglish.

"Yes, they have one over there," he answered, pointing to the ground, "but we are not sure you should climb up there. What would happen if you got hurt?"

"Who else is going to do it?" I asked. "I've used a machete before."

"For God's sake let's do something," interjected one of the men still straining on a rope.

"Bueno. Let him give it a try," said the leader of the utility crew.

I grabbed the machete and started climbing the tree. Its trunk was warm, but not too hot to climb. My hands and clothes were immediately covered with black soot. When I got to the desired limb, I saw that it was bigger than I had guessed from below, about three inches across where I needed to cut it. I started hacking. The wood was very hard and difficult to cut and I wasn't progressing very fast. I started a wedged-shaped cut, like one would do with an axe. After finding the sweet spot on the blade, I doubled the intensity of my swing. I was nearly through. Finally, the limb broke, but hung on, dangling. With one final swing, it was severed and fell to the ground, freeing the tangled wires.

The ropers pulled the pole upright, and there was a cheer from the whole crew. I descended, smudged and glad to have a chance to help. Power was restored across the break within the hour. We returned to the park, dirty and hungry. There was no hot meal that

Figure 9:9 Dealing with the charred and downed electricity poles

night. The workers had all gone home in the afternoon. I ate some trail mix instead.

Restoring Paradise: Project Summary

The government of Costa Rica has already approved the repurchase of lands now privately owned in and around their national parks with a goal of bringing the total of government-owned and protected sites up to the level of 25 percent of the nation. They currently own only 12 percent. While MIRENEM, the Ministry of Natural Resources and Mines, is authorized to increase their parklands, they cannot afford to buy the rest.

My proposal is that the United States assist the government of Costa Rica by stepping in and buying 10 percent of Costa Rica. Most of the land would be unforested, marginal ranchland now owned by private citizens in Costa Rica, many eager to sell. The long-term goal would be to consolidate, reforest and protect in perpetuity lands in and around existing wet and dry tropical forests in eight designated conservation areas.

This reforestation project could remove over 100 million tons of carbon from the world's atmosphere (367 million tons of carbon dioxide). It would be a bold step forward for the U.S. at a time when environmentalists are clamoring for America to do something in the absence of a commitment from the U.S. to meet the proposed voluntary standards for carbon dioxide emissions agreed to by other nations in Rio de Janeiro and Kyoto. The project could cost $1 billion over the next 20 years, or $50 million per year, which, while an impressive figure, is relatively little when you consider that our federal budget is $2.3 trillion and the payments would be spread over two decades. Indeed, the figure does not even represent the total interest paid to the U.S. each year on debts owed by the Costa Rican government. The U.S. could also forgive part of this Costa Rican debt, in a debt-for-carbon-sequestration trade, enough to reduce Costa Rica's U.S. debt payable by $25 million per year. The U.S. could then require Costa Rica to apply that $25 million of interest toward this project, matching the U.S. dollars, and making it a U.S./Costa Rican partnership.

The land could be acquired by a new nonprofit organization set up in Costa Rica that could act as a land trust for the venture. About half of the money would be needed to buy the land sought, while the balance would need to go toward several critical aspects of the venture that would insure that the reforestation commitment would be in perpetuity. These other areas would include park management (including rangers, park administrative staff, property managers, lawyers, accountants and fire brigades), infrastructure (including roads, office buildings, housing, lodges, water and sewer plants, etc.) and regional scientific research centers (working in conjunction with InBio to continue the massive effort of surveying all the native flora and fauna in the country). Protecting ten percent of a nation is a rich idea. This project could serve as the international model for creating a sustainable reforestation effort on the level of a whole nation. Never in U.S. history has any environmental activity been undertaken on such a grand scale.

Costa Rica has long been known for its progressive leadership in the areas of peace, the humanities and the environment. Business in Costa Rica moves more slowly and gracefully than it does in the United States, and the banking system and government agencies are trustworthy. Costa Rica, which has been a democracy for over 200 years and has never nationalized its foreign businesses, can immediately implement a tropical forest project with a strong probability of success without undue complications due to political or infrastructure difficulties.

Although the Costa Rican government leads the world in the legislative steps it has taken to declare large areas of its land national parks or conservation areas, it does not have the initial capital required to complete its land acquisitions and manage the properties in a sustainable manner. However, due to the political and educational steps taken over the past thirty years, Costa Rica has prepared its general population to accept the idea that it is worth preserving its ecological assets. Eco-tourism has already become a booming business in Costa Rica. The country has already been the site of tens of millions of dollars of protection and reforestation efforts, and the infrastructure is already in place in both the government and non-governmental agencies to accomplish these projects on a piece-by-piece basis. This places reforestation efforts in Costa Rica at an advantage over all other developing countries in the world. Costa Rica today is clearly well placed to react responsibly to offers of financial assistance in any major tropical reforestation project.

This proposed project is in a unique position to benefit from the timing of market conditions that are now occurring. Most of the land that is targeted for acquisition is marginal cattle ranchland that is uneconomical in today's depressed world cattle market. Consequently, most of the owners are eager to sell their land and invest the proceeds in new business ventures. However, some of the land is located in coastal areas of prime commercial recreational development, and, as is the case with the corridor in Ohio, each year millions of dollars are being invested to develop these areas in ways that will permanently remove them from possible reforestation. It is critical that these areas be acquired in the next few years before they are permanently lost.

A further benefit of Costa Rica is the fact that over the past 20 years foresters have proven that they can reestablish both wet and dry tropical forest on lands within or adjacent to existing forests.

Much has been written about how land deforested through slash-and-burn farming methods in the Amazonian bioregion turns to desert within a few years, never again to recover. However, the topsoil in Costa Rica is thicker to start with, and while the grasses have depleted the soil of minerals, they have also protected it from erosion. Foresters have now shown that the trees—once they have been helped for the few years it takes for them to grow taller than the grass—will successfully compete with the grass for survival. The foresters' experience in Costa Rica is an opportunity for the immediate consolidation and reforestation of the large tracts of the country's former forestlands on a scale never before accomplished by any other nation.

This project aspires to purchase up to 500,000 hectares (1,235,000 acres) that would permanently remove over 100 million tons of carbon from the world's atmosphere. In terms of global greenhouse gases, the equivalent amount of carbon dioxide removed from the atmosphere by this project would be 367 million tons. The benefits to wildlife of such a venture would be incalculable.

One of the most important aspects of this proposal is the inclusion of many administrative and social programs necessary to insure that each of the eight targeted conservation area projects receives maximum community support. Ultimately, this would become a massive sociological and educational program requiring changes in the population's lifestyles. Some citizens would have to be relocated, others would have to learn to discontinue hunting and trapping and burning in areas they may have used for generations. The loss of such employment would be compensated for by the many jobs that would be created by the park expansions and necessary reforestation, as well as by the input of cash into the economy from the land purchases.

Any project proposal offered in the developing countries of the world without such social and educational considerations is destined to fail. It is not enough just to throw dollars at buying land and planting trees; it is also critical to finance the responsible management of the land for decades to come. A successful project will need to fully protect the land from logging, farming, hunting and fires. Intensive educational programs will be needed to retrain a whole generation about their responsibility to value and protect the forested areas.

A Call to Action: What is needed for this idea to become a reality are a few citizens to take it on and be its champion. We need President Bush and his staff members to read this project proposal. Are you the one to help them do that? The Republican administration needs one major national and one international environmental project to point to so they can say that, in the absence of other specific contributions to the reduction of greenhouse gases, they are doing their part. We need the leaders of both the United States House of Representatives and Senate to read this proposal. Are you the one to give this book to your Representative or Senator with this section highlighted?

That said, we cannot and do not need to wait for our government in order to proceed. We need donors who see the practicality of this project to help start the initial funding so we can set up the organization needed to begin to move ahead. We can acquire all the necessary governmental approvals and letters of support in Costa Rica ahead of time. Let's start. Are you ready to help me? If so, email me at david@davidakidd.org to get involved.

These are just a few of the ways you can be a proactivist—from the most intimate to the largest and most expansive. There are no shortages of environmental projects to work on. I want to emphasize that this list is not meant to be a compendium of every type of environmental problem or possible activity needed in America and the world. It is meant only to offer a sample. We didn't scratch the surface. As you can see, though, at every stage of the activism I have tried to think big and have not been afraid to get involved. I hope I have communicated something of the enthusiasm and urgency with which all these endeavors can, and must, be implemented. You can do the same as an activist for the environment or any cause you wish to undertake. That said, in the next section I will discuss the dangers that can happen when you decide to take on too much without proper planning—both within yourself and for your project: burnout and stress.

10: How to Avoid Activist Burnout and Cope with Stress

FOR THREE DECADES as a community activist I have thought deeply about how to effect responsible and sustainable change in the world. During that time, as you have read, I have performed my own sustained community action in the not-for-profit sector—in tree planting, vegetarian and animal activism, nonviolence training, teaching workshops and consulting with other groups—and I expect to have another thirty years of productive service. At the same time, however, I have watched scores of other well-meaning activists burn themselves out and thereby remove themselves from community action. As a result, I have developed some information and even begun to teach about what I call sustainable activism in local and national workshops.

This chapter contains some of the insights that have arisen from those who have participated in my workshops. Obviously, the concepts contained in this chapter might be easier to absorb in a life-changing way in a six-hour workshop than in a chapter that takes twenty minutes to read, but I hope to give you the highlights so that you will not only be able to begin your career as a community activist, but continue it for the rest of your life.

Sustainable Activism

I believe in setting goals high. As activists, we must endeavor to act in such a way that every action we perform is the most conducive to developing both ourselves and our environment, and bringing about the eventual success of our project. To use an organic metaphor, that means creating a nurturing environment around us, for those who support us and even those who don't. Anything less than that is less than ideal, because a situation where both parties feel they have won is more desirable than one where one party has lost. This "evolution-ary action" is also sustainable action, because non-evolutionary action results in the eventual self-destruction of the actor, and there-fore cannot be sustained.

Why should we even be concerned about this? The first reason is to make sure we are on our right path.

The Buddhist and Hindu idea of karma is particularly relevant here. The elementary law of karma indicates that we pay a price for our actions. What if we zealously performed a lifetime of action only to discover that we have not only succeeded in harming others, but, just as bad, have harmed ourselves? That would create a negative karma for which we would have to pay a price. On the other hand, the result of successful action is personal fulfillment, happiness and the ability to continue our work, which is also a function of karma. Successful action is good for our personal evolution. Throughout my life, I have tried to make sure these simple laws govern my actions. Actions that serve to hurt others while helping me are not spiritually in my best interest, nor are they in the interest of the subject of my actions. Conversely, actions that help others while hurting me are also not in my best interest, nor are they in the interest of the subject of my actions. I don't need to become a martyr.

I understand that these thoughts may be very difficult for some people who are involved on the front lines (and, as I found out at Hegins, sometimes they really *feel* like front lines) of contentious issues of environmental or animal rights activism, or any controver-sial cause about which they feel passionate. There are clearly those who are making a lot of money off the backs and labor of animals and through despoiling the beauty of the natural world. We are all complicit in some way with the deaths of ten billion animals who are killed each year in the United States for food. I can hear the question now, as I heard it over the years, "Are you saying we should stand back and simply send those people our love?"

I am not suggesting that we wimp out and refuse to stand up to violence or cruelty; in fact, quite the opposite. This book is about taking action, and doing it for a lifetime. What I am suggesting is that there is a way to perform our actions without having them become self-destructive. How we perform our action is just as critical as the action itself. If we do it wrongly, we may end up being no different from those perpetrating the very violence we oppose.

Action based on anger is not only not sustainable, it is suicidal. We will eventually burn out, eaten up by our own rage. If we act from love rather than hatred, then not only will we not burn out from the unsustainable emotions that anger breeds in us, but we will more effectively bring about change. If we act from love, we can get up every day with a renewed sense of energy and purpose. When based in love, our work energizes and heals us. We become indefatigable.

Anger has its place. Occasionally, it is necessary to be angry to motivate those who have become callused with indifference and who do not respond to a message that is couched less intensely. Nevertheless, that anger should be focused and short, and the speech that accompanies it should still be considered and not self-destructive.

Not only is wrong action ineffective and debilitating, but it also causes stress. Stress in our nervous system causes us to become limited and inflexible and makes our behavior pinched and inauthentic. A healthy, stress-free nervous system is capable of both acting and reacting with true unconditionality and provides us with immediate benefits. As we respond to our environment, likewise it responds to us. In this way, acting from love will generate more support for your cause. The way to avoid stress in your environment is to become stress-free yourself. In the next few sections I will show you what stress is, and in the next chapter we'll explore how I learned to deal with it.

Discovering Stress

An Overview

In my discussion of stress, I am not going to give an elaborate description of how the nervous system works, since I am not a physiologist. Instead, I am going to talk in analogies and with examples about what stress is and the reactive patterns that arise once we have acquired stress. These are the patterns that make us react to things and take away our ability to act freely. Seeing them helps us to know when we have stress. I will then offer a few ways to solve the problem of stress. Please note that it is not enough to just learn to cope with stress. We should want to be free of it completely.

The first path to becoming free of stress is on the level of the mind, and involves changing our worldview—literally changing our patterns of thinking. Worldviews are belief patterns so deeply rooted in us that we don't really know they exist. What our worldview consists of is the way we see ourselves and others in our actions. In this regard, most people have not learned how to separate the actor from the action. The way we experience or think about time and space is also important to our worldview, and below you'll see how working on both can help us deal with stress and anger. We'll also talk about how our expectations of others fit into our worldview, and how critical communication can be.

The second pathway to freedom is on the level of feelings and the spiritual path. Having a personal belief system has helped many people deal with their stress. Developing a personal meditation program and taking time to be in nature are also remedies to be considered and will be discussed below.

The Stress Syndrome

Although most people don't have a clue what stress is, almost everyone can describe its symptoms. Stress wasn't even discovered or, more accurately, described scientifically until the mid-1900s, when a Canadian doctor named Hans Selye first described the stress syndrome in the human body. Dr. Selye said that stress was any kind of imbalance in the physiology, and he went on to identify two kinds of stress: *eu*-stress and *dis*-stress.

Eustress is the good kind of stress. The prefix *eu* comes from Greek, meaning *well* or *good*, as in "euphoria." Eustress is that normal imbalance that needs to exist in us so we can survive. For example, there is a chemical imbalance in our digestive system that causes one compound to act on another in order to digest food so we can assimilate its nutritional components. Digestion is the body's attempt to move chemically from imbalance to balance. Likewise, there is a positive-negative electrical imbalance that allows an electrical impulse to jump across the gaps, or synapses, in our nervous system. Without that imbalance, our nervous system could not send messages throughout the body. These imbalances are eustress.

The kind of stress that most of us mean when we have problems is distress. Distress is any kind of abnormal imbalance in the nervous system. Distress is caused when the nervous system is asked to cope with a situation that is more than it can bear at that time, causing an overload. Any overload to the system causes distress. Distress then triggers our built-in emergency response, called our "fight or flight" response.

When most people think about their nervous system, they are referring to the autonomic nervous system. This is the system that controls involuntary functions. These include the heartbeat, breathing, digestion, glandular activity, and contraction and dilation of blood vessels. Actually, the autonomic system has two parts to it, the sympathetic and parasympathetic systems, which are designed to balance one another. The sympathetic system is our survival system. It stimulates the body and is responsible for secreting stress hormones. The parasympathetic system relaxes the body. It secretes hormones to slow the heart and speed up digestion. Sustainable action and long life are based on us operating primarily in our parasympathetic nervous system. Using the sympathetic system is destructive and wears us out. It was meant for emergencies only.

How We Accumulate Stress

The best way I've found to explain how stress accumulates in the body is to use the following analogy. Imagine that your nervous system is like a large light bulb. Each person's body represents a different wattage capacity. Some people have 50-watt nervous systems, while others have 1,000-watt nervous systems. Most people function within a certain range—let us say for argument, 300 to 500 watts. A person with an operating range from 50 to 100 watts feels and senses at a very refined level. However, if that person is exposed to loud noise (like a rock band) or to a smoky room (like a bar), he or she will instantly get a headache, and will usually flee immediately from such a sensory overload.

A person with a 300 to 500 range won't share or even comprehend this experience, since he or she starts out at a level where the sensibilities are coarser and can tolerate sensory experiences in a much higher range. If your body has a range of 500 to 1,000 watts, you might not even begin to have fun until the music on your sound system is turned up and you can feel the vibrations from the speakers through your feet. You can party until dawn and still be strong enough to keep going the next day. Such a heavy sensory load does not cause you stress. However, it does make it hard for you to relate well to someone with lower-wattage sensibilities. If we understand our differences in this way, it is hardly surprising that some people cannot communicate easily with each other: We literally live within different frequency ranges. Some people shut down before others even begin to feel. Still others only begin to wake up after another has shut down. Our long-term goal should be to be flexible enough to feel at the finest levels while simultaneously being strong and stable enough to enjoy life at its most intense levels.

Now imagine a stressful situation. Each situation represents a certain demand on our system, which can also be measured in watts. What if a certain problem creates 200 watts of potential stress, and we have a 300-watt system? The answer is that we can cope and no stress is accumulated. However, if a 200-watt problem comes and we only have a 100-watt nervous system, overload occurs. We deal with the first 100 watts of the problem, but then we can't take it anymore. We try to turn away from the problem, and say things like "I don't want to hear about it. I don't want to think about it." The problem lies in the fact that the other 100 watts doesn't disappear. It is still hanging out there for us. The part we couldn't cope with is the overload that causes stress. The stress that we do not deal with always locates itself somewhere in our body—no matter whether the stress is physical, mental or emotional. The stress may later appear in the mind or heart as a result, but it starts in the body.

Physical stress is the easiest to understand. If my head bangs into a wall, my skull is overloaded (let's call it a 500-watt problem and I have a 100-watt nervous system). Not only do I kill 500,000 brain cells, but I incur 400 watts of stress overload and get a headache. Or imagine that I lift a box that is too heavy and strain my back muscles. Clearly, we can see that physical problems such as these can create physical stresses.

Mental or emotional stresses, however, are more difficult to comprehend, since many people do not believe that an emotional or mental condition can manifest itself in the body. However, any massage therapist can tell you what kind of stress their clients have and where that stress is located. Stress retains its flavor, and good massage therapists can often identify the type of stress they are massaging out of the body by the actual emotional state that suddenly comes up in their client. When the therapist releases anger, the patient becomes angry; likewise, grief, sadness and fear are all enmeshed in the fabric of the body. Therapists have even reported that different parts of the body store up different negative moods. They also store up positive moods. A mother who is overwhelmed by joy at her daughter's wedding and cries might have had 1,000 watts of joy, but only a 500-watt nervous system. Good events can cause overload just as easily as bad events.

Throughout our lives we will be exposed to major problems that come with a great deal of stress. These may include the act of being born, being physically or sexually abused, getting married, getting divorced, buying or selling a house, moving, losing a job, changing careers or suffering the loss of a pet or loved one. These are the 1,000-watt problems. We all know people who have had to face several of these major stresses at once. A human being can only take so many of these, without dealing with them over the long term, before his or her system can no longer cope and serious illness or even death results.

Our solutions, then, are either to avoid stress by not being around it in the first place, or to strengthen our nervous system so we will be better able to cope with it. We can learn to do both.

Fight or Flight Response
Remember a time when you were called on to speak in class and did-n't feel prepared? You stood up, your neck and cheeks went red, your armpits and forehead suddenly broke out in a sweat and you experienced such a shortness of breath that you could hardly speak. That's the stress response in the body, and it's called the "fight or flight" response.

Our body has a built-in emergency response mechanism that was designed to save our lives. The "fight or flight" mechanism is one of our most primitive systems. It helped prehistoric humans escape or fight off predators, and it remains very active today.

When facing a stressful situation, our body's first response is to switch from the parasympathetic to the sympathetic mode of functioning. The adrenal glands, sitting on top of each kidney, release hormones, immediately stopping nearly all of the blood flow to our digestion and redirecting it to the skeletal muscles in the arms and legs. Our strength increases, our breathing intensifies, our heart speeds up and we sweat. All of this is to make us stronger, faster and cool while our internal engine runs in high gear. Our body is preparing us to fight for our life or run like heck. Extremely effective though this system has proven over the millennia, this "emergency back-up system" is terribly destructive. After the threat has disappeared, we are left shaking, and the chemicals secreted by the adrenal glands are very damaging to our health.

Because of the stress we encounter in our fast-paced daily lives, and thanks to a chronic lack of sleep, most people can only make it through the day by using their "fight or flight" system all the time. We drink coffee and tea, smoke cigarettes, take pills and even yell at each other to stimulate our "fight or flight" system. Have you ever heard someone say, "What I need is a good fight?" These stress chemicals are habit-forming. They wake us up and give us a rush. Lacking natural energy, many worn-out people run on their emergency back-up system until it too becomes completely exhausted. That behavior may be able to last for ten or twenty years, but after that people are not only utterly burned out but suffering from chronic fatigue. The "fight or flight" mechanism should be saved for real emergencies only.

Reactive Patterns
One story will suffice to show what happens when stress goes untreated. There was a woman named Mary who lived in the Carolinas with two small children. She had a pretty patio, completely decorated in yellow. One day, while sitting on the patio, Mary received a telephone call informing her that her husband and both of his parents had been killed in a small plane crash. You can imagine that she went through the whole range of stresses: horror, fear, grief, anger, and finally, loneliness.

For the rest of her life, Mary hated the color yellow, although she didn't know why. She also hated the sound of the phone ringing. Years afterward, when her teenage daughter showed Mary her new dress, her mother said, "That's a nice pattern, but you don't look good in yellow. Go back and get the same thing in any other color." Similarly, when the phone rang at work, Mary would often say, "Don't worry about it, it's probably bad news anyway." Since Mary was in charge of a sales department, this was not a good response. When she finally recognized these patterns of reaction in herself, Mary started to be able to deal with her reactive patterns and be more positive.

The obvious point to be made here is that our stresses, once incurred, can cause us to react when we encounter similar environmental stimuli. When the actual stress is embedded in our memory, so also is its emotional content. That stress then exists like a string hanging out of us. Anyone or anything may accidentally pull our string, and instantly we will react with the emotion that may have been locked into us even decades before. These are reactive patterns.

Reactive patterns can define a person's whole personality. For example, extreme patterns can lead to an extreme sense of victimization. A person with such reactive behavior might describe his or her day like this: "I went to the bank and the teller there really pissed me off. Then I went to the grocery store and the clerk there made me mad. You just can't find good help these days. Later, when I talked to my mom on the phone we started yelling at each other. What a day! Why is everyone out to get me and always trying to make me mad?" People in this predicament have strings hanging out all over them. No matter where they go, they cannot avoid having someone accidentally pull one of them.

Even if we are not personally as reactive as the victim described above, we can see how having a reactive pattern takes away our freedom. With so many reactive patterns, we become so engaged in automatically reacting to situations that we no longer are able to simply act. Instead of being real actors, we have become reactors, victims of our own stress.

Understanding that we have reactive patterns helps us to know that we too must have some deeply rooted stresses in us. Whether we are five or fifty, we can have these stress patterns embedded in our bodies. Once established, these stresses color our every feeling, thought, word and action. Recognizing them is the first step to doing something about them, while failing to deal with them will ultimately cause us to age more rapidly and eventually burn out.

As we eliminate our stress, we expand the range of our nervous system, both at the top end and the bottom. The result is that we can be sensitive enough to feel the finest, most refined sensation and at the same time be strong enough to endure the the most intense sensations. This applies not only to negative experiences, but also to experiences of pleasure. We can only endure as much pleasure as we can pain. That's not only more fun but another reason to want to live a full life, with a healthy and fully functional nervous system.

Activist Burnout

Burnout is caused when we perform our day-to-day actions only using our emergency back-up system. If we do it over a long enough period, we simply exhaust our back-up systems and ourselves. This is particularly a problem with activists, who have a tendency to take it upon themselves to launch a crusade over some issue. Newly converted to a cause, or ego-driven to the extent that they feel only they can solve the problem, these activists work tirelessly, impressing everyone with their depth of knowledge and sincere commitment. Then, suddenly, they stop working and drop completely out of sight. This happens *a lot*. When you ask the previously indefatigable activists where they have been, their response is often something like the following: "I don't want to hear about it anymore. Don't call me. I don't want to talk about it, just leave me alone." That's burnout. This is not to say that these activists don't still feel a commitment to the project, and may even feel guilty about not being able to complete their work. But their bodies are telling them that they cannot endure the daily stress any longer and they are, quite literally, unable to continue. This problem is not confined to activists. Students often drop out of college for the same reasons, and people quit successful careers because of it. People end relationships because of it. All of us in this hectic day and age are at risk.

As I said at the beginning of this chapter, the ideal of activism is to learn how to perform our action so that it is sustainable. Unfortunately for the individuals involved (including both volunteers and working activists) and for the institutions employing them, most people are working against their own biological clock—the time when they will eventually exhaust themselves. Our round-the-clock way of living in the industrialized world almost guarantees it. Amazingly, some people even have come to believe that such stress is good for us, and we find ourselves ludicrously comparing our stress-related problems, proud of the suffering we have endured, a virtual martyr complex.

But burnout is not only unnecessary, it is counterproductive and irresponsible. There are too many good programs available to help us reduce or eliminate stress-related burnout to allow it to get us down. In my opinion, stress management techniques for the staff of any organization, nonprofit or for-profit, should be an integral part of every strategic plan. To fail to include them is to fail to plan for the longevity of the organization. Unfortunately, most people spend more time planning for their vacation every year than planning how to take care of themselves through a stress management program. Vacations help relieve stress, but they do not eliminate it. In fact, many people return from their vacation more tired than when they left.

As I indicated earlier, one of the easiest changes we can make that will help us to perform sustainable action is to re-program our basic worldviews so that we can begin to act differently in the world. I will now discuss how you can do that. My observations come from 28 years of experience in teaching stress management courses to thousands of clients.

Changing Our Worldview: Taking Responsibility for Ourselves

One of the most self-defeating of the worldviews we unconsciously learn is that of conditional love. Conditional love is the belief that we are responsible for other people's happiness and sadness, and they are responsible for ours. It expresses itself as "I will love you if you love me back in a certain way that I expect. Conversely, to obtain your love, I must love you back in the way you expect."

We learn conditional love when we are young, and it harms us throughout our whole lives. We are taught, usually by our parents, that we are responsible for other people, and we reasonably conclude that other people are responsible for us. This is not the truth. We are each responsible for ourselves. As children we are often told, "You are bad!" or "You make me angry," a situation that gives young children enormous power when they realize that their actions can actually make another person angry or happy. But it also places a great burden on them, because they realize that they carry the full responsibility for their parents' happiness with them.

The net result is that children grow up thinking they have power over others and that others have power over them. We try to keep others happy; we even manipulate them to like us, or drive them crazy to keep them feeling powerless. This pattern of belief is the root of codependence and causes all of us in some way to enable negative behaviors in others and others to do the same to us.

It is my belief that such codependence is one of the reasons why so many relationships fail. How many couples join together and even affirm that they are each responsible for the other's happiness? Such relationships can only result in failure or unhappiness, because no one can ever totally fulfill your every desire. At some level you have to be responsible for your own inner happiness. If you take on that responsibility for yourself and meet someone who has done the same, then you are a couple who have the most to give to each other without conditions.

The truth is that no one can ever make you angry. Your anger and how you respond to any situation is entirely dependent upon the condition of your nervous system. Let me give you an example. One evening after work, while you are highly stressed, you accidentally drop a glass in the sink and break it while doing dishes. You yell, throw the towel and stomp around the kitchen frustrated about how unfair the world is because everything is always happening to you. On another day, when you are rested and fresh, you might break another glass in exactly the same way. On that day you look down, realize your carelessness, feel stupid and resolve to be more cautious while you carefully pick up the broken glass. On this second day there is no anger, no feeling of victimization. Yet the very different responses come from the same person—you—in the same place experiencing the same events. The only difference is the state of the nervous system.

I remember watching my wife one day as she entered the kitchen and found that our three-year-old daughter had colored all over the refrigerator and part of the wall. She raised her voice sternly. "You are bad," she said. "You make me angry."

"I think you need to meditate," Sara responded to her mother. Sara had already watched for years as her mom and dad meditated twice daily and had observed that while we might come home tired and grouchy before meditation, we were usually calm and relaxed afterwards.

"No, I don't," my wife replied. "You were bad, and you need to wash off this refrigerator right now and stop coloring on it." I thought about this classic exchange for years. My daughter was right, of course—at least about making her mother angry.

Being responsible for our own actions means that how we respond to any situation or person has to do with *us*, and not the other person or event. Those individuals are responsible for their actions and reactions, and we are responsible for our actions and reactions. This means that no one can "make" us angry. Our anger response is either a choice we make or an automatic response that has to do with our stresses. In either case, it is *our* anger, not *theirs*.

Even if someone hits us, we have a choice—to respond with violence or to turn the other cheek. Once more, I want to make it clear that I am not saying we should be indifferent to violence and let everyone walk all over us. That would not be for our highest good or theirs. The assailant still has to answer for his or her behavior, and may need to be corrected immediately. But we have a choice of response—a choice of love or anger. Never underestimate how hard it is to change such a worldview, or how massive a transformation can occur once you have begun to change it.

Changing Our Worldview: Bad Actions Equal Bad Person

Another misconception we learn when we are very young is that our behavior is the same as our self-image. This is not true. When our parents say, "You are bad," they usually mean "What you did is bad." They meant to condemn your action, not you personally. However, the language our parents use was garnered from their own parents and their language from theirs, so this worldview has become almost a part of the very definition of the parent-child relationship.

Such a common mistake in language is hard enough to find, let alone correct. However, this language also leads to conditional behavior. What we really mean to say when we tell a child that he or she is bad is, "I love you, and most of the time you behave very well. But right now your behavior is not right. What you did was wrong, and you will have to be punished for it (i.e., clean the refrigerator)." But how clearly do we think when a child who misbehaves triggers our ancient worldviews and stresses or someone shouts at us?

When you go up against someone performing an action that is obviously cruel or violent, such as torturing an animal, it can feel very personal. For many, it would be a real challenge to see the good in that person at that moment, and be able to love them. I understand how hard it can be; I've been there. It is a cop-out for us to simply say that "I am right and he is wrong" or "I am good and he is evil." While easier, that kind of thinking is simplistic and immature. Life is much more complex than that. To love that person unconditionally is exactly what we need to do. We need to uphold that person's integrity. If we cannot love the outer person, then we need to love them on their soul level, even while we object to their action. We need to believe that somewhere deep inside them there is a being that is inherently good. I want to emphasize again: Changing the way we respond to others is not just for their benefit, *it is for ours*. We need to learn to respond in a way that does not harm them and, at the same time, does not harm us.

Giving Away Our Power

As part of the conventional process of growing up with these worldviews, we are usually taught to give our power away to others. It amazes me that even in America, where we are taught that we have no formal class system, we are surrounded by people who unconsciously either look up or down at others. We may all be guilty of this in one way or another. This bigotry, and occasionally sexism or racism, is so built into our thinking that we seldom know it is happening. However, it is self-evidently not right, because when it happens to us or we do it to others, we don't feel comfortable. Unfortunately, because of the way the problem is embedded within us, the situation isn't always very balanced: We quite often feel fine when it is we who are taking the power or being given it, but not when it is taken away from us or when we give it away.

For example, how many times have you been introduced to someone who has either great wealth or great power in society, and you allowed yourself to be instantly intimidated by them? "He's better than I am," you start to think, or "There isn't anything I could say to that person that would be of value," or "His time is more valuable than mine." Sometimes we put people on a pedestal either because we have poor self-esteem or so that we can worship them or show them off to others. We believe this gives us power. But it is not good for the other person, and definitely not good for us—neither putting people down nor raising them up is good for anyone, because when you worship someone else you are putting yourself down. You do them harm when you give away your power like that, and you harm yourself in the process. If they are wise, they will not accept your power or let you take theirs.

Changing our Worldview: Redefining Our Sense of Time

Although our planet has more means of communication at its disposal than ever before, it is my belief that one of the biggest problems we face today is a failure to communicate effectively. Good communication is a constant challenge—as good as I am in this area, it certainly remains one of my own weakest links.

In order to communicate effectively you need to have everybody together—whether physically in the same room or through some means of technology. The second and most important step is that once you are together, you need to be in the same time zone. By "time zone" I do not mean the part of the country or world you live in. I mean that some people do not live in the present time, but instead conduct their lives in the past or in the future and are simply not communicating in the same dimension of time. If you are trying to communicate with someone who lives in the past while you are in the present there are two options: Either you need to go back to the past to talk to them, or they need to come to the present to talk with you. Otherwise, you will both fail to communicate—every time.

The ideal, of course, is to learn to be in the present, what ancient teachings call "being in the moment." True happiness can only occur when you are living in the moment, because happiness that is based in the past or future is imaginary and therefore not able to last. All negative emotions and unhappiness exist when we are not living in the moment. There is no anger or fear, no guilt, shame, grief or sorrow when you are in the moment. These emotions are always found in the past or future. In order to give you a sense of what I mean, let me highlight two of those emotions: anger and fear.

Think first about anger. Can you anticipate anger in the future? Not usually. That's because the future has not happened yet. Can you suddenly concoct anger in the present? No. That's because in the present there is only the "right now." Nothing is happening to be angry about. In short, anger can only be felt in retrospect; we have to look back to feel anger. Therefore, one major source of anger is living in the past. Something in the past that people see as unfair or unjust causes them to react with anger. It is as if they get stuck in the past, entangled in the web of their own reactive patterns. If they suddenly return to the here and now, however, their anger will often go away. When it returns, they have temporarily slipped back into the past time zone.

Now let's think about fear. Fear is not experienced in the present tense; it can only be experienced in the future—even if that future is only a fraction of a second ahead of the present moment. There is no fear right *now*. It is in the next moment. By bringing a fearful person back to the moment, we can dispel that fear instantly. If we want to communicate with such a person, we need to either go into his or her future or bring the person back into our present.

Other emotions that are rooted in the past are guilt, grief and shame. All of them depend on our dwelling on things that have already happened. The emotions that depend on looking into the future are worry and paranoia. People who worry all the time are stuck in the future. When they run out of things to worry about in their own lives, they quickly move on to worry about the lives of their friends and family. Usually, there is no anger in the future. However, I've seen people with so much anger who were so good at imagining a negative future outcome in their relationships that they could summon anger at their partner for something that they thought they "might" do in the future. See how we are? It may be that we are innocently drawn to the past or future in order to help us to process the stress related to specific emotions. We just weren't meant to get stuck there. The lesson is that our true fulfillment and happiness exists only in the present, not in the past or future.

Being out of the present is not something to blame yourself for. It is a habit that the nervous system learns, and for many it is a necessary survival technique. It helps us cope with pain by allowing us to escape it until we are strong enough to deal with it. However, when we become aware of this process happening, our role is to gently bring ourselves (or others) back into the present moment until we (or they) can rehabituate to it.

Changing Our Worldview: Having Realistic Expectations

Once we are all established in the same time zone, we can begin to communicate. Communication is necessary so that we all have the same expectations. I often teach that anger is caused by expectations that are not met. People who live in the past, and therefore dwell on their unfulfilled expectations, may account for much of the remaining anger on this planet.

If we expect something to happen and it does not, we get angry. Yet, we need to ask ourselves: Were our expectations realistic? Or were they the result of an overactive imagination or fantasy? Did we communicate our expectations to the other person we were working with? If we didn't, then isn't it unfair to be angry with someone for not fulfilling an expectation they knew nothing about? As you might imagine, the last problem happens all too often.

For example, what if you ask someone to meet you and the other person agrees and then doesn't show up? Was your expectation met? No. Do you have the right to be disappointed? Yes. In our culture, courtesy demands that the other person should have made an attempt to let you know that he or she was not going to be able to meet you or would be late.

Now, what if you knew I was going to be at an event and you decided that you would also go to the event, meet with me, and then we'd go out afterward for food and perhaps a movie? You turn up, and I am not there; or I'm at the event but have other plans and can't go and eat or see a movie with you. Should you be upset? No. Not only did I not know about your expectation, but I had not agreed to it. Therefore, your expectation was false or unrealistic. All this seems quite logical when we examine it, but I am sure you know many instances when such a situation—and the consequent disappointment—has happened to you or to someone who expected something from you without your knowledge.

These kinds of false expectations happen all the time with couples, particularly about sex. It's very common for one member of the couple to start imagining a romantic evening ending in sex. The fantasy might go on all day. Unfortunately, the other partner has had a tiring day and is grouchy, hungry or completely focused on something else and misses all the body language and cues, such as romantic candlelight, that the lonely partner is sending out. As a result, someone gets his or her feelings hurt and feels unappreciated. It would have been much easier to have talked and made realistic plans. You don't have to be explicit to negotiate sex—or whatever you wish—with your partner, but we all know enough to make it obvious what we need. You could say, "I've been feeling romantic, and I want us to spend some time alone tonight." If you live with a workaholic, you may need to get a spot in his or her appointment book; or, better yet, sit down together and schedule your personal time on your partner's calendar for the whole month in advance. By setting up clear lines of communication and clear expectations you not only establish the justification to be upset should your expectations not be met but also decrease the chances that those expectations will not be met. This of course does not eliminate the possibility of spontaneous behaviors. It just gets the basic needs covered.

It may also help to lower your expectations. How many times have you had a habitual liar promise to do something for you and not deliver? It amazes me when people get upset over a habitual liar or a drunkard not making good on a pledge. By nature, we want to trust everyone, but some people have not earned that trust. Part of recognizing the unconditional in our lives is being honest enough to factor into a relationship the right for the other person to fail, especially when history has shown it to be a trend.

Even better than lower expectations would be not having any expectations at all. This is the hardest task we face: completely unconditional giving. Where you would have asked for something, reduce that demand to nothing. That way, anything that you get will come as a bonus and be much more appreciated. Of course, this doesn't mean we should discount our friends as worthless. What it means is that we accept full responsibility for ourselves and take any help we receive as an unexpected blessing.

By making our expectations realistic, we stand less of a chance of setting ourselves up to be hurt and to incur stress. We also have a better opportunity of communicating with our partners, friends and associates so that they know better what our expectations are and have a chance to agree or disagree to it. Everyone feels better when everything is out in the open and all expectations are clear and agreed upon.

Changing Our Worldview: Redefining our Sense of Space
We interpret our experience on this planet in terms of time and space. We usually sense time as a linear function, the sequential ticking away of seconds and minutes, days and weeks. For most people our sense of space is limited to how big our body is in relation to other objects and bodies and how much room we need to get around wherever we go. In nature, many animals have whiskers in proportion to their body size to help keep them from getting into situations where they might get stuck. In humans, this sense, however, is not always reliable. Many people have a completely false sense of their body size. Some thin people see themselves as fat, and some overweight people see themselves as thin.

There is, however, another sense of space available to us that only some people have been able to experience. You will recall that, while on leave from Viet Nam, I had an experience where I felt myself becoming larger. Many would consider that expanded sense of the self as bigger than the body a "mystical experience," as though it is a visitation from outside our body or realm of consciousness, perhaps a mere hallucination. They are wrong. There need not be anything unbelievable about a sense of our own unboundedness, for humankind has the faculty to experience the infinity of space. Indeed, the number and depth of religious traditions and philosophical schools that have developed ideas about an individual's experience of infinity testifies that such an experience is available to all human beings. People who have had such experiences have evoked a Higher Self, an inner Being, a World Soul, Transcendence—yet they are all referring to the same sense. Eastern traditions refer to the establishment of the mind in this field of life as *enlightenment*, or *Nirvana*. Western Christian mystics have called it *Illumination*. Individuals in every culture, in every religion and in every age have written about such experiences, but they are seldom understood.

The reason why it is beneficial to allow one's mind to establish itself at this highest level of expansion is not only so that the Self is conceived of as unbounded space, but because it is only from this level that we can come to appreciate that we are a part of a greater whole. Only at this level can we understand that everything and everyone else is a part of us. Yet this Transcendence is not an intellectual understanding; it is a direct perceptual experience. The same Transcendence we experience is within everyone and everything at its deepest core. Given that understanding, how can we then see anyone as our enemy? How can we hate ourselves? Realizing our Oneness is our greatest mystical truth. If everyone understood this and experienced their mystical Union, wars and strife would immediately cease.

Developing a Personal Creed
Another way to handle stress better in our life is to realize that we are not responsible for everything around us. We need to assume responsibility for our actions, but we are never responsible for the outcomes of those actions. If we fail to accomplish our goal, and we have per-

formed good actions, then we need not burden ourselves with the additional stress of self-condemnation. Turning over the outcome of our action is another way to handle stressful situations more effectively. What happened to me when I went to Viet Nam is an example of this. I went to Viet Nam an agnostic. What that meant for me was that I believed in God, but I didn't care about any particular organized religion. In fact, when we were required to select our religious choice so it could be printed on our metal dog tags, I chose "No Pref." Most of the men I was with thought that meant I was an atheist, although a few knew the difference between an atheist and an agnostic. By signing up for "No Pref" I meant to say that I didn't really care who prayed over me in the event of my death or injury. When I returned to the United States in July 1972, I was no longer an agnostic. I had by then developed my own personal creed—something I believed in. What I was not sure about was what organized religion, if any, I might find to fit with my new belief system.

After my nineteen months in Viet Nam, I was probably about as stressed out as most of the men who did only one tour over there. Although a combat veteran, I considered myself better off than most because I hadn't had much personal contact with the enemy. Except for perimeter ground probes, the shots fired at me had been relatively inaccurate and impersonal. Nevertheless, I returned highly stressed and with some obvious reactive patterns. (You will recall, for instance, that shortly after returning home, I hit the floor of my parents' dining room in Ohio when I heard a truck backfire.) I was full of mixed emotions. I was proud for doing my job well and serving my country, but ashamed to have been a part of some of the war experiences. I was also disillusioned because I felt that the United States should never have gone to Viet Nam in the first place. I was excited about being a civilian once again after the over-controlled and over-managed life in the military, but I was also anxious about re-entering civilian life and facing major educational and career choices.

Fundamentally, however, I had an overwhelming sense of isolation from not being able to talk with anyone back home about my experiences and emotions of the last nineteen months. Unlike in other wars, few units sent to Viet Nam were trained, shipped out and returned together. That meant that each person returned when his or her year was up, often alone. Units that returned together had some days or weeks to process their experiences, hash out the good and bad of it, and become somewhat, as it were, "decompressed" before going to their homes. Even my brother, another Nam veteran, and I could not find the words to compare notes or share our experiences. We were reduced to veiled references or oblique jokes that might refer to the possible experiences we had had.

Nevertheless, I considered myself better off than many because I felt a true exhilaration simply from being alive. I also carried a quiet but supreme confidence that came from *knowing*, and not just believing, that there was a Supreme Intelligence governing the Universe and that I, and therefore all of humankind, had the possibility of making a direct personal contact with It. I knew this from my personal experiences to date. By then my creed consisted of a sincere belief in the existence of God and the possibility of the establishment of a personal, direct and intimate experience of the presence of God by any human with a functioning nervous system, regardless of his or her professed faith or belief system. (Looking back, I guess that I came home from the war as a Theosophist, although I didn't know that then.) Simply having the quiet knowledge of a higher power takes a burden off one's shoulders. I believed that my creed helped me deal with a considerable amount—although not the whole—of my war-related stress.

What is critical about having a belief system is that it needs to be original and personal. It is not enough to adopt a creed that someone else has written for you to believe and have it be meaningful in your personal life. If this means that six billion people will develop six billion versions of what they believe God to be, then that's exactly what needs to happen. Each version of that creed will be right for each of us at that time in our life and our evolution. What is useful is that our creed, once written down, will change and evolve along with us over the years. But it has to be personal, and based on your experiences and understandings.

Social Alienation

In spite of my personal creed, I think I was no different from many Viet Nam veterans in that I was scary to a few people. I came back possessed of a fierce intensity and with one of those ten-mile stares that comes from being under fire. In addition, I felt alienated from my old friends' ways of having fun. The same guys I had left behind three years earlier were still going to the same bars and making the same jokes about the same women. The only difference was that they now had longer hair and bell-bottomed pants, and smoked a little of that weak stateside reefer. It seemed so trite. Just weeks earlier, everything I had done had been a matter of life and death. Suddenly, nothing I did much mattered to anyone.

I tried to fit in for about a month. In the first week, my friends dragged me downtown one night to King Arthur's, a local college pub, where I hoped to be normal and fit in for an evening. There was little chance of that. I still had a very short military haircut and unfashionable, outdated clothes. I agreed to one drink to celebrate my return (alive). I asked for a mixed drink. The bartender asked for an I.D, something that hadn't happened to me in three years. I gave him my military one and he told me I wasn't old enough to buy a mixed drink. (In Ohio at the time, you had to be twenty-one to buy high–alcohol content beer—7 percent—or mixed drinks.) I had forgotten. Even though I felt thirty, I was in fact only twenty. I laughed, incredulous.

I leaned over and spoke to the bartender. "You know, it seems ironic to me," I said, "that our government has decided that I was old enough to travel around the world for the last three years in the Army—where I drank and got laid in fourteen different countries and in ten different languages, and spent nineteen months getting shot at—but am not mature enough to have a drink in Ohio." He laughed and bought me a drink. Maybe, I thought, things are going to be all right after all. It was at least an improvement over the hippie kids who had spat on me in the San Diego airport when I passed through in uniform when I was being discharged.

I grew my hair long and stopped going out to bars. I shopped for textbooks to prepare for college in the fall and started work in the same forging factory I had worked in before the service. They had held a place for me, as required for veterans. I worked the midnight shift at the hammer shop and went to college during the day.

Remembering my commitment to God, I felt certain that my destiny, and maybe my career, lay in some aspect of organized church work. Having shunned, like my parents, most churches all my life, I felt for the first time that I could really belong to one and relate to the people there. After all, in my case, I felt I had really been "saved."

However, it didn't work out like that. After a few months in a church that my grandmother had attended, our oldest familial church connection, I learned some stark lessons. First, the activities of the church appeared to be mostly about perpetuating the activities of the church. Second, no one there ever asked or seemed to care about me or my experiences. Third, we were told that we weren't worthy of having an original personal experience or relationship with God and that to have just a "contented faith" in God was enough to expect. We were told that all the big experiences had been reserved for Jesus, or some of the better saints, and anyone who said otherwise was being blasphemous. Eventually, I learned which of the elders were sleeping with which of the church members' wives, and who was involved in the latest plot to overthrow or undermine the authority of the minister. As you can imagine, I was fairly disillusioned and promptly left. I decided that organized religion—or at least that one at that time— was not my path to enlightenment. I crossed off that career choice.

Maybe, I reasoned, my right venue was to be involved in community service. I was told I was too young to join the Chamber of Commerce, so I joined a local chapter of a younger men's community service organization. They raised money in some projects and then spent it on others. After a few months of observing this, I proposed a project. There seemed to be a definite lack of children's entertainment in our community, I suggested. Why not bring a troupe of children's entertainers from Cleveland and sell tickets as a fundraiser?

The event went well, but lost a little money, as projected for the first year. Once the project bills were settled, my boss in the organization became very insistent that I write a detailed summary of the project for future reference. Nagging was not a good tactic for this vet. Working through the night and going to school through the day, I could either sleep or do homework in the evenings, but not both. I was very tired all the time. I suggested that if he wanted a report, I would talk to him for a few minutes and he could write it himself. I didn't have the time. I was verbally chastised for my irresponsibility.

A few weeks later I went along with the club members on a bus trip to Cleveland for a ball game—a trip where some men were drunk before we left and mooned and shouted at women in other vehicles. To these older, supposedly responsible young businessmen, I was a party pooper. I wanted nothing to do with that, so I quit. I wished them well, but my time was too precious for such inane forms of supposed relaxation. Again, I was learning through the process of elimination what I did not want to do for my service.

As I have said, better communication will reduce stress in us and others. To communicate well, our goal must be to be strong inside but flexible enough to reach out to the full range of personalities—whether these belong to people who are mind-centered, body-centered or centered within their emotions. We need balance and the ability to flow within our full range of thoughts and senses for ideal communications. Once we can understand this, we can start communicating with more patience and tolerance.

Using Nature: The School of the Outdoors

Being in nature is healing. Being outdoors helps to remind us of God as the creator, maintainer and destroyer of all. Within nature we can sense the infinity of both time and space. When I look at the sky I am instantly filled with its endlessness and reminded of the hugeness of our own inner Being. When I sit by a flowing river bubbling down over some rocks, within seconds I hear the eternity of time flowing in the never-ending running water. Plants and animals remind us of our own human ability to evolve and adapt to new places and environments. Being drawn to these higher thoughts heals us unconsciously. I am glad that research now exists that shows that being within nature or even near plants and flowing water can help to heal the body. Our immune systems are strengthened when we are exposed to nature. People are happier and get sick less often. Science confirms my own experiences.

There is an old Eastern parable that says that our relationship with others influences how we relate to nature. I'd like you to try to understand it without getting caught up in its old-fashioned ideas about gender roles. I'm sure it can be comfortably adapted to fit in with a more contemporary definition of relationships. It goes like this: How we relate to our mother determines how we relate to Mother Nature. If we love our mother, we will love Mother Earth. We will enjoy being outdoors. If we trust our earthly mother, we will trust ourselves to be alone in the woods. If we hate our mother, we will not like being in the outdoors. If we don't trust our mother, we will be afraid of the woods.

How we love our father determines how we love God. If we love our father, we will love God. If we trust our father and know he is always there for us, we will trust God to be there for us when we need Him as well. If we hate our earthly father, we will surely hate God. We may even become atheists. If we don't trust our father, or if he was cruel to us, then we don't trust God, and will expect God to be cruel to us as well. In short, how we love our mother determines how we love Mother Nature, and how we love our father determines how we love God. Think about this story and begin to apply it to people you know. You may have to question some of them. Try first the ones who have very deep positive or negative feelings about either God or Nature. Ask them about their relationships with their parents. I've done this, and in hundreds of cases there has almost always been a connection.

The obvious lesson to learn here is that, if we have some feeling of conditionality with our parents, we cannot live a whole life. We cannot hate one man, whether our earthly father or our ex-husband, and completely love our current husband. Likewise, we cannot hate one woman, whether our mother or our ex-wife, and completely love our current wife. The old patterns of hate and anger get in the way of our new attempts to love.

This is why, I believe, nearly every spiritual tradition in every culture in every time has taught us to honor our mother and father. It doesn't matter how our parents treated us; we need to love them fully and unconditionally. Honoring them is not simply for their good; it is for our own good. If our parents did things we are angry or resentful about, however bad, forgiving them is for our own good, not theirs. Through forgiveness, we are not letting them off the hook. They will still pay a price for their actions someday. But by practicing forgiveness, we ourselves might escape paying the same price—and by releasing old reactive patterns, we may escape repeating their behaviors with our children.

It sometimes helps us to move forward on this tough issue by rationalizing that our parents probably did the best they knew how. If they had known a better way to act as parents, they probably would have done that instead. But their behavior was learned from their parents and colored by their personal stress patterns. Do you want to hold on to the same patterns of conditional love and pass them on to your children?

11: An Ancient Technique of Stress Management

If we think of defeat, that's what we get. If we're undecided, then nothing at all will happen for us. We must just pick something great to do and do it. Never think of failure at all, for as we think now, that's what we get.—Maharishi Mahesh Yogi

THE FIRST WOMAN I started dating after getting out of the Army was Kathy. It was 1972 and she was nineteen and I was twenty-one. Having graduated early from high school, Kathy had already attended Case Western Reserve University in Cleveland for two years before burning out and returning to Canton for a break to decide what field to select as her major. Her IQ was intimidating, over 160. I concluded that she must have thought I was good-looking, because I certainly couldn't keep up with her in a conversation.

One day Kathy said to me, "You're no fun anymore. All you ever want to do is sleep." It was true. I usually recovered from my grueling week of working midnights in a factory while going to college all day by getting a full day of sleep on Saturdays. Sunday was for homework. All that was left was Saturday night.

"There's a lecture coming up about a technique of meditation that might help you get more rest," Kathy continued. "Would you be interested in going to it?"

"Absolutely," I responded. "I'll try anything that might help."

Kathy told me she had learned about this meditation technique in college. It was called the Transcendental Meditation Program or TM for short. I had never heard of it. Kathy told me TM was a spiritual development technique that was great for stress management and had been brought to the United States in 1959 by a teacher from the Himalayan region of India, Maharishi Mahesh Yogi. TM was not actually a practice of Hinduism, but was derived from the same ancient writings called the Vedas that formed some of the roots of Hinduism. Evidently, the technique was a more generic practice and much older than Hinduism. Therefore, anyone from any religion, culture or language could practice it. This was fine by me, since, after my experience at church, I didn't feel like I belonged to any one religion anyway. At that point I didn't care whether or not it was a religious practice, as long as it worked. So I went along to the free public lecture at the library.

The speaker's name was Brenda, and she had been trained by Maharishi. She was based out of Chicago and was traveling a circuit to teach classes across the Midwest. This was her second visit to Canton. She hoped to teach more students each trip, some of whom might eventually go and become trained as teachers. Then it was hoped each community would have its own trained teachers.

Brenda's message was simple. Everyone could learn TM because it was very easy. Five-year-olds could do it, she said, and so could one-hundred-year-olds. What was involved was sitting upright with the eyes closed. You didn't need any props; no one would even know what you were doing. It was just a thought process, so there was no chanting or noise. Brenda explained that after the two free introductory lectures we would be learning to meditate over a four-day period, two hours each day. Then we would need to start the practice of TM twice each day for twenty minutes, before breakfast and before dinner. "TM is very deep," Brenda said. "Each twenty-minute meditation is considered equivalent to two or three hours of sleep." Since I was exhausted and this sounded like exactly the high-tech rest I needed, I agreed to take the class.

I learned to practice TM the next weekend. It was easy. In my first meditation I went so deep that I felt I was floating in space. I completely lost track of time as well. "TM takes the mind to its inner Being," Brenda told us. To transcend, she says, means to "go beyond." We were being trained to "go beyond" thinking to the source of all thoughts—our inner Being.

Being is that level of perfect silence that exists beyond all thoughts and feelings. It is the nothingness that is the foundation of the universe, beyond and before all creation. Being is to human consciousness what the unified field is to creation. Brenda taught us that this field of Being can be directly experienced by the human nervous system, and TM offered a really easy way to get there fast on a regular basis.

Wait a minute, I thought to myself in the class. Maybe this Being was the very same cosmic Presence I had experienced several times before in Viet Nam and with my friend Kandy. There couldn't possibly be two different nothingnesses, two transcendences. Not having been successful at finding my way back to those peak experiences in the last year, it was a thrill to have accidentally discovered a simple method of contacting that inner space within me on a regular basis twice daily. Serendipity is alive and well, I thought. It was also great to learn for the first time some new and proper words to describe my spiritual experiences. Now it would be easier to talk about.

The Benefits of the TM Program for Stress Management

In her TM class, Brenda explained that it was only recently (in 1970) that it had begun to be researched scientifically. It was important for me to understand, however, that even without any scientific research, the benefits of TM would continue to be the same as they had been for thousands of years. It had already been tried and tested, and had withstood the test of time.

Ironically, Maharishi had come to North America at the height of the Cold War in the 1950s to explain that he had a program to offer for the creation of world peace. However, most of his audiences in the United States and the world had clearly cared more about the personal benefits of TM than spiritual growth, let alone the accomplishment of such an abstract goal as world peace. Maharishi discovered that people wanted to learn TM because it reduced their insomnia, but not because it might save the world from a nuclear holocaust. So Maharishi encouraged independent scientific studies to be made in research universities to prove the benefits of TM.

I learned that some of the benefits discovered to that date included a reduction of insomnia, more energy, improved memory, faster reaction time and a deeply relaxed body, as evidenced by a significantly slower heartbeat and breath rate during meditation. You could also increase your IQ and get higher grades in school.

After starting TM, I immediately felt better. However, I couldn't quite put a handle on the specific changes. The problem with such self-analysis is that your deeper self changes inside with your outer changes. So it is hard to take yourself back to how you were before you practiced TM to be able to see the contrasts and differences that have occurred. In spite of that, within weeks I could see a difference at school. I was more rested, yet energetic. I could concentrate longer when reading or listening. My memory had improved. Before, as I read my text, my mind would drift off completely in the middle of the page. Typically, my eyes would automatically continue to scan back and forth across the page until I got to the bottom, then they would stop. Then I would realize that while my eyes were moving, my mind had wandered on to a completely different thought and was daydreaming. I could read a page like that three or four times and still not be able to say what was on it. Studying was a chore.

After only a few weeks of TM, I only needed to read or hear something once and I knew it fully. My college grades went up seven quarters in a row. While that says a lot about TM, it says even more about where my grades were when I started TM! Skeptical friends have told me that I just grew up in college and so my study habits improved, but that's not true. I was a twenty-one-year-old in classes with eighteen-year-olds. And I *wanted* an education, while many of the students were there because they wanted the 2-S college deferment, which would allow them to avoid being drafted into the military. Again, as a war veteran, I already felt ten years older than my age, and was often more mature than some of the professors and graduate students who were teaching me.

At that time, the scientific literature showed that in surveys with tens of thousands of students, whatever grades one got as a freshman in college were usually consistent for the entire four years. Very few people suddenly improved or got worse. So when researchers on TM found that nearly 2,000 college student practitioners suddenly experienced dramatically improved grade point averages, it was highly statistically significant.

There was another benefit for which I was immediately grateful. My job on the forging shop hammer crew was dangerous; I couldn't afford a mistake. I was already well known for being able to lean against an industrial-sized fan during a break and fall asleep standing up before the next job started. Fellow crew members were used to coming over to wake me up to go back to work. Often, I found pranksters had tied my shoestrings together while I'd been napping. After taking TM, however, my fatigue vanished so completely that I began to carry a textbook to work to study during longer breaks.

Within three months of taking my TM class, I went on a weekend workshop, called a "residence course." It was held in a beautiful Jesuit retreat center near Canton that was called Loyola of the Lakes. In one weekend, the classes and extra meditations, some in groups, were as profound for me as a whole month of meditating had been. I felt so wonderful after that course that I immediately decided to become a teacher of TM. I wanted to share this knowledge with my friends. Besides, Canton needed a full-time teacher. Maybe, I thought, I could teach TM while finishing college and get out of the factory. If one weekend was such a pleasant experience, I wondered what it would be like to go on a six-month teacher-training course (TTC). I immediately took steps to sign up.

After two years of college, I finally quit my midnight factory job. The next week my brother bid to get on the same hammer crew, but he broke several ribs in an injury on the job within a few months, and quit. My uncle, having worked at the shop for decades, then took my old job. Within months, he tragically lost the bottom half of one leg from a die that slid out of a massive hammer. I was grateful to have gotten out when I did.

Signs of my apparent Post-Traumatic Stress Disorder (PTSD) diminished. PTSD was the newly discovered name for that age-old syndrome of stressful situations producing reactions that could appear later. I had been having the usual symptoms of PTSD: night sweats and nightmares; sudden, inexplicable fear in sleep; flashbacks both asleep and while awake; sensory dislocations caused by sudden loud noises (or specific sounds like the *whap whap whap* of helicopters) and a host of reactive patterns in activity. All of these vanished within months of taking TM.

I also avoided some of the other PTSD symptoms that eventually developed in many Viet Nam vets: an inability to hold a job; high levels of drug and alcohol abuse and jail time; abnormal psychological and emotional profiles and higher than normal sickness and suicide rates. I did eventually end up getting divorced, and was unable to make a serious commitment in other relationships for the next twenty years. Maybe I didn't leave Viet Nam wholly behind, but TM certainly helped.

The real test for me in 1972 came when I talked with someone about the war. Before taking TM, the slightest conversation or even a question about Viet Nam that I refused to answer was enough to bring back a whole rush of sensory overloads and ensure nightmares and sweats the next time I slept. Before I took TM, I felt like everyone I met was constantly pulling those strings I talked about in the last chapter that trigger reactive behaviors. After starting TM, however, that behavior dissolved. I stopped overreacting to *all* sensory input, not just questions about Viet Nam. Suddenly it all seemed behind me.

In fact, I changed so much in my first year of doing TM that it took me quite a while to re-learn who I really was. I had an identity crisis of major proportion. In the process, I had to let go of many of my friends who had self-destructive habits, like drinking and drugs, and began to hang out with new friends with more wholesome lifestyles. I found that I was more content than ever before in my life. Eventually, I settled down and began to appreciate the new me.

There has been a growing body of scientific research each year on the TM technique. Some of the benefits of TM found so far include:

Deep relaxation—The initial studies, published in *Science* (1970) and the *American Journal of Physiology* (1971), introduced the concept of a state of restful alertness during the TM technique. The unique physiological characteristics of this state included reductions in plasma cortisol, plasma lactate, skin conductance (a measure of relaxation) and breath rate. Studies also indicated reduced heart rates, oxygen consumption and base metabolism. TM was shown to induce a genuine state of profound rest, an exciting and unique discovery in Western scientific research.

Brain Integration—People practicing TM become more whole-brained. Most people spend most of their time living and working from just one side of their brain. Being whole-brained means that one begins to experience more activity in all the parts of one's brain. Researchers have found that in TM special brainwave patterns, called beta spindles, sweep across the brain, demonstrating coherence between the front and rear lobes and the left and right hemispheres. These coherent brain wave patterns have been associated with improved intelligence and problem solving, and appear to be cumulative. The longer we meditate, the more they occur. Other findings show increased blood flow and increased oxygen to the brain during meditation, which might account for improved long- and short-term memory studies. There are also dramatic increases in brainwave activity and blood flow in the frontal lobe, a finding associated with reduction of violent tendencies—a promising find for those wishing to rehabilitate violent prisoners.

Reduction of heart disease, cancer and neurological disease—Heart disease and cancer kill more Americans than everything else combined. In long-term studies by Blue Cross, a health insurance company, people who practiced Transcendental Meditation experienced decreased hospital admissions compared to controls in all major disease categories. These included 87 percent fewer admissions for heart disease than their average insurance client, 55 percent fewer for tumors, 87 percent fewer for neurological diseases, 63 percent fewer for injuries, and 30 percent fewer for infectious diseases. The overall average reflected 53 percent fewer inpatient hospital admissions for all age groups combined and 68 percent fewer inpatient admissions for adults 40 years and over. When TM was combined with TM-advanced programs including Ayurvedic herbal remedies and dietary recommendations, the totals reflected 92 percent lower health care costs. Meditators lived longer and were healthier.

Reduced use of alcohol and cigarettes—I've now taught hundreds of students. Thousands have come through the Canton TM Center I co-founded and chaired. Again and again, many of our meditators have reported reducing their use and abuse of both alcohol and cigarettes. It makes sense. Sometimes smokers pick up a cigarette and light it as a result of rising tension. It's a reflex habit to stressful stimuli, a reactive pattern. When meditators suddenly calm down, that pattern is released, and they find that they don't reach for a cigarette as often. Most don't notice the change happening but are surprised to find cigarettes left over at the end of their day. For those who smoke even two packs a day, TM could pay for itself in just over one year if it just causes you to cut your smoking in half. The same experiences apply to drinking. Not only do meditators drink less alcohol, but TM has been used as an adjunct therapy in national alcohol treatment facilities. It is not used to "dry out" alcoholics; rather, TM helps recovering alcoholics cope with the stresses and strains of the "real world" and reduces their chances of going back to the bottle. I have had many alcoholics tell me that TM literally has saved their life.

Reduced depression—I am told by physicians that one-third of America is on anti-depressants. TM has repeatedly demonstrated that it quickly reduces depression and, when individuals do have downturns, those downturns are not as deep and do not last as long. With TM, the roller-coaster effect of mood swings smoothes out over time.

Increased IQ and memory—TM studies show that IQ goes up in meditators. Surprisingly, it doesn't matter at what age one starts TM to get this benefit. Both long-term and short-term memory is increased. As you have read, this was my personal experience.

Increased resistance to disease—Studies have shown that if blood is drawn just before and after meditation, dramatic and measurable changes occur. One of these changes is a marked increase in white blood-cell counts. This is an indicator of increased immune system health. This makes sense, since stress weakens the immune system. Other blood work shows lower serum cholesterol levels after meditation. Both indicators are related to the reduction of stress.

Taking the Next Step

As I indicated earlier, when I began TM there was not much research on its benefits. However, within a few years, scores of well-documented and independent studies were published from many universities in many different countries. They revealed that TM was much more valuable than I had ever imagined. As of 2003, there are over 600 published studies on TM and it has been verified as the world's premier meditation technique from a scientific research basis. So TM is the Cadillac of meditation systems. To me, TM would be just as valuable without any research. What is more important than any of that research is that there is a long tradition, both written and oral, of Vedic knowledge that outlines not only how to meditate but also how one can grow to enlightenment from the experience, step by step. Unfortunately, there are no shortcuts. TM cannot be taught from a book or tape. A trained instructor is necessary.

Some months after becoming a TM meditator, I realized that somehow I had stumbled onto a path that led me back down the very road I had committed to find and take while in Viet Nam. As you will recall, I had made a promise to try to find a path that would lead me back to the experience of the presence of God, to habituate to that experience and then share it with others. I was certain by then that TM was already opening me up to a greater appreciation of my spiritual and religious values. As I began to understand TM, I concluded that contact with the Transcendent clearly represented contact at the least with the absolute, impersonal side of God, the omnipresent Nothingness. I knew it would be fun to watch to see whether my experience grew into a renewed personal experience of God as well, and how it affected others.

In the middle of my sophomore year of college, I dropped out of school and trekked to Europe to train as a teacher of TM. My family was dismayed. How could I drop out of college, they asked? I promised to return. To me TM was a job-training course with a personal spiritual bent.

On the TM course, 1,500 people from around the world attended the first three months in Belgium and France, were made teachers and then went home. I stayed a second three months with about 250 others in Vittel, France. The TM movement found it cheaper to board us in European resort cities than to have the courses in the United States. We were moved back and forth between winter resorts in the summer and summer resorts in the winter. Most of that Phase II group then became teachers and went home. However, I was still having fun. So I called home to have my car sold and stayed three more months with 18 others in a small advanced course in Arosa, Switzerland. We were privileged to be able to see Maharishi almost every day or night in those last months.

In the teacher-training courses, the prospective teachers focus on two aspects of knowledge: understanding and experiences. The actual coursework of knowledge was six and a half days a week, with Thursday mornings off. Every day from mid-morning to about 9 p.m., minus mealtimes, we attended lectures on topics ranging from lecture-training to understanding people's experiences to the philosophy of enlightenment. Of course, at some point, we began to learn the intricacies of how to actually teach the seven-step TM class. The course was fairly intensive.

In addition to the classes on understanding, we were given plenty of opportunities to deepen our own personal experiences of meditation. The typical day included two meditations mixed with Hatha yoga for hours in our rooms morning and evening, with another group meditation before lunch. Eventually longer periods of meditation were offered in a structured program, with short periods of silence.

My personal meditations deepened to the point of fascination. Each one was different, and I looked forward to every one of them. Indeed, rather than tiring of it all, I wanted more. Maharishi had lectured about the refinement of perception that could occur when we begin to evolve into a more refined nervous system on the path to enlightenment. He said that heaven was a state of mind, not just a location where someone could go after death. So why wait for it? He suggested that we could refine our perceptions to the point of enjoying celestial sight, hearing, taste, smell and touch while still living in our bodies. In such a state, one would be living the reality of "heaven on earth" while still alive. Experienced from such a higher state of consciousness, every perception is heightened and creates waves of joy.

Regarding my own refinement of perception, one particular experience comes to mind. After some months of the TTC, I was spending part of every day deeply aware of the sense of space within me that comes when we begin to have Transcendental Consciousness along with quiet activity. That is called *witnessing*, because our Higher (Universal) Self is witnessing our lower (Individual) Self go through its daily activities. It was a bit disorienting at first, but very pleasant.

I was sitting on my bed in my hotel room in Vittel in meditation one afternoon when I heard a bird begin to sing on my patio balcony. Suddenly I was swept up on waves of bliss from the bird's song. It was so incredibly beautiful. I knew I had never heard anything like it before in my life. It must be something special to Europe, I thought. I could hear tones and sub-tones in the melody that I had never experienced before. A few weeks earlier I had heard the sound of a cuckoo nearby after dinner, and had gone outside and seen it calling in the evening light. That was a first for me; before I had only heard mechanical ones on clocks. Knowing that this bird might be yet another new species for me to observe, I made an exception to the rigid course rule of not interrupting meditations for any reason and sneaked over to the patio door to see what kind of bird was making such a beautiful sound. It was a common crow. Such is the power of meditation.

Witnessing plus sensory input creates bliss. This is why gurus teach that enlightenment is a state of bliss-consciousness. Everything creates bliss in that state.

Near the middle of my TTC, after moving to Zinal, Switzerland, I finally accessed and dealt with most of the major stresses that had been bottled up inside me from my war experiences. Conveniently, Swiss Army teams on skis chose a week during my course to conduct maneuvers up-valley from us, and to detonate grenades and dynamite and shoot machine guns in the mountains. In addition to their training, they were systematically knocking down all of the potential avalanches before the start of the ski season. Most of the course members complained about the resulting noises, but I found them serendipitous and provocative. The whole experience reminded me of the time I dreamed about an accident and an ambulance drove by my house (for real) to fit its sound effects perfectly into my dream.

My meditations that week were filled with intense memories of every stressful event I went through in the army, with the Swiss Army providing sound effects. Sweeping moods of fear, anger, resentment, guilt, excitement, joy, hours of tears and even laughter consumed me that week. Every time I heard an explosion or gunfire I was thrown back into another experience. I am convinced that I was purged of vast amounts of emotional garbage that week. Meditation provided the process, and the army, as it has always done, provided the emotional trigger.

That week provided an interesting experience for me because it was clear that, in the vast majority of cases, the TM program did not cause one to think about the stress one was releasing. We could find ourselves thinking about what we might want to do today at the same time as we were releasing the stress we had picked up from falling off a bicycle at the age of ten. In this way, most meditators are saved from the psychological trauma of having to actually relive their stress while releasing it. The release of my war experiences was an exception to that rule.

After completing TTC, I stayed in Switzerland to work on the TM international staff. I was eventually sent to Livigno, Italy to assist with a teacher-training course in progress in an alpine ski resort town across the border from St. Moritz.

Start up of Canton TM Center

While in Italy, I met my wife-to-be, Karen, a registered nurse/TM teacher from Kansas. Months later, she returned with me to Canton to marry. We started a full-time TM Center in Canton and began to offer classes. Within five years, I finished college while teaching TM full time. This was the first of many community nonprofit organizations I would become involved in over the next thirty years.

We had three children, all girls and all born at home. Although a part-time nurse at a local hospital, Karen did not believe that birthing was a disease. She adamantly refused to give birth in a hospital. Hospitals were for emergencies and major illnesses, she believed, and I agreed. Both local hospitals also disliked natural births then, and often preempted the mothers during the labor to make them take medications or get a C-section. We found an old-fashioned doctor to come to the house, Ralph Vance. He helped Karen deliver Sara, our first, and then, three years later, with his help, I was able to deliver Stephanie, and later, Annie. The home deliveries remain on my short list of my most spiritual experiences. They were definitely magical moments, experiences often missed in the clinical hospital settings. The resulting publicity of our children's home births led to a number of home births in Canton. Today, area hospitals have new home-birthing rooms that offer a full range of natural birthing techniques.

I was able to chair the Canton TM Center from 1974 until 1992. At that time, when my "free tree" project was beginning to take off, Brad, one of my earlier TM students who had become a teacher, returned to Canton to take over local center activities. TM was the first of many organizations I became involved in that were engaged in improving the environment.

I see TM as the premier technique for environmental improvement. Most of us think of the environment as something outside of us. But that is only half the truth. The rest of our environment consists of all that is going on inside our body and soul. How can we call ourselves "environmentalists" while we allow ourselves to pollute our inner environment? TM promotes sustainable action. Practicing TM is an ideal environmental action, and there is a clear link for me between my wanting to teach TM and planting three million trees in my community.

The Canton TM Center has taught over 2,000 students over the last thirty years. Nearly a dozen different teachers have come to Canton to work after their teacher training before going off to start their own centers. There are many wonderful stories of individuals whose lives were dramatically changed as a result of taking the course—people who have been able to reduce or stop their alcohol, cigarette and drug abuse. What often surprised me was that people on tranquilizers ended up over-medicated after taking the TM course, and we encouraged these folks to return to their physician frequently to get their dosages reduced as they became more naturally tranquil. Often, they were weaned off their drugs completely.

One particularly dramatic case concerned a man named Ralph who lived in a small Appalachian town along the Ohio river. Ralph's family was well known, and he owned a historic Victorian hotel as the family business. However, he had a wife who was a mean alcoholic and who created an almost unbearably stressful situation every night. Over the years, Ralph had developed critically severe migraines. He never knew when they would come, and when they did, he would be bedridden for days or even weeks. The slightest movement caused him unbearable pain. Not surprisingly, his pharmacist had given him increasingly harder drugs over the years to fight the pain. Surprisingly, the pharmacist had himself been using some of the same medications from Ralph's prescriptions, and when I met both of them after my introductory lecture, they both confessed to being hopelessly addicted to the same powerful morphine-based drug. Could TM help, they asked?

Both took the course. Ralph's headaches went away and never returned. I stayed in touch with him. He said that one day it seemed that a migraine was about to start again, but it had dissolved in his afternoon meditation and never returned. His health had improved, he had kicked his drug habit and for the first time in years he seemed to believe that he had a future. He sold his hotel, put his wife in rehab, moved to Florida and took up sailing. I never heard from the pharmacist again, except that he wrote me a card with a message on it. "You saved my life," he said.

One woman who learned TM in the Canton Center found it easy to give up the use of drugs almost immediately. Her comment was straightforward: "Compared to the various drugs I have taken," she said, "TM is the best 'high' I have ever experienced. Besides, it's long-lasting and has no harmful side effects." In my experience of teaching I have found that most people who smoke pot find that after a few weeks of TM they are so "naturally high" that the same pot that used to "lift them up" actually "brings them down." It is no longer fun at that point. While even the thought of giving up pot was difficult to consider at first, by the time they did give it up it was no real loss in their life.

TM may be great in special situations, but it is even better for the average person who doesn't have a lot of major problems (heavy baggage) holding them back. Such an individual can move ahead in his or her personal evolution of consciousness faster without having to spend years getting rid of past garbage in the system. I like to say that TM is an all-natural, all-organic program; it contains no impurities and has no known negative side effects. It is clearly designed for the natural health advocate!

Having said all these good things about TM, I have to add that the TM Program does not have a corner on the Transcendence market. There have been great people of all cultures in all ages who have written about their personal contact with Transcendental consciousness, and most of them were not involved in the TM technique. TM may offer the slickest, most scientific and immediate results known to-date, but what is most important here is for everyone to choose a personal path for spiritual growth and stress management, and stick with it.

Maharishi's Five Contributions to the World

There are several major contributions that Maharishi has made to the world while teaching the TM program on every continent. The first was his offer of the knowledge of TM to the whole world. Before his departure from India to teach worldwide, that knowledge had been mainly confined to isolated areas of the Himalayas. Maharishi's second major contribution to the world was his teaching that TM can be for everyone and not just for recluses. (Formerly, only monastics had the opportunity to study and regularly practice the technique.) His third contribution was the unique idea of integrating TM into daily life in such a way that the benefits came promptly and helped the average person reach enlightenment. His solution was the systematic twice-daily practice now familiar to all TMers. Fourth, Maharishi has offered a comprehensive explanation of how the development of consciousness can occur as we grow from ignorance of our higher Self to enlightenment that is simple to understand and practical in its inspirational value. Finally, and the world doesn't know it yet, but Maharishi has been collecting the world's experts on other ancient Vedic technologies, and is currently engaged in creating locations in India where tens of thousands of Vedic scholars will sit together and perform practices that will raise human consciousness and help to create world peace. This one stroke, after the initial teaching of TM itself, may be his greatest legacy to the world. To me it represents the highest ideal of environmentalism.

Bringing TM out of the Mountains

I want to spend time with each of these contributions so you can understand their magnitude. Transcendental Meditation is an ancient technique, dating back thousands of years. No one can say exactly where it began or by whom it was first practiced, but it has been part of an oral tradition handed down generation after generation from master to student. This ancient Vedic tradition included most of the most revered teachers of Vedic knowledge in India—people like Vasishtha, Vyasa, Govinda and Shankara. However, the knowledge was kept in remote parts of the Himalayas.

The most recent modern-day custodian of the knowledge was Maharishi's teacher, Sri Brahmananda Saraswati, or Guru Dev. Before Maharishi brought the knowledge of TM around the world, one had to practically—and in the ancient days, literally—give up all of one's possessions and become a monk to learn to meditate. The general teaching was that to become enlightened one needed to completely remove oneself from the stress of the world by renouncing it.

In India, people are divided into two fields of community life: householders and recluses. Householders are men and women who hold worldly jobs and have families, while recluses are rarely married and, if they are, are mostly celibate. Sometimes married monks are permitted to procreate, then go back to being celibate. Since ancient times, this has not been considered improper, and was how the Brahman, or highest, caste was able to have offspring to teach to be Brahmans and continue the oral tradition. Guru Dev chose to be a celibate Brahman.

The most secret knowledge was given only to the monks and kept closely guarded. It was felt that the teachings needed to be kept in their pure form—hence the secret nature of the instruction process. Furthermore, one usually needed long practice of meditation to reach enlightenment. So if only monks had the time to put into their practice, then it was not necessary to teach the masses who needed to work and raise families and could therefore not reach enlightenment.

The only hope for householders to reach enlightenment was to raise their families, finish their careers and then go into an ashram or retreat center and, under the guidance of a teacher, meditate long hours to try to get to enlightenment before dying. The most householders could hope for was to select a guru who would teach them some of the easier and less demanding techniques and then try to visit their guru's ashram (retreat center) for several weeks each year to meditate. Meanwhile, most individual growth would be limited to that provided by the grace and blessings of their teacher. Only once they had raised their families and retired from work could they go off to the ashram full time and dedicate themselves to seeking enlightenment.

Maharishi changed that concept completely. A few years after Guru Dev passed on, Maharishi traveled to the south of India to visit a temple. What Maharishi observed was that people living in the world were unhappy and stressed and that they needed to be free from suffering. Under the inspiration of his late teacher, Maharishi began to teach anyone who wanted to learn to meditate. Soon he was being asked to travel from town to town across India to teach. That is how the world TM movement began. Initially, Maharishi was not popular among some of the custodians of the ancient tradition for taking the knowledge out of the remote valleys where it had been kept.

Maharishi taught that we each need to dip into the Transcendent by meditating each morning and afternoon and so developed the concept of having people meditate about twenty minutes each morning and evening. From there we can emerge feeling refreshed and awake. This way, we would get the rest and increased energy just when we needed it the most. Each meditation produces an effect that lasts for hours. If we meditate in the morning, whether or not we've had a good night's sleep, we start the day more alert and energized. Then, before supper, we meditate again to prepare ourselves for the next six or eight hours of evening activity. Meditate and act; then meditate and act.

In this way, I've calculated, twenty minutes twice a day adds up to the same amount of time spent meditating to reach enlightenment each year as the average seeker got in India by going away several weeks to an ashram. For comparison's sake, let's imagine that in your life you were able to go each year to a retreat center and meditate for eight hours a day for six weeks, with weekends off. Each year, these six weeks of 40 hours of meditating would result in 240 hours of meditation. Comparatively, by meditating with TM twice a day for twenty minutes for one year we also meditate over 240 hours. So TM's structured program of twice-daily meditation offers both men and women the opportunity to get the same benefit of long retreats in a much more accessible structure. The time adds up and is a very powerful tool. Its effect is also cumulative.

Integration through Balancing Meditation and Action
Another positive aspect of twice-daily meditation sessions is that we get the meditation when we need it. Rather than meditating all at once each year while on retreats, Maharishi reasoned, why not accomplish the same thing a little bit each day? This simple change to the practice fit the more rapid and demanding lifestyle of the world's householders, especially in the West. It also enabled householders to make it through the day each day and be nicer—more tolerant, patient and kind—to each other. At the end of each day, we could dip in again to refresh ourselves and be better prepared to enjoy our families.

Maharishi explained further that we needed to train the nervous system to habituate to the experience of Transcendence. By dipping into deep meditation twice each day, then coming out and allowing that experience to fade away in activity, we were helping to stabilize the ability to maintain pure consciousness in all of our activity. One of Maharishi's best-known analogies used in teaching TM is the example of dyeing a cloth a new color. If you had a white cloth that you wanted to dye orange, then the process would be to dip the cloth into a vat of orange dye, then remove it and let it dry. The orange color would fade in the sun as the cloth dried. But a little bit of the color would become stuck in the cloth. By repeatedly dipping the cloth into the dye and then drying it in the sun, each day more color would be made steadfast until the full value of the orange color was reached. Likewise, as meditators, by dipping our human nervous system into the full value of the Transcendent each day, then allowing those attributes to wear off over several hours of activity, something is made steadfast. That something is consciousness. In each meditation we release stress, become more flexible and are better able to maintain the Transcendental Consciousness for longer periods of time through the day. One day, when we dip into meditation and come out, we will bring the full sunshine of the Transcendence with us, and it will not go away. It will have become steadfast. This is the definition of enlightenment.

With this understanding, all action, whether we are engaged in rigorous work all day or reading a book, becomes a path to enlightenment. The important thing, according to Maharishi, is to meditate first, then go out and do something. The ideal is to perform action that is wholesome, life supporting and good for ourselves and the world. It doesn't matter whether we are a dishwasher or a congressperson or a nun: We all have an equal chance to grow to enlightenment by carefully giving our nervous system the experience of Transcendence alternated with daily activity. That's how Transcendence is stabilized.

Understanding of States of Consciousness

Another of Maharishi's contributions to the world has been his teaching of the philosophy behind the TM program. His detailed explanation of the concept that there are different states of human consciousness has helped millions understand their personal spiritual experiences.

One of the most ancient and perplexing metaphysical issues debated for millennia has concerned misunderstanding about whether enlightenment is to be experienced as a state of duality or unity. Maharishi has taught that the first state of enlightenment, Cosmic Consciousness, is a state of duality. In that state, one experiences the Transcendence within us, our inner Self, as unbounded awareness, but the outer world is still a very separate, gross physical state. However, as one lives in this initial state of enlightenment, it evolves. Eventually we become able to perceive on finer levels until we can actually sense the Transcendence in everyone and everything else. At that time, Unity Consciousness dawns. We can see everything in terms of our deepest inner Self. In that state life is lived in Oneness. Maharishi's simplified explanation is that "Knowledge is structured in Consciousness," and that "Knowledge is different in different states of consciousness." For

metaphysicians, this is a brilliant understanding that has been offered
to the world's knowledge of the evolution of humankind.

Vedic Scholars for World Peace
In addition to the individual benefits of TM, research has been gathered that shows conclusively that when the TM technique is practiced
in large groups along with one of the TM advanced programs, communities experience a reduction of crime, accidents and overall sickness, and positive events increase. This discovery in the 1970s has led
Maharishi to send groups of thousands of highly trained technicians
to hold group meditation courses in various troubled areas of the
world over the last two decades.

The advanced program is called the TM Siddhi Program. The *sid-
dhis* are specific ancient practices that produce dramatic effects on
both individuals and the environment when practiced from the level
of the Transcendent. Someday, the world will catch up to the fact that
every major war and even the fall of the Berlin Wall and the breakup
of the Soviet Union have been profoundly affected by the tactical
application of these technologies around the world. Additionally,
Maharishi has refined other ancient techniques called *yagyas* that can
be practiced in large groups. These programs have the ability to affect
world consciousness when practiced by thousands of meditators with
the ability to operate from the Transcendent.

For many years, Maharishi has pleaded with leaders of governments around the world to help fund the creation of a meditator community that could, for the first time in history, put together tens of
thousands of experts who could help to create world peace and raise
world consciousness through their collective practice of these ancient
technologies. While some have admired Maharishi for the scientific
basis of his proposal, the idea has not been adapted because no one
wants to be known as the person who diverted military dollars to the
creation of a meditation program to create peace. On April 12, 1999,
in a full-page advertisement run in the *Wall Street Journal*,
International Herald Tribune, and the London *Financial Times*,
Maharishi wrote to the world's governmental leaders, "Can you imag-

ine if bombs began to fall in Washington, D.C., and destroy the high-rises of the money markets of New York? Will NATO be able to prevent this? When this happens it will be beyond the power even of the wealthy to save the situation." With the attack by terrorists on September 11, 2001, and the subsequent declaration of war on terrorism, we have entered a new era of stress in the world's collective consciousness. Viewpoints are becoming polarized and hardened. The result is the creation of an environment conducive to world war and major mistakes and overreactions by world leaders.

Always focused on world peace, in 2002, Maharishi took his appeal instead to the wealthy meditators of the world. Quietly, the $100 million needed was raised by a few scores of individual donors to build just such a community and fill it with 40,000 Vedic scholars, technically called *pundits*, who would be responsible for raising world consciousness. In the known history of humankind, never have these technologies been practiced simultaneously by so many. But, then, never in recorded history have we had so many living on the planet at one time. What an unprecedented outpouring of generosity to offer to humankind!

Publicity for this historic event may come through the back door. A junior U.S. Congressman, Dennis Kucinich of Cleveland, Ohio, has proposed that the U.S. create a new cabinet position for a Minister of Peace to lead a new federal government Department of Peace. This new department would explore scientifically proven technologies to create peace instead of war. Congressman Kucinich has chosen to run for President of the United States in 2004, bringing his ideas about peace into the light of national media attention and public debate. Maharishi's program could be one of the proposals that could obtain media scrutiny and exposure under his banner.

In any case, in the next couple of years we will see the possibility of rising world consciousness as a result of the commencement of this massive program. This project represents one of the most ambitious and altruistic environmental actions ever attempted. The funding and launching of this new Vedic pundit project represents Maharishi's greatest hour in his selfless offering of nearly fifty years of service to humankind.

12: The Future of Proactivism

ACTIVISM HAS A great future. When they were younger, my daughters lamented that all the best ideas had already been thought of, that all the best inventions had already been invented and all the best activist causes had already been protested and acted on. There was nothing left for them to be involved with.

Clearly, they were wrong. As colorful and full of activism as the 1960s were, they addressed only the tip of the iceberg of new issues. My most thoughtful guess is that some of the most dramatic changes that will occur in our world's cultures, religions, political and economic systems haven't even been thought of yet. We have a long way to go to arrive at a world with an ideal society in every nation. In fact, what we now need are millions of new activists, young and old, to meet the world's changing needs.

We don't even have to dream up future projects to keep everyone busy: We already have enough problems right now that need a dramatic increase in the number of activists operating on the local, state, national and international levels. If you look, for example, at our unchecked population growth and the resultant world hunger, homelessness, massive

deforestation and wildfires, air, water and soil pollution and a loom-
ing energy crisis, you'll see that there are a plethora of areas where
you could make a difference right now. Since you know these problems exist, there must, by definition, be room for and a need for more
activists. Indeed, during the next decade, a large segment of our population will enter their senior years. The post-World War II "baby
boomers" are beginning to retire and will initiate a massive increase
in the need for elder care both in and out of health care facilities. We
will need activists more than ever. Fortunately, many of them will be
strong enough to jump in to help.

As I said in my introduction, America is not a finished product.
We are still reinventing America every day, and we have an opportunity to grow our country into whatever we want it to be. We need to
do this because it is clear that if people of greater consciousness do
not take charge of what path we are to go down, then people of less-
er consciousness, motivated entirely by individual or corporate greed,
will certainly lead us in a direction that instead serves their needs.

In proactivism, consciousness equals responsibility. As I have said,
it will not be our governments or even our elected legislators who will
take responsibility for solving our social problems; it will be private
citizen activists who will conceive and implement these changes.
Government works reactively, not proactively; it responds to wheels
that squeak. Whether you are a ten-year-old who writes to complain
to a government agency or a ninety-year-old like Grannie D., who
walked across the United States to protest environmental and social
injustice, you can be that squeaky wheel. The responsibility ultimately lies with those who are awake enough to be aware of the problems.
And if you understand the problems, then you are qualified to help
implement the changes necessary to arrive at a new solution.

The best summation I've found of the coming climax of the collision between population growth and natural resources on the planet
is in the book *The Last Hours of Ancient Sunlight* by Thom Hartmann.
In his book, he makes a compelling argument for why we need to
change our thinking and the way we live. His entire book explains the
need for activists in the coming decades.

Hartmann points out that never in recorded history have so many people lived on this planet together. For the first two hundred thousand years of modern humanity, there were about five million people on this planet. Ninety percent of all population growth has occurred in the last one-tenth of one percent of all of human history. This growth started with the discovery and widespread use of domestication of livestock and the Agricultural Revolution, which showed us how to farm with greater productivity. The resulting increase in food supply has led to a larger population.

Hartmann says we are going to run out of coal and oil by mid-century. The problem is that six billion inhabitants live today in a world that can at best sustain a population of only 250 million to one billion without coal or oil. I've often wondered whether we have reached the crossover point of sustainability, and I had already learned from Werner Fornos of the World Population Institute that we had done so in large metropolitan areas. Now Thom Hartmann says we have done this globally. And at the current rate of growth, according to current estimates by the United Nations, by the year 2050 we will have over nine billion humans on this planet. All of us in the West who have lived on this planet over the last 200 years have done so by borrowing from our stored reserves of energy in the form of coal and oil reserves. The resulting increased productivity and efficiency yielded from oil and gas usage has allowed us the luxury of growing more humans and living the fat and gluttonous lives we currently lead in America. This era will not—indeed, *cannot*—last.

Hartmann argues that these ancient reserves, our savings account of stored energy on the planet, will be almost completely depleted in the next thirty years. At that time, we as a planetary population will have to choose. We will have the ability either to grow food to feed everyone, leaving billions in cold climates freezing to death in the winters, or to use the land to grow wood for heat to stay warm, leaving billions to face starvation. What will it be, food or heat? Something will have to give, or we will have massive numbers of humans dying. Most of us will live to see this day come. If we do not, our children certainly will.

Hartmann also indicates to us that short of the discovery of new sustainable technologies, the inevitable collision between our accelerating population growth and limited resources on the planet will not only occur but will likely result in an Earth-shaking sociological implosion. This will come directly as a result of the exhaustion of the oil and coal reserves that have allowed the population growth to occur in the first place. It will take major changes in every aspect of human life to facilitate our coexistence in a sustainable manner. The failure for us to move as a species in unison in the direction of sustainability can only result in massive famine, social, political and economic upheaval, devastating wars and catastrophic levels of loss of human life.

We cannot be content to save humanity without also saving the planet. We need a healthy planet because there is currently no place else for us to go. Nor can we be content to save the planet without saving the humans. I still believe that we as humans are capable of being better than collapsing into another global confrontation over dwindling resources. We still have a chance to change. We have a few short decades to figure out our problems and turn them around. To do this we will need a new calm and coherence in world human consciousness and an army of activists to implement changes necessary for the survival of humanity. This is why I am calling for millions of proactivists, dedicated to the survival of both our species and the planet. We humans and our planet will need to arrive at our new destination together.

The Metaphysics of Activism
The proactivism I am calling for is based on love. Activism based on love instead of fear is sustainable. Fear only exists when we allow ourselves to live life in a future tense. Any new understanding must start with the concept that the "future" is now. When we bring ourselves to live our lives in this moment, we find that both past and future do not exist. Or, better said, they only exist in this moment. Only from this perspective can we begin to grasp the concept that

there is no future "evil" to fear. Each new moment is simply the now. That's our basis for all action.

I want the theme for this millennium to be "There is no fear." Fear comes from our lower Self, from ego. Fear is an affirmation that there is no God. When living in a conscious awareness of the presence of God within and around us, there is no fear. If we truly believe there is a God, there can be no place or time where God, and therefore Divine Order, is not present. And everything is truly in Divine Order, even if we are not able to comprehend that idea while in the midst of seeming chaos. Fearing the future is a sign of a lack of faith in God. Fear of the future is blasphemous.

Our philosophy of action needs to be based on the dual concepts of sustainability and giving. By sustainability I mean that we need to simplify our lifestyles not to live beyond our annual renewable income of food, water and energy. We need to share what abundance we have, knowing that more will come. Hoarding by any individuals or nations will disrupt the ability to supply the world with all the necessary resources for a peaceful coexistence.

Proactivism, as I have said, is good spiritual work. If we work from love and not hate, our efforts will be evolutionary for both ourselves and the people whose actions we may oppose.

Time—Our Most Precious Natural Resource

There is one resource that is not renewable, and that is time. While in the cosmic sense eternity may be timeless, full of an infinity of hours, individually we are working against a biological clock to accomplish as many wholesome tasks as possible in our limited lifetime. There is no time to waste in procrastination. When we face our mortality, it often wakes us up to the limited time we have remaining. Sometimes it takes the death of a loved one to shock us out of our stupor. Or we may personally have a tumor that turns out to be benign, experience sudden chest pains, have a serious car accident or undergo a surgery that causes us to realize that we have come close to death. Or we may be sent to war. Every moment of life becomes more precious to those facing death.

For over thirty years, I have remembered each day to be grateful for having survived my time in Viet Nam. Frankly, I am *still* surprised to be alive. I have during this time tried to be the best activist I can be.

Nature continues to remind me that life is precious. In the last two years, my house has been broken into three times. Three times someone has gone into my basement while I was away and disconnected the flue on my gas hot water tank, with the idea of filling my house with odorless and deadly carbon monoxide. One time they even loosened the nut on my gas line to the water heater, hoping to blow me up. Fortunately, my old basement is literally too drafty to allow fumes to build up, and I have escaped harm. Another time in the last three years I was chased across town by a van full of men who were casing my house. Such direct attacks, along with telephone threats over the last thirty years and numerous acts of vandalism, tend to get your attention.

In February 2002, the very week I started writing this book, I was struck by lightning. The previous year I had moved into the City of Canton, but I kept my office in my old residence in Plain Township. On the phone while sitting on the couch with a friend, the 120-foot oak tree a few feet outside my living room window was struck by lightning in a freakish winter storm, for the second time in two years. The energy from the strike jumped into the house and blew out my TV, jumped across two surge protectors, fried the ethernet card in my computer and burned out three phones and some wiring, while zapping me with a shock to the ear. I was surprised, but not injured. All of these incidents simply make me more resolved to accomplish as much as I can in the time I have remaining. The lightning told me, quite literally, it was time to work faster. We never know when it may be time to leave.

The Politics of Activism

Politics is a bad word in the United States today, and to be a politician is often considered the lowest of professions. If you're one of those who hates politics and politicians, I have the same bad news for you now as I had at the beginning of the book regarding activism. You

Figure 12:1 Campaign button

already *are* a politician. If you are reading this book, you are already being political. In fact, everything you do is political. If you have opinions or talk to anyone, you are political. When you talk with your spouse, you are being political. When you negotiate with your teacher or boss, you are being political. If you have opinions and try to follow them to help make a difference in any circumstance, you are being political. Therefore, you are a politician. My advice to you is: Get over it! Activism equals politics. Let's get used to the words. Your first choice as an activist is whether you will work through the existing system or completely ignore it or try to tear it down. If you are still disturbed by the words "politics" and "politicians" then there is only one way to bring the words out of the gutter and make them respectable and dignified again: Get involved in politics and make it better.

After 30 years in the nonprofit sector, in October 2001 I decided to get off my environmental high horse and go out into my community and seek the opportunity to hold a responsible political office. I moved into Canton and gathered enough signatures to be placed on the ballot in the November 2002 election as an Independent candidate for a seat in the Ohio House of Representatives. The theme of my election campaign was "Bringing the Light of Consciousness to Politics." I was an Independent running against both a Republican first-timer and a Democratic incumbent, and I promoted the idea that I was "A Candidate for All the Voters." During the campaign, I found there was a huge upsurge of interest in supporting Independents. People were very tired of the same old two-party politics. I created a

Figure 12:2 The "Tree Man"

campaign committee, recruited volunteers, raised money, printed materials and organized my campaign for the next few months.

I came in third (out of three), with a very respectable 18 percent of the vote in a heavily partisan district. I didn't win, but I made my mark and met a lot of remarkable people along the way, who influenced and were influenced by my thinking. My effort to be political is not over. If I believe all that I have written (and I do), then I have no choice but to move ahead to obtain a position of responsibility where I can begin to shape those policies that will affect our future and the futures of our upcoming generations. It is time to bring new ideas to government.

If you think the planet matters, if you are tired of the same old standoffs in politics, and if you believe, as I do, that individuals and communities can work together to bring about change, then get involved in your community and even run for office. I hope I have shown in this book that it can be done—that if you organize yourself, have the right motivations, plan ahead, think big and work thoroughly and meticulously you can do anything you set your mind to. Our planet desperately needs people who see their lives bound up with the other human and living beings to step forward and challenge all of us to make a difference, whether it is by planting trees or becoming vegetarian, or stopping violence wherever and to whomever it occurs. It means recognizing that a higher consciousness is calling to us to achieve the very best we can achieve and reach higher than we can imagine. It means acting from love and not from fear; it means being in the moment and not dwelling in the past or worrying about the future. It means looking out at the vast infinity of the stars and making an agreement that your life will be dedicated to the realization of the Divine Will for the planet. Our world is so beautiful, so rich and diverse and expressive of vitality and abundance; why do we want to destroy it and the other beings who share it with us? Why would we want to do something to our home, which so clearly wants us to flourish and in which, by polluting and defiling, we are killing ourselves?

Even though *Growing America* has come to an end, growing America has not. Indeed, we haven't really begun. There are so many crises for us to turn into opportunities, and so many problems that can be turned into solutions, that we can't afford not to be optimistic and excited about what lies ahead for humanity, even as our situation becomes more and more dire. I have provided some ideas of what can be done and suggestions on how to carry them out. In the appendices are some organizations you may wish to join or help. But the answer lies with *you*. *You* may be the person to do the project that you've only dreamed about; as I have said, if you've dreamed of it, then it's your responsibility to make it happen. And there is no age barrier to such activism. I was twenty when I made my life commitment, and over thirty years later that commitment still stands. God has kept me alive—as He keeps you alive—for a purpose. Discover that purpose, and act.

Appendix 1
A Practical Call to Action—Earth Share

Please contact either the Earth Share National office, one of its national member organizations or one of its state affiliates listed below to invite them to conduct a workplace giving campaign in your place of employment.

National Office

Earth Share
7735 Old Georgetown Road
Suite 900
Bethesda, MD 20814
800-875-3863
240-333-0300
www.earthshare.org

Earth Share National Member Charities

African Wildlife Foundation

1400 16th Street NW, Suite 120
Washington, D.C. 20036
888-4-WILDLIFE
www.awf.org
Foremost authority on African wildlife, dedicated to protecting elephants, mountain gorillas and other endangered species through innovative, practical programs developed with the people of Africa.

American Farmland Trust

1200 18th Street NW, Suite 800
Washington, D.C. 20036
202-331-7300
www.farmland.org
Works to stop the loss of America's farmland to sprawling development by working with communities on smarter growth that includes local family farms. Advocates environmentally healthy farming practices.

American Forests

910 17th Street NW, Suite 600
Washington, D.C. 20006
800-368-5748
www.americanforests.org
Funds private and public land reforestation projects; provides satellite imagery of tree loss to cities; educates the public on the value of tree and forests.

American Rivers

1025 Vermont Avenue NW
Suite 720
Washington, D.C. 20005

877-4-RIVERS
www.americanrivers.org
Works to protect and restore America's rivers through public education and by ensuring safe drinking water and recreational opportunities, and preserving fish and wildlife habitat.

Beyond Pesticides
701 E Street southeastern, Suite 200
Washington, D.C. 20003
202-543-5450
www.beyondpesticides.org
Prevents pesticide poisoning of our environment, homes, workplaces, schools, food and water through a practical information clearinghouse on toxic hazards and non-chemical pest control.

Center for Health, Environment & Justice
P.O. Box 6806
Falls Church, VA 22046
703-237-2249
www.chej.org
Empowers families protecting their children, and communities protecting public health, from toxic chemicals in drinking water, air, food. Assists with information, community organizing and coalition-building.

Clean Water Fund
4455 Connecticut Avenue NW
Suite A300-16
Washington, D.C. 20008-2328
202-895-0432
www.cleanwaterfund.org
We all live downstream. Neighborhood-based action and education for clean, safe water. Sensible solutions for people and environment: safe drinking water, pollution prevention, resource conservation.

The Conservation Fund
1800 North Kent Street, Suite 1120
Arlington, VA 22209
703-525-6300
www.conservationfund.org
Preserving America's outdoor heritage: over 3.2 million acres protected since 1985! 1000 acres preserved daily. Efficient! 95 percent of funds go directly to mission.

Conservation International
1919 M Street NW, Suite 600
Washington, D.C. 20036
800-406-2306
www.conservation.org
Works to conserve Earth's living heritage, our global biodiversity, and to demonstrate that human societies are able to live harmoniously with nature.

Defenders of Wildlife
1101 14th Street NW, Suite 1400
Washington, D.C. 20005
202-682-9400
www.defenders.org
Working since 1947 to save America's precious wild animals and threatened habitat for our children and future generations through education, citizen action and scientific research.

Earth Day Network
1616 P Street NW, Suite 200
Washington, D.C. 20036
202-518-0044
www.earthday.net
Promotes peace, justice and a sustainable future through education and events. EDN supports community efforts to improve public health and the environment around the world.

Earthjustice (formerly Sierra Club Legal Defense Fund)
426 17th Street, 6th Floor
Oakland, CA 94612
510-550-6700
www.earthjustice.org
Protects people, wildlife and natural resources by providing free legal representation to citizen groups to enforce our environmental laws.

Environmental and Energy Study Institute
122 C Street NW, Suite 630
Washington, D.C. 20001
202-628-1400
www.eesi.org
Develops and promotes innovative policies on climate change, clean air, transportation, renewable energy/energy efficiency technologies, and sprawl. Promotes policymaker action through education, advocacy and coalition building.

Environmental Alliance for Senior Involvement
9292 Old Dumfries Rd, P.O. Box 250
Catlett, VA 20119-1934
540-788-3274
www.easi.org
EASI coordinates and connects teams of active senior Americans who lead multi-generational, community-based environmental efforts toward a healthy environmental legacy for future generations.

Environmental Defense
257 Park Avenue South
New York, NY 10010
800-684-3322
www.edf.org
Creates lasting and fair solutions to com-
plex environmental challenges. Our areas of concentration are preserving biodiversity, stabilizing climate, protecting health and safeguarding oceans.

Environmental Law Institute
1616 P Street NW, Suite 200
Washington, D.C. 20036
202-939-3800
www.eli.org
Environmental law that works for you: community-based education + research on national problems = solutions to protect people and nature. Independent and non-partisan.

Friends of the Earth
1025 Vermont Avenue NW, Suite 300
Washington, D.C. 20005
202-783-7400
www.foe.org
Focuses on the root causes of environmental degradation by exposing wasteful federal spending and tax subsidies for corporate polluters, and empowers citizens to take action.

INFORM, Inc.
120 Wall Street, 16th Floor
New York, NY 10005-4001
212-361-2400
www.informinc.org
Promotes innovative business practices today that will leave a resource-rich and healthy world for our children tomorrow.

Izaak Walton League of America
707 Conservation Lane
Gaithersburg, MD 20878
800-IKE-LINE
www.iwla.org
Hunters, anglers and others preserving outdoor America's future—wildlife,

habitat, clean air and water. Initiatives include watershed protection, energy efficiency, sustainable communities. 325+ volunteer chapters.

Land Trust Alliance
1331 H Street NW, Suite 400
Washington, D.C. 20005
202-638-4725
www.lt.org
Helping people protect forest, farms, waterways and natural, historic and undeveloped places in their own communities. Leads, educates and assists 1,200+ grassroots conservation organizations nationwide.

National Audubon Society
700 Broadway
New York, NY 10003
212-979-3000
www.audubon.org
Works to protect birds, wildlife and their habitats, including our oceans. Educational outreach programs instruct and inspire future conservationists. Audubon Centers offer outdoor experiences.

National Parks Conservation Association
1300 19th Street NW, Suite 300
Washington, D.C. 20036
800-NAT-PARK
www.npca.org
Preserves national parks from Grand Canyon to Gettysburg; protects endangered wildlife and cultural sites; promotes new parks; defends parks against pollution, inappropriate development and overcrowding.

National Wildlife Federation
11100 Wildlife Center Dr.
Reston, VA 20190-5362
800-332-4949, ext. 4016
703-438-6000
www.nwf.org
Protects species including wolves, Florida panthers, grizzly bears and bald eagles; protects and restores habitat for people and wildlife; educates youth through classroom/outdoor education.

Natural Resources Defense Council
40 West 20th Street
New York, NY 10011
212-727-2700
www.nrdc.org
NRDC saved Baja's whales, Canada's Spirit Bears, California's sequoias. Defends embattled wildlife, wilderness, coasts, rivers and clean air across America and around the globe.

The Nature Conservancy
4245 North Fairfax Drive
Suite 100
Arlington, VA 22203-1606
703-841-5300
http://nature.org
Buys and protects land to save our world's rare plants and animals from extinction. Results: 10 million acres protected—rain forests, prairies, wetlands, mountains, beaches.

The Peregrine Fund
566 West Flying Hawk Lane
Boise, ID 83709
208-362-3716
www.peregrinefund.org
Saves eagles, condors, falcons and other endangered birds through research, breeding and conservation programs.

Helps preserve rain forests. Educates children and adults about nature and science.

Pesticide Action Network
49 Powell Street, Suite 500
San Francisco, CA 94102
415-981-1771
http://panna.igc.org
Works to eliminate poisonous pesticides. Links consumer, labor, health, environmental and agriculture groups internationally to advance safer, ecologically sound pest control alternatives.

Rails-to-Trails Conservancy
1100 17th Street NW, 10th Floor
Washington, D.C. 20036
202-331-9696
www.railtrails.org
Converts thousands of miles of unused railroad corridors into public trails for walking, bicycling, hiking, skating, horseback riding, cross-country skiing, wildlife habitats and nature appreciation.

Rainforest Alliance
665 Broadway, Suite 500
New York, NY 10012-2331
888-MY-EARTH
www.rainforest-alliance.org
Conserves endangered forest ecosystems and the wildlife and people that live within them by transforming land use, business practices and consumer behavior.

Rocky Mountain Institute
1739 Snowmass Creek Road
Snowmass, CO 81654-9199
970-927-3851
www.rmi.org
Delivers practical information that helps citizens, businesses, governments save energy and natural resources, prevent pollution, strengthen communities. Doing more with less, its solutions invigorate economies.

Safe Energy Communication Council
1717 Massachusetts Avenue NW
Suite 106
Washington, D.C. 20036
202-483-8491
www.safeenergy.org
Promotes environmentally safe, affordable energy. Fights for energy efficiency and renewable energy like solar and windpower. Educates communities about nuclear power and waste dangers.

Scenic America
801 Pennsylvania Avenue SE
Suite 300
Washington, D.C. 20003
202-543-6200
www.scenic.org
Protects natural beauty, fights billboard blight, saves America's special places. Our education and advocacy preserve thousands of miles of roads and hundreds of communities.

The Sierra Club Foundation
85 Second Street, Suite 750
San Francisco, CA 94105-3456
800-216-2110
www.sierraclub.org/foundation
Fights to preserve wilderness and protect environmental quality worldwide through a powerful combination of education, scientific research, publishing and litigation.

Student Conservation Association
689 River Road, P.O. Box 550
Charlestown, NH 03603
603-543-1700
www.thesca.org
Over 1,200,000 hours of environmental service yearly, with high school and college volunteers working in parks, forests, refuges nationwide. Building trails, saving wildlife, helping visitors.

Surfrider Foundation
P.O. Box 6010
San Clemente, CA 92674-6010
800-743-SURF
www.surfrider.org
Protects and preserves the world's oceans, waves and beaches through conservation, activism, research and education. Activities include water quality monitoring, environmental education and grassroots activism.

Trust for Public Land
116 New Montgomery Street
4th Floor
San Francisco, CA 94105
800-714-LAND
www.tpl.org
Conserves land for people to improve the quality of life in our communities and to protect our natural and historic resources for future generations.

Union of Concerned Scientists
2 Brattle Square, P.O. Box 9105
Cambridge, MA 02238-9105
800-666-8276
www.ucsusa.org
Scientists and citizens working together to reduce air pollution, prevent global warming, protect endangered species, reduce nuclear arsenals and ensure safety of our food system.

U.S. PIRG Education Fund
218 D Street southeastern
Washington, D.C. 20003
202-546-9707
http://uspirg.org/uspirgeducation-fund.htm
PIRG protects public health and the environment. We organize citizens against threats to clean air and water, to prevent global warming and preserve natural resources.

The Wilderness Society
1615 M Street NW
Washington, D.C. 20036
800-THE-WILD
www.wilderness.org
Works to protect the nation's wilderness and wildlife so that people can enjoy clean air and water and the beauty of America's natural heritage.

Wildlife Conservation Society
2300 Southern Blvd.
Bronx, NY 10460-1099
718-220-6891
www.wcs.org
Saves endangered species and threatened ecosystems in 50 countries; teaches ecology and inspires care for wildlife through the Bronx Zoo and national science education programs.

World Wildlife Fund
1250 24th Street NW
Washington, D.C. 20037
202-293-4800
www.worldwildlife.org
Protects endangered wildlife and their threatened habitats by providing emergency assistance and long-term support to parks and nature reserves, and through anti-poaching activities on five continents.

Earth Share State Affiliates

Please visit Earth Share's affiliates' Web sites to view lists of their member groups and to learn more about what they do!

Earth Share of California
49 Powell Street, Suite 510
San Francisco, CA 94102
800-368-1819
esca@earthshareca.org
www.earthshareca.org

Earth Share of Florida
535 Central Ave., Suite 410
St. Petersburg, FL 33701-3703
877-539-4794
info@earthshare.org
www.earthshareofflorida.org

Earth Share of Georgia
1447 Peachtree St, Suite 214
Atlanta, GA 30309
404-873-3173
elicia@earthsharega.org
www.earthsharega.org

Earth Share of Illinois
220 South State Street, Suite 432
Chicago, IL 60604-2002
312-922-9040
steve@earthshare-illinois.org
www.earthshare-illinois.org

Earth Share of Indiana
P.O. Box 1523
Indianapolis, IN 46206
317-971-2416
trails@indianatrails.org
www.earthshareindiana.org

Earth Share of Michigan
P.O. Box 363
6380 Drumheller Road
Bath, MI 48808-0363
517-641-7200
lorraine@earthsharemichigan.org
www.earthsharemichigan.org

Earth Share of Missouri
1915 Alfred Avenue
St. Louis, MO 63110
314-771-6668
info@earthsharemo.org
www.earthsharemo.org

Earth Share of New England
325 Huntington Avenue, Box 27
Boston, MA 02115
877-207-5756
info@earthshare.org
www.greenfornewengland.org

Earth Share of New Jersey
P.O. Box 191
Middletown, NJ 07748
908-872-3400
ken@earthsharenj.org
www.earthsharenj.org

Earth Share of New York
201 E 42nd Street, Suite 3200
New York, NY 10017
800-230-3369
info@earthshare.org
www.earthshareny.org

Earth Share of North Carolina
331 W. Main Street, Suite 602
Durham, NC 27702
919-687-4840
800-200-6311
jill@earthsharenc.org
www.earthsharenc.org

Earth Share of Ohio
3528 North High Street
Suite E
Columbus, OH 43214-4090
614-263-6367
info@earthshareofohio.org
www.earthshareofohio.org

Earth Share of Oregon
P.O. Box 40333
Portland, OR 97240
503-223-9015
info@earthshare-oregon.org
www.earthshare-oregon.org

Earth Share of Texas
814 W. 23rd Street
Austin, TX 78705
800-GREENTX
estx@earthshare-texas.org
www.earthshare-texas.org

Earth Share of Washington
1402 Third Avenue, Suite 525
Seattle, WA 98101
206-622-9840
eswinformation@esw.org
www.esw.org

Earth Share of Australia
P.O. Box 227
Bangalow, NSW
2479 Australia
www.earthshare.org.au

Environmental Fund for Arizona
644 N. Country Club Drive
Mesa, AZ 85201
480-969-3682
www.efaz.org
Please Note: Earth Share also collaborates with the Environmental Fund for Arizona; although EF-AZ is not an Earth Share affiliate, it may be an option in some Earth Share campaigns for AZ-based employees.

Other Volunteer-Based Organizations

Association of Junior League International
132 West 31st Street, 11th Floor
New York, NY 10011-3406
212-951-8300
www.ajli.org

International Rotary
One Rotary Center
1560 Sherman Avenue
Evanston, IL 60201
847-866-3000
www.rotary.org

Junior Chamber International
16120 Chesterfield Parkway West
Chesterfield, MO 63017
636-449-3100
800-905-5499
www.jci.cc

John McConnell
Earth Trustees Inc.
4924 East Kentucky Circle
Denver, CO 80246
303-758-7687
www.earthsite.org

Knights of Columbus
Supreme Office
One Columbus Plaza
P.O. Box 1760
New Haven, CT 06510-3226
203-752-4000
www.kofc.org

League of Women Voters
1730 M Street NW, Suite 1000
Washington, D.C. 20036-4508
202-429-1965
www.lwv.org

Lions Clubs International
300 West 22nd Street
Oak Brook, IL 60523
800-221-4792
www.lionsclubs.org

National Tree Trust
1120 G Street NW #770
Washington, D.C. 20005
202-628-8733
www.nationaltreetrust.org

Ruritan National, Inc.
P.O. Box 487
Dublin, VA 24084
877-787-8727
www.ruritan.org

United States Junior Chamber
of Commerce (JayCees)
P.O. Box 7
Tulsa, OK 74102-0007
800-JAYCEES
918-584-2481
www.usjaycees.org

Appendix 2
Recommended Reading

Animal Rights

Mason, Jim. *An Unnatural Order: Why We Are Destroying the Planet and Each Other* (New York: Continuum, 1997).

Newkirk, Ingrid. *Free the Animals: The Amazing True Story of the Animal Liberation Front* (New York: Lantern Books, 2001).

Regan, Tom. *The Case for Animal Rights* (Berkeley: University of California Press, 1983).

Singer, Peter. *Animal Liberation* (New York: Ecco Books, 2001).

Environmentalism

Brown, Lester R. Christopher Flavin and Sandra Postel. *Saving the Planet: How to Shape an Environmentally Sustainable Global Economy* (New York: W. W. Norton, 1991).

Caldicott, Dr. Helen. *The New Nuclear Danger: George W. Bush's Military-Industrial Complex* (New York: The New Press 2002).

DeVall, Bill and George Sessions. *Deep Ecology* (Layton, Utah: Peregrine Smith Books, 1985)

Hartmann, Thom. *The Last Hours of Ancient Sunlight: Waking Up to Personal and Global Transformation* (New York: Three Rivers Press, 2000).

Hawken, Paul. *The Ecology of Commerce: A Declaration of Sustainability* (New York: HarperCollins Publishers, 1993).

. *Natural Capitalism: Creating the Next Industrial Revolution* (New York: Back Bay Books, 2000).

Nonviolence

Merton, Thomas, ed. *Gandhi on Non-Violence* (New York: W. W. Norton, 1965).

Gandhi, M. K. *Non-Violent Resistance: Satyagraha* (Mineola, New York: Dover Publications, 2001).

Reforestation
Little, Charles E. *The Dying of the Trees: The Pandemic of America's Forests* (New York: Penguin, 1997)
Giono, Jean. *The Man Who Planted Trees* (White River Bridge Junction, Vermont: Chelsea Green Publishing Company 1985).
Richter, Conrad. *The Trees* (New York: Knopf, 1991).

Social Change/Politics
Cleveland, Clyde J. and Edward F. Noyes. *Restoring the Heart of America: A Return to Government by the People* (Fairfield, Iowa: Better Books, 2002).
Gladwell, Malcolm. *The Tipping Point: How Little Things Can Make a Difference* (New York: Little, Brown & Company, 2000).
Hock, Dee. *Birth of the Chaordic Age* (San Francisco: Berrett-Koehler Publishing, 1999).
McLaughlin, Corinne and Gordon Davidson. *Spiritual Politics: Changing the World from the Inside Out* (New York: Ballantine, 1994).
Rifkin, Jeremy. *The Hydrogen Economy: The Creation of the Worldwide Energy Web and the Redistribution of Power on Earth* (New York: Tarcher, 2002).
Roth, Robert. *A Reason to Vote* (New York: St. Martin's Press, 1999).
Schlosser, Eric. *Fast Food Nation: The Dark Side of the All-American Meal* (New York: Perennial, 2001).
Williamson, Marianne. *Healing of America* (New York: Simon & Schuster, 1997).

Spiritual Development
Butterworth, Eric and David F. Miller. *Spiritual Economics: The Principles and Process of True Prosperity* (Unity Village, Missouri: Unity Books, 1993).
Cady, H. Emilie. *Lessons in Truth* (Unity Village, Missouri: Unity Books, 1995).
Dass, Ram. *Be Here Now* (New York: Crown Publishers, 1971).
Fox, Emmet. *The Sermon on the Mount: The Key to Success in Life and the Lord's Prayer: An Interpretation* (San Francisco: HarperSanFrancisco, 1989).
Hesse, Hermann. *Siddhartha* (New York: Bantam, 1971).

Spalding, Baird T. *Life and Teachings of the Masters of the Far East* (Camarillo, CA: DeVorss and Co, 1996).

Williamson, Marianne. *A Return to Love: Reflections on the Principles of "A Course in Miracles"* (New York: HarperCollins, 1996).

Zukav, Gary. *The Seat of the Soul* (New York: Fireside, 1990).

Transcendental Meditation Program

Denniston, Denise. *The Transcendental Meditation TM Book: How to Enjoy the Rest of Your Life* (Fairfield Press, 1986).

Mahesh Yogi, Maharishi. *Science of Being and Art of Living* (New York: Meridian, 1995).

Olsen, Helena & Roland. *His Holiness Maharishi Mahesh Yogi: A Living Saint for the New Millennium* (New York: Samhita Productions, 2001).

Reddy, Kumuda, M.D., and Linda Egenes. *Conquering Chronic Disease Through Maharishi Vedic Medicine* (New York: Samhita Productions, 2002).

Roth, Robert. *Transcendental Meditation* (New York: Primus, 1994).

Vegetarianism

Kasin, Miriam. *The Age of Enlightenment Cookbook* (Arco Publishing, 1980).

Lappé, Frances Moore. *Diet for a Small Planet* (New York: Ballantine Books, 20th Anniversary Edition, 1991).

Lyman, Howard. *Mad Cowboy: Plain Truth from the Cattle Rancher Who Won't Eat Meat* (New York: Touchstone, 2001).

Marcus, Erik. *Vegan: The New Ethics of Eating* (Ithaca, New York: McBooks Press, 1998).

Moran, Victoria. *The Love-Powered Diet: When Will-Power Is Not Enough* (Novato, California: New World Library, 1992).

Raymond, Jennifer. *The Peaceful Palate: Fine Vegetarian Cuisine* (Novato, California: New World Library, 1992).

Rhodes, Richard. *Deadly Feasts: The "Prion" Controversy and the Public's Health* (New York: Touchstone, 1998).

Rifkin, Jeremy. *Beyond Beef: The Rise and Fall of the Cattle Culture* (New York: Penguin Books, 1992).

Robbins, John. *Diet for a New America: How Your Food Choices Affect Your Health, Happiness and the Future of Life on Earth* (Novato, California: H. J. Kramer, 2000)

——. *The Food Revolution: How Your Diet Can Help Save Your Life and Our World* (Berkeley, California: Conari Press, 2001)

Viet Nam

Karnow, Stanley. *Vietnam: A History* (New York: Viking, 1983).

Fall, Bernard B. *Street without Joy* (Mechanicsburg, Pennsylvania: Stackpole Books, 1994).

Fall, Bernard and Don Oberdorfer. *Last Reflections on a War: Bernard B. Fall's Last Comments on Vietnam* (Mechanicsburg, Pennsylvania: Stackpole Books, 2000).

Appendix 3
Recommended Web Sites

Animal Advocacy
Association of Veterinarians for Animal Rights (www.avar.org)
Endangered Species Coalition (www.stopextinction.org)
The Fund for Animals (www.fund.org)
Global Resource Action Center for the Environment (www.gracelinks.org)
Humane Society of the United States (HSUS) (www.hsus.org)
In Defense of Animals (www.ida.org)
Last Chance for Animals (www.lcanimal.org)
People for the Ethical Treatment of Animals (PETA) (www.peta.org)
United Poultry Concerns (www.upc-online.org)

Environmentalism
Circle of Life Foundation (www.circleoflifefoundation.org)
Earth Island Institute (www.earthisland.org)
Friends of the Earth (www.foe.org)
The Natural Step (www.naturalstep.org)
Redefining Progress (www.rprogress.org)
Rocky Mountain Institute (www.rmi.org)

Reforestation
ACT TreeLink: The Community Forestry Resource (www.treelink.org)
Friends of Trees (www.friendsoftrees.org)
National Alliance for Community Trees (ACT) (www.actrees.org)
National Arbor Day Foundation (www.arborday.org)
The National Tree Trust (www.nationaltreetrust.org)
Trees Are My Friends (www.treesaremyfriends.org)
USDA Forest Service, Cooperative Forestry (www.fs.fed.us/spf/coop)

Transcendental Meditation Program & TM Schools and Universities
To learn TM in the U.S.: 1-800-LEARN-TM or www.tm.org

Maharishi School of the Age of Enlightenment (U.S.) (K to 12)
    (www.maharishischooliowa.org)
Maharishi University of Management (U.S.) (www.mum.edu)
Maharishi Vedic University (www.maharishi.org)
Maharishi Open University (www.mou.org)

Vegetarianism

Alliance for Bio-Integrity (www.bio-integrity.org)
American Dietetic Association Position Paper on Vegetarianism
    (www.eatright.com/adap1197)
Dr. T. Colin Campbell (www.nutrition.cornell.edu/faculty/campbell.html)
EarthSave International (www.earthsave.org)
Farm Animal Reform Movement (www.farmusa.org)
Farm Sanctuary (www.farmsanctuary.org)
The Fund for Animals (www.fund.org)
GoVeg Campaign, People for the Ethical Treatment of Animals
    (www.goveg.com)
Humane Society of the United States (www.hsus.org)
International Vegetarian Union (www.ivu.org)
Dr. John McDougall (www.drmcdougall.com)
North American Vegetarian Society (www.navs-online.org)
Physicians Committee for Responsible Medicine (www.pcrm.org)
Satya (www.satyamag.com)
Union of Concerned Scientists (www.ucsusa.org)
Vegetarian Resource Group (www.vrg.org)
VegNews (www.vegnews.com)
VegSource (www.vegsource.com)
Worldwatch Institute (www.worldwatch.org)

Volunteerism

AmeriCorps (https://recruit.cns.gov)
Corporation for National and Community Service (CNCS) (www.nation-
    alservice.org)
Environmental Alliance for Senior Involvement (www.easi.org)
Learn and Serve America (www.learnandserve.org)
Peace Corps (http://peacecorps.org)
Senior Corps (www.seniorcorps.org)

Appendix 4
Awards and Recognitions Received

Awards and Recognitions Received for American Free Tree Program, Inc., the Stark Free Tree Program and founder David A. Kidd

April 1989
   Citation of Merit Award, Ohio Conservation Congress
March 1990
   National Recognition Award, Northern Ohio Windstar Connection
April 1990
   Project Award, The National Arbor Day Foundation
June 1990
   Ohio Magazine article, "Ohioans: The Man Who Plants Trees"
September 1990
   Maharishi Award, Maharishi International University
October 1990
   Teddy Roosevelt Conservation Award (presented by President George H. W. Bush)
September 1991
   Full page advertorial, "Free Trees for a Plentiful Future" in *Time* magazine, donated by Amway Corporation
January 1992
   Buckeye Award, International Society of Arboriculture (Ohio Chapter)
March 1992
   Certificate of Recognition (presented by Mrs. Barbara Bush, Springfield, Ohio)
October 1992
   Paul Harris Fellowship Award, given by Canton (Ohio) Rotary Club
February 1993
   Stark County Marketing Executive of the Year, Sales and Marketing Executives of Stark County, Ohio

March 1993
> Conservation Award for Outstanding Individual in Private Service, Ohio Forestry Association, Inc.

July 1994
> Daisy Sticksel Conservation Award, Ohio Association of Garden Clubs

September 1994
> National Society Daughters of the American Revolution Conservation Award

April 1995
> Non-member Individual Award, Environmental Education Council of Ohio

February 1996
> Forest Conservationist Award, The League of Ohio Sportsmen, The National Wildlife Federation

July 1996
> Outstanding Volunteer Project Award, Ohio Department of Natural Resources

October 1996
> Distinguished Alumni Award, Kent State University Stark Campus Alumni Council

February 1997
> National Award for Environmental Sustainability, Forests/Rangelands Award, Renew America

December 1999/January 2000
> *Satya* magazine article, "The Man Who Plants Trees"

September 2002
> Golden Carrot Award Vegetarian Club of Canton on its 16th anniversary

Other Features

Alabama Wild, November 1997

E: The Environmental Magazine, March/April 1993

Guide to the Green Scene 1995, The Earth Day Coalition

How on Earth!, January 1995

Odyssey, April 1992

Orion Nature Quarterly, Autumn 1990

Stand Up and Be Counted: The Volunteer Resource Book by Judy Knipe (New York: Simon & Schuster) October 1992

Time, September 21, 1991

Vegetarian Times, December 1993

Vegetarian Voice, Vol. 18, no 4, Winter 1992–93

Contact the Author

ᵈkidd @ TM. org

To Contact David A. Kidd

Kidd & Associates
3500 26th Street NW
Canton, Oh 44708
Telephone: 330.453-2387
E-mail: david@davidakidd.org
www.davidakidd.org

To Contact David Kidd to Speak to Your Group
I am happy to travel to speak on *Growing America* and various related topics. You can go to my Web site to see a current list of lectures available. Just send an e-mail or call to set up a lecture.

To Contact David to Offer a Workshop or Consultation
Again, at www.davidakidd.org, just select "Consulting Information" to learn about the services available from David Kidd or my associates around the country. We offer organizational structure and organizational development consulting and team-building workshops.

To Become a "Free Tree" Ambassador
You can become my "free tree" ambassador for your area and start your own "free tree" project. Please go to my Web site at www.davidakidd.org and check out the "Free tree" section. My wish is to have individuals start projects and report to me each year on how many trees they have distributed. I will tally the results on my Web site.

To Become a Greenspace Ambassador
You can become my greenspace ambassador for your area. I want motivated individuals to seek out potential greenspace in their own communities that can be placed in a land trust and held in protection for the benefit of both wildlife and humans. Please go to my Web site at www.davidakidd.org and check out the "Greenspace" section.